A PARENT'S GUIDE TO EXPLORING FUN PLACES IN TENNESSEE WITH CHILDREN. . .YEAR ROUND!

Kids Love Publications
1985 Dina Court
Powell, Ohio 43065
www.kidslovepublications.com

Dedicated to the Families
of Tennessee

For the latest major updates corresponding to the pages in this book visit our website:

www.kidslovepublications.com

ISBN# 0-9726854-2-1

KIDS ♥ TENNESSEE ™   Kids Love Publications

TABLE OF CONTENTS

State Map

(With Major Routes and Cities Marked)

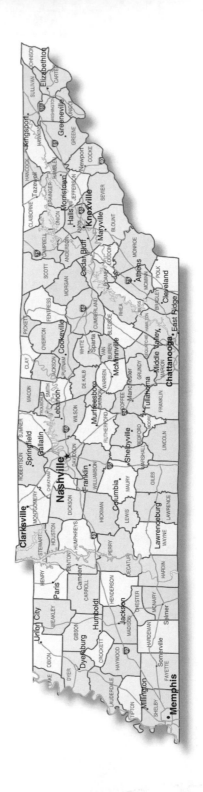

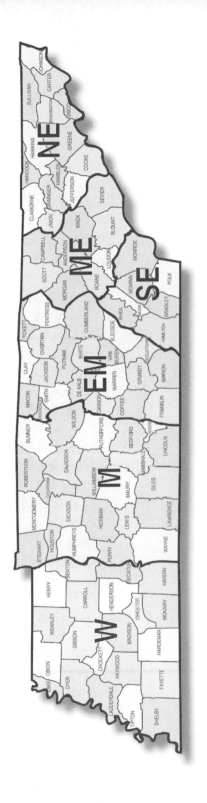

Chapter Area Map

CITY INDEX (Listed by City & Area)

CITY INDEX (Listed by City & Area)

Acknowledgements

We are most thankful to be blessed with our parents, Barbara (Darrall) Callahan & George and Catherine Zavatsky who help us every way they can – researching, proofing and babysitting. More importantly, they are great sounding boards and offer unconditional support. So many places around Tennessee remind us of family vacations years ago…

We also want to express our thanks to the many Convention & Visitor Bureaus' staff for providing the attention to detail that helps to complete a project. We felt very welcome during our travels in Tennessee and would be proud to call it home!

Our own kids, Jenny and Daniel, were delightful and fun children during our trips across the state. What a joy it is to be their parents…we couldn't do it without them as our "kid-testers"!

We both sincerely thank each other – our partnership has created an even greater business/personal "marriage" with lots of exciting moments, laughs, and new adventures in life woven throughout. Above all, we praise the Lord for His so many blessings through the last few years. God does answer prayer…all prayer, *eventually*!

We think Tennessee is a wonderful, friendly area of the country with more activities than you could imagine. Our sincere wish is that this book will help everyone "fall in love" with Tennessee.

In a Hundred Years…

It will not matter, The size of my bank account…
The kind of house that I lived in, the kind of car that I drove…
But what will matter is…
That the world may be different
Because I was important in the life of a child.

-    *author unknown*

HOW TO USE THIS BOOK

If you are excited about discovering Tennessee, this is the book for you and your family! We've spent over a thousand hours doing all the scouting, collecting and compiling (*and most often visiting!*) so that you could spend less time searching and more time having fun.

Here are a few hints to make your adventures run smoothly:

- ❑ Consider the **child's age** before deciding to take a visit.
- ❑ Know **directions** and parking. Call ahead (or visit the company's website) if you have questions *and* bring this book. Also, don't forget your camera! *(please honor rules regarding use).*
- ❑ **Estimate the duration** of the trip. Bring small surprises (favorite juice boxes) travel books, and toys.
- ❑ Call ahead for **reservations** or details, if necessary.
- ❑ Most listings are **closed major holidays** unless noted.
- ❑ Make a **family "treasure chest"**. Decorate a big box or use an old popcorn tin. Store memorabilia from a fun outing, journals, pictures, brochures and souvenirs. Once a year, look through the "treasure chest" and reminisce. "Kids Love Travel Memories!" is an excellent travel journal & scrapbook that your family can create. *(See the order form in back of this book).*
- ❑ Plan **picnics** along the way. Many State History sites and state parks are scattered throughout Tennessee. Allow time for a rural/scenic route to take advantage of these free picnic facilities.
- ❑ Some activities, especially tours, require **groups** of 10 or more. To participate, you may either ask to be part of another tour group or get a group together yourself (neighbors, friends, organizations). If you arrange a group outing, most places offer discounts.
- ❑ For the latest **updates** corresponding to the pages in this book, visit our website: **www.kidslovepublications.com.**
- ❑ Each chapter represents an area of the state. Each listing is further identified by city, zip code, and place/event name. Our popular **Activity Index** in the back of the book **lists places by Activity Heading** (i.e. State History, Tours, Outdoors, Museums, etc.).

MISSION STATEMENT

At first glance, you may think that this is a book that just lists hundreds of places to travel. While it is true that we've invested thousands of hours of exhaustive research (*and drove over 4000 miles in Tennessee*) to prepare this travel resource...just listing places to travel is <u>not</u> the mission statement of these projects.

As children, Michele and I were able to travel extensively throughout the United States. We consider these family times some of the greatest memories we cherish today. We, quite frankly, felt that most children had this opportunity to travel with their family as we did. However, as we became adults and started our own family, we found that this wasn't necessarily the case. We continually heard friends express several concerns when deciding how to spend "quality" and "quantity" family time. 1) What to do? 2) Where to do it? 3) How much will it cost? 4) How do I know that my kids will enjoy it?

Interestingly enough, as we compare our experiences with our families when we were kids, many of our fondest memories were not made at an expensive attraction, but rather when it was least expected.

It is our belief and mission statement that if you as a family will study and <u>use</u> the contained information <u>to create family memories,</u> these memories will grow a stronger, tighter family. Our ultimate mission statement is, that your children will develop a love and a passion for quality family experiences that they can pass to another generation of family travelers.

We thank you for purchasing this book, and we hope to see you on the road (*and hearing your travel stories!*) God bless your journeys and happy exploring!

George, Michele, Jenny and Daniel

GENERAL INFORMATION

Call *(or visit the websites)* for the services of interest. Request to be added to their mailing lists.

- ❑ Tennessee Department of Tourist Development, Nashville. (800) GO2-TENN or **www.tnvacation.com**
- ❑ Tennessee Department of Environment/Conservation, Bureau of Parks/Recreation, Nashville. (423) 532-0001 or (800) 421-6683.
- ❑ Tennessee's Civil War Heritage Trail: A Path Divided. Tennessee Historical Commission, Nashville. (615) 532-1550 or **www.state.tn.us/environment/hist/**
- ❑ Tennessee Historical Commission, Nashville. (615) 532-1550
- ❑ Tennessee Wildlife Resources Agency, Agriculture Center, Nashville. (615) 781-6500 or (800) 372-3928
- ❑ Tennessee State Parks, Nashville. (888) TN-Parks or **www.tnstateparks.com**
- ❑ Llama Trekking, Tennessee Overhill (423) 263-7232.
- ❑ Music Highway - Interstate 40 between Memphis and Nashville. (888) 243-9769.
- ❑ Pick Tennessee Products, **www.picktnproducts.org**.
- ❑ Whitewater Rafting/Kayaking, **www.chattanoogafun.com**
- ❑ **M** - Clarksville Convention & Visitors Bureau, Clarksville. (800) 530-2487 or **www.clarksville.tn.us**
- ❑ **M** - Sumner County Convention & Visitors Bureau, Gallatin. (888) 301-7866 or **www.sumnercountytourism.com**
- ❑ **M** - Wilson County Convention & Visitors Bureau, Lebanon. (800) 789-1327 or **www.wilsoncountycvb.com**

- ❑ **M** - Rutherford County Convention & Visitors Bureau, Murfreesboro. (800) 716-7560 or **www.rutherfordchamber.org**.
- ❑ **M**- Nashville Convention & Visitors Bureau, Nashville. **www.nashvillecvb.com**
- ❑ **ME** - Gatlinburg Dept of Tourism, Gatlinburg. (800) 568-4748 or **www.gatlinburg.com**
- ❑ **ME** - Knox County Parks & Rec., Knoxville. (865) 215-2346
- ❑ **ME** - Knoxville Tourism & Sports Corporation, Knoxville. (800) 727-8045 or **www.knoxtsc.com**
- ❑ **ME** - Pigeon Forge Dept of Tourism, Pigeon Forge. (800) 251-9100 or **www.mypigeonforge.com**
- ❑ **NE** - Johnson City Convention & Visitors Bureau, Johnson City. (423) 461-8002 or **www.johnsoncitychamber.com**
- ❑ **SE** - Hamilton County Parks & Rec, Chattanooga. (423) 842-0177.
- ❑ **SE** - Bradley County Recreation Dept., Cleveland. (423) 476-0582.
- ❑ **SE** - Smoky Mountain Convention & Visitors Bureau, Townsend. (865) 448-6134 or **www.smokymountains.org**
- ❑ **W** - West Region Department of Tourism, Jackson. (731) 426-0888 or **www.tnvacation.com**
- ❑ **W** - Cultural Development Foundation of Memphis. Provide productions to school-aged children and families in the performing arts. (901) 327-9578.
- ❑ **W** - Memphis Convention & Visitors Bureau, Memphis. (901) 543-5300 or **www.memphistravel.com**
- ❑ **W** - Memphis Division of Park Services, Memphis. (901) 454-5200 or **www.ci.memphis.tn.us/divisions/park.cfm**

Check out these businesses / services in your area for tour ideas:

AIRPORTS

All children love to visit the airport! Why not take a tour and understand all the jobs it takes to run an airport? Tour the terminal, baggage claim, gates and security / currency exchange. Maybe you'll even get to board a plane.

ANIMAL SHELTERS

Great for the would-be pet owner. Not only will you see many cats and dogs available for adoption, but a guide will show you the clinic and explain the needs of a pet. Be prepared to have the children "fall in love" with one of the animals while they are there!

BANKS

Take a "behind the scenes" look at automated teller machines, bank vaults and drive-thru window chutes. You may want to take this tour and then open a savings account for your child.

CITY HALLS

Halls of Fame, City Council Chambers & Meeting Room, Mayor's Office and famous statues.

ELECTRIC COMPANY / POWER PLANTS

Modern science has created many ways to generate electricity today, but what really goes on with the "flip of a switch". Because coal can be dirty, wear old, comfortable clothes. Coal furnaces heat water, which produces steam, that propels turbines, that drives generators, that make electricity.

FIRE STATIONS

Many Open Houses in October, Fire Prevention Month. Take a look into the life of the firefighters servicing your area and try on their gear. See where they hang out, sleep and eat. Hop aboard a real-life fire engine truck and learn fire safety too.

HOSPITALS

Some Children's Hospitals offer pre-surgery and general tours.

NEWSPAPERS

You'll be amazed at all the new technology. See monster printers and robotics. See samples in the layout department and maybe try to put together your own page. After seeing a newspaper made, most companies give you a free copy (dated that day) as your souvenir. National Newspaper Week is in October.

RESTAURANTS

PIZZA HUT & PAPA JOHN'S

❑ Participating locations

Telephone the store manager. Best days are Monday, Tuesday and Wednesday mid-afternoon. Minimum of 10 people. Small charge per person. All children love pizza – especially when they can create their own! As the children tour the kitchen, they learn how to make a pizza, bake it, and then eat it. The admission charge generally includes lots of creatively made pizzas, beverage and coloring book.

KRISPY KREME DONUTS

❑ Participating locations

Get an "inside look" and learn the techniques that make these donuts some of our favorites! Watch the dough being made in "giant" mixers, being formed into donuts and taking a "trip" through the fryer. Seeing them being iced and topped with colorful sprinkles is always a favorite with the kids. Contact your local store manager. They prefer Monday or Tuesday. Free.

SUPERMARKETS

Kids are fascinated to go behind the scenes of the same store where Mom and Dad shop. Usually you will see them grind meat, walk into large freezer rooms, watch cakes and bread bake and receive free samples along the way. Maybe you'll even get to pet a live lobster!

TV / RADIO STATIONS

Studios, newsrooms, Fox kids clubs. Why do weathermen never wear blue clothes on TV? What makes a "DJ's" voice sound so deep and smooth?

WATER TREATMENT PLANTS

A giant science experiment! You can watch seven stages of water treatment. The favorite is usually the wall of bright buttons flashing as workers monitor the different processes.

U.S. MAIN POST OFFICES

Did you know Ben Franklin was the first Postmaster General (over 200 years ago)? Most interesting is the high-speed automated mail processing equipment. Learn how to address envelopes so they will be sent quicker (there are secrets). To make your tour more interesting, have your children write a letter to themselves and address it with colorful markers. Mail it earlier that day and they will stay interested trying to locate their letter in all the high-speed machinery.

Chapter 1
Area - Eastern Middle (EM)

Our Favorites...

* State Park Hiking - Rock Formations & Falls

* South Cumberland State Recreation Area - Monteagle

* Falls Creek Falls State Park Resort - Pikeville

* Dutch Maid Bakery - Tracy City

Fun aboard the Falls Creek Falls Swinging Bridge!

FALLS MILL

134 Falls Mill Road (1 mile north of U.S. 64 at Old Salem)

Belvidere 37306

❑ Phone: (931) 469-7161 **Web: www.fallsmill.com**
❑ Hours: Monday-Saturday 9:00am-4:00pm, Sunday 12:30-4:00pm
   except closed Wednesdays and Thanksgiving, Christmas and
   New Years.
❑ Admission: $1.00-$3.00.

Built as a cotton and woolen factory in 1873, the mill was later
converted to a cotton gin, then a wood-working shop before its
present use as a grist mill. Falls Mill is open to the public every
day except Wednesdays. Visitors begin with an introductory
history of the mill and then take a self-guided tour of the buildings
and scenic grounds.

CORDELL HULL BIRTHPLACE & MUSEUM STATE PARK

1300 Cordell Hull Memorial Drive (1.5 miles off Hwy 111 on
SR 325)

Byrdstown 38549

❑ Phone: (931) 864-3247
   Web: www.state.tn.us/environment/parks/cordell/
❑ Hours: Wednesday-Monday 8:00am-4:00pm.

The site consists of Hull's original log cabin birthplace, an
activities center and a museum housing documents and artifacts.
The collection includes his Nobel Peace Prize that is on display.
President Roosevelt praised Secretary Hull as "the one person in
all the world who has done the most to make this great plan for
peace an effective fact." The 1945 Nobel Prize for Peace was
given to Hull in recognition of his work in the Western
Hemispheres, for his international trade agreements, and for his
efforts in establishing the United Nations.

CUMBERLAND MOUNTAIN STATE PARK

24 Office Drive (I-40 exit 317, Hwy 127, 9 miles south of town)

Crossville 38555

❑   Phone: (931) 484-6138 or (800) 250-8618 cabins
      Web: www.state.tn.us/environment/parks/cumbmtn/
❑   Hours: 7:00am-10:00pm.
❑   Miscellaneous: Concert in the Park summertime series.

Centered on Cumberland Mountain (elev. 2,000 feet), it is America's largest forested plateau. The Homestead Museum, located one mile from the park, depicts the Cumberland Homestead Community of the 1930's. Rustic cabins are nestled in the woods at Cumberland Mountain State Park and have fully equipped kitchens, cable TV, fireplaces (except single cabins), linens, picnic tables and grills. The restaurant is open for lunch and dinner. The park's pride, catfish is served on Fridays. The park offers several miles of moderate trails around the lake, creek and in the woods. Other activities: camping, golfing, swimming, fishing and boating.

CUMBERLAND COUNTY PLAYHOUSE

221 Tennessee Avenue

Crossville 38557

❑   Phone: (931) 484-5000. **Web: www.ccplayhouse.com**

With two indoor stages and one outdoor theatre, the Cumberland County Playhouse is one of the premier Southern pro theaters. Considered "Tennessee's Family Theater", they perform shows like Carousel and Scrooge and family music concerts. Tickets typically range $10.00-$20.00.

OZONE FALLS

(I-40 exit 329, follow US 70 east)

Crossville 38557

❑   Phone: (931) 484-6138

A "hidden" waterfall which is accessible to almost everyone, Ozone Falls lies just a couple of miles from I-40 and it is a 100+ foot waterfall with a nice basin and pool at the base. A steep trail located 70 yards west of the parking area will lead you to the base of the falls and allows you to walk behind the falls.

DUNLAP COKE OVENS PARK

114 Walnut Street, downtown

Dunlap 37327

❑   Phone: (423) 949-2156

Web: www.bledsoe.net/cokeovens/tours.htm

The walking tour around the Coke Ovens Park offers the visitor an opportunity to spend some time walking through the quiet woods discovering the ruins of a once great industrial complex. The more strenuous Incline Hike includes climbing the 3900 foot incline to the top of the bluffs to explore the area where coal was once mined. Stop by the museum first to borrow a hand carved walking stick.

CIVIL WAR TOUR/ BATTLE OF HARTSVILLE PRESERVATION

240 Broadway

Hartsville 37074

❑   Phone: (615) 374-9243 (C of C)

Self-guided tour includes 17 stops related to Gen. John Hunt Morgan and the Battle of Hartsville. Brochure and map available at the chamber office.

LIVING HISTORY MUSEUM OF TROUSDALE COUNTY

101 White Oak Street

Hartsville 37074

❑   Phone: (615) 374-9243

Complete farm setting with a furnished house, barn, corn crib and an outhouse (over 100 years old) showing how the tobacco farmer lived in the 1930s. Growing tobacco and tools on display.

STANDING STONE STATE PARK

1674 Standing Stone Park Hwy (I-40 exit 288, Hwy 111N to Hwy 52W to Hwy 136)

Hilham 38568

❑   Phone: (931) 823-6347 or (800) 713-5157 cabins
      Web: www.state.tn.us/environment/parks/standstn/
❑   Hours: Day use park closes at sunset.

The rustic park is noted for its outstanding scenery, spring wildflowers, fossils and other natural diversity. The park takes its name from the "Standing Stone," an eight-foot tall rock standing upright on a sandstone ledge, which was supposedly used as a boundary line between two separate Indian nations. The park is known for its annual National Rolley Hole Marble Competition each September. Standing Stone State Park has an Olympic size pool with one low dive and a kiddie pool. The pool is located within walking distance of cabins and camping via a paved foot trail. Also, located next to the pool is the Recreation Hall, tennis courts, volleyball and basketball courts. Ten miles of hiking trails wind through the wilds where hikers can observe diversity in plant and animal life from the trails as they trek across swinging bridges. Standing Stone is equipped with four types of cabins: Rustic, Timberlodge, Modern and Overton Lodge (group lodge). Other activities: camping, fishing, and boating.

PICKETT STATE PARK

4605 Pickett Park Highway (Hwy 154, northeast of town)

Jamestown 38556

❑   Phone: (931) 879-5821 or (877) 260-0010 cabins
     Web: www.state.tn.us/environment/parks/pickett/
❑   Hours: Office: 8:00am-4:30pm. Park: 7:30am-dark.

Situated in a remote area of the Cumberland Mountains, the
17,372-acre Pickett State Park and Forest possess a combination of
scenic, botanical and geological wonders found nowhere else in
Tennessee.   Of particular interest are the uncommon rock
formations, natural bridges, numerous caves and remains of
ancient Indian occupation. Pickett features five chalets, five rustic
stone cottages and five wooden cottages ideally suited for
vacations. Each is completely equipped for housekeeping. Other
Activities: Camping,   boating,   fishing,   swimming   and
hiking/horseback trails.

OLD STONE FORT STATE ARCHAEOLOGICAL PARK

732 Stone Fort Drive (I-24 turn southwest at the Highway 53, Exit
110 and follow the signs)

Manchester 37855

❑   Phone: (931) 723-5073
     Web: www.state.tn.us/environment/parks/stoneft/
❑   Hours: Park: Daily 8:00am-sunset. Museum: 8:00am-4:30pm.

An earth and stone enclosure built as a sacred site by prehistoric
Indians about 2,000 years ago. The Visitor Center and exhibit hall
complex includes exhibits relating to the history, archaeology, and
legends surrounding the Old Stone Fort and its builders, the
Woodland Indians. Other Activities: camping, hiking and fishing.

CUMBERLAND CAVERNS

1437 Cumberland Caverns Road (7 miles southeast of town on
Hwy 8 or Hwy 55, from US 70 or I-24)

McMinnville 37110

❑   Phone: (931) 668-4396. **Web: www.cumberlandcaverns.com**
❑   Hours: Daily 9:00am-6:00pm (May-October). Spelunking and
     group tours rest of year by reservation.
❑   Tours: Tours leave at the top of each hour. The first tour leaves at
     9:00 am and the last tour leaves at 5:00 pm. The tour lasts
     approximately 1½ hours.

Tennessee's largest cave is so big they have an underground
ballroom complete with chandelier and organ music for group
meals. Most all the rooms on tour are large and some of the
formations include shapes described as the Twin Trolls, the Three
Chessmen or Moby Dick. The tour includes a look at an 1812 saltpeter
mine, pools and waterfalls. An original underground pageant of light
and sound, "God of the Mountain", is shown on every tour.

SOUTH CUMBERLAND STATE RECREATION AREA

Rte. 1, US 41 (3 miles from I-24 between Monteagle and Tracy
City)

Monteagle 37356

❑   Phone: (931) 924-2980 or 924-2956
     Web: www.state.tn.us/environment/parks/socumb/
❑   Hours: Sunrise to sunset.

FIERY GIZZARD TRAIL, LITTLE GIZZARD CREEK SMALL
WILD AREA - 2.2 mile west of Foster Falls. Vistas of the
Cumberland. Hike down into Laurel Branch gorge. Primitive
camping. FOSTER FALLS SMALL WILD AREA (423-942-
5759) - 60 feet waterfall plunges into a deep pool. Mountain laurel,
azaleas and hemlocks grow above the falls, along the sandstone
overlook and in the gorge below. Picnic, camping and hiking.
CARTER STATE NATURAL AREA - 140 acres with LOST
COVE CAVE - impressive cave mouth (100ft. Wide, 80 ft. high)

with cave stream and a cold drafting air. It is necessary to climb up and down over large rocks and wade thru a stream in order to traverse the remainder of the cove. The Great Stone Door, a 100-foot-deep crevice at the crest of the plateau, guards the western access to the trail system.

ALVIN C. YORK STATE HISTORIC AREA

(7 miles north of Jamestown on SR 127)

Pall Mall 38577

❑ Phone: (931) 879-3657
    www.state.tn.us/environment/parks/sgtyork/museum.htm
❑ Hours: Open year-round daylight hours for park. Home open Saturday-Sunday 9:00am-5:00pm.
❑ Admission: FREE

The historic area is a memorial to the man General Pershing called the "greatest soldier of the World War" and the places Alvin knew and loved all his life are here: his family home and farm, the rock ledge where he married his beloved "Miss Gracie"; the church he helped to build, and the post office/general store he built and operated. In the area are scenic views of Wolf River and a gristmill. The York homesite museum includes a collection of wartime and personal mementos, including historical photographs, family portraits and personal items.

FALL CREEK FALLS STATE PARK RESORT

Route 3 (entered from Hwy 111 or Hwy 30)

Pikeville 37367

❑ Phone: (423) 881-5298 (866) 836-3297 reservations
    Web: www.state.tn.us/environment/parks/fallcrek/
❑ Hours: Open 24 hours, roads to Falls close at dark.

Fall Creek Falls is the highest waterfall east of the Rocky Mountains, plunging 256 feet into a shaded pool at the base of its gorge. The park's other falls, (Piney, Cane Creek, and Cane Creek

Cascades), though smaller, are just as impressive. Some are waterfalls, cascades, sparkling streams, or gorges. The park offers hiking trails, bicycle trails, horseback riding, swimming pools (one at the Inn, one near campgrounds), canoeing, paddle boats and golf plus an inn/restaurant (great views, all rooms waterfront w/ good Southern cuisine buffets served) and cabins, camping. The overlook (short) trails to each fall are mostly manageable, but the hiking trails to the bottom (under the Falls) or to the Piney Falls Suspension are somewhat strenuous! We recommend them (age 8+ for safety) but wear sturdy, rugged shoes and maybe bring a flashlight. There are many steep paths made of layered rock. What an adventure, though! Be sure to stop at the tunnel of cold air at Fall Creek Falls. Stop by the Nature Center to chat with rangers and look thru displays. The Village Green has shops and recreation areas. You'll find many seasonal, daily family activities meet at the Nature Center or Village Green. The kids might get to meet their first salamander or baby snake on the trail!

ROCK ISLAND STATE RUSTIC PARK

82 Beach Road (Rte. 287)

Rock Island 38581

- ❑   Phone: (931) 686-2471 or (800) 713-6065 cabins
      Web: www.state.tn.us/environment/parks/rockis/
- ❑   Hours: 7:30am – 10:00pm.
- ❑   Admission: $3.00 per vehicle.

Rock Island's cascading Great Falls forms a spectacular backdrop for a natural beach, located on the headwaters of Center Hill Lake. Picnic areas, boat launch, camping and cabins available. The park's Blue Hole is good for fishing.

EDGAR EVINS STATE PARK

1630 Edgar Evins State Park Road (I-40 at exit 268 at State Hwy. 96 and Center Hill Lake)

Silver Point 38582

- ❑   Phone: (931) 858-2114 or (800) 250-8619
      Web: www.state.tn.us/environment/parks/edgar/

❑   Hours: 6:00am-10:30pm.

❑   Admission: $3.00 per vehicle, per day.

Located north of Smithville on the forested hillsides of Center Hill
Reservoir, the park mostly attracts water enthusiasts. The park has
cabins, campsite, boat launch ramps, marina, pool for cabin guests,
lake swimming, hiking, and playgrounds. A popular fall cruise
extends 50 miles upstream to Rock Island State Park.

BURGESS FALLS STATE NATURAL AREA

4000 Burgess Falls Drive (SR 155, north of town)

Sparta 38583

❑   Phone: (931) 432-5312

   Web: www.state.tn.us/environment/parks/burgess/

❑   Hours: 8:00am until 30 minutes before sundown when gates
   close. Park is closed when the river is high or when there is snow
   on the roads and/or trails.

A stream-side nature trail winds beside Falling Water River to the
plunging Burgess Falls. A $3 per vehicle, per day access fee is
charged at this park. Also fishing and hiking offered.

VIRGIN FALLS STATE NATURAL AREA

(Hwy 70, follow signs to Scott Gulf Road), **Sparta** 38583

❑   Phone: (931) 836-3552 (local C of C)

   Web: www.state.tn.us/environment/nh/natareas/virgin/

❑   Admission: FREE

Formed by an underground stream that emerges from a cave, drops
over a 110 foot cliff and disappears into a cave at the bottom. The
natural area is operated as a Bowater Pocket Wilderness Area and
has 8 miles of hiking trails and backcountry camping. Virgin Falls
is located within the greater Scott's Gulf region and adjacent to the
BRIDGESTONE / FIRESTONE CENTENNIAL WILDERNESS
(Eastland Rd, www.centennialwilderness.com). The 10,000 acre gift
from the company has hiking trails to Cancy Fork River and bluffs
overlooking the gorge.

DUTCH MAID BAKERY & MUSEUM

111 Main Street (I-24 west to US 41 north at Jasper, head into town)

Tracy City 37387

- ❑   Phone: (931) 592-3171. **Web: www.dutch-maid.com**
- ❑   Hours: Daily 9:00am-6:00pm (CST). Employees bake on Tuesdays, Thursdays and Saturdays. Closed Thanksgiving and Christmas.
- ❑   Admission: FREE
- ❑   Miscellaneous: Now take you baked goodies down the road to Foster Falls for a snack with a view!

Tennessee's oldest family operated bakery, established in 1902 by Swiss immigrants. Old World recipe breads and famous "applesauce" fruitcakes are baked year-round. Most of the Dutch Maid Bakery's equipment dates back to the 1920s, and the recipes are from the 1880s. The old Bakery is actually a functioning museum. The primary mixers date from 1929 and 1945, the oven 1923, and the old bread slicer/bagger from 1916. When new parts are required, they have to be made. Salt Rising bread prep requires 22-24 hours from starter to sponge, mix, mold, proof, bake, cool, dry, slice and bag. On your short, casual tour, you'll learn how they measure only by weight, how they don't bake by time, but by color and even get a chance to walk in the "rising room". Many people travel to Tracy City to taste the salt-rising bread, sugar plum cake and the "sock it to me cake". Remember, "Brot" is German for bread.

FIRESTONE POTTERY

707 North Fork Lane (north of Gainesborough, near SR56)

Whitleyville 38562

- ❑   Phone: (931) 621-3456. **Web: www.firestonepottery.com**

Come and visit. Many customers come to the pottery site, often bringing a picnic lunch to enjoy by a little waterfall or in the gardens. See them at work in the studio and gain special insight into the mysteries and delights of pottery making. Each piece is hand-crafted and offers a special message from the Bible. FREE. Call first to see when the husband-and-wife team are in the studio crafting.

TIMS FORD STATE PARK
570 Tims Ford Drive (Hwy 130 or Hwy 64)
Winchester 37390

❑   Phone: (931) 962-1183or (800) 471-5295 cabins
     Web: www.state.tn.us/environment/parks/timsford/
❑   Hours: Recreation Center (games and pool) open Tuesday
     through Sunday 10:00am-6:00pm (summer); open on weekends
     only in the Spring and Fall
❑   Admission: $3.00 per vehicle, per day.

Tims Ford State Park, located on the Tims Ford Reservoir in the
rolling hills of southern middle Tennessee, is an outstanding
recreational area and fishing paradise. The lake offers recreational
facilities for camping, swimming, fishing, boating, bicycle and
hiking trails and water-skiing. Stay in one of the rustic cabins or
stop by the marina for boating launches or eateries. Every other
Saturday night, they welcome "Pickin and Grinnin" entertainment
to come visit and perform.

Chapter 2
Area - Middle (M)

Our Favorites...

* Historic Collinsville - Clarksville

* Uncle Charlie's Old Amish Village - Ethridge

* Carter House - Franklin

* Mansker's Station, Historic - Goodlettsville

* Trinity Music City - Hendersonville

* Cracker Barrel Headquarters - Lebanon

* Discovery Center at Murfree Spring - Murfreesboro

* County Music Hall of Fame - Nashville (& Broadway St)

* Opryland - Hotel, Opry, Museum, Opry Mills,
General Jackson Showboat - Nashville

* Purity Dairies - Nashville

* Hermitage, The - Nashville (Hermitage)

* Sam Davis Home - Smyrna

Future Stars at the famous Grand Ole Opry!

PORT ROYAL STATE PARK

3300 Old Clarksville Hwy (off Hwy. 76, five miles E of I-24, Exit 11)

Adams 37010

❏   Phone: (931) 358-9696

Web: www.state.tn.us/environment/parks/proyal/

❏   Hours: 8:00am-sundown.

The site of one of the state's earliest communities, the park is a place of quiet beauty featuring a hiking trail, picnicking, canoeing and fishing. It has a covered bridge spanning the Red River. MUSEUM: Exhibits display artifacts, tools, and weapons from aboriginal peoples (Cherokee on their way on the Trail of Tears) through frontier life and the Civil War period to present day tobacco farming. An exhibit also details the history of the Port Royal Covered Bridge.

MONTGOMERY BELL STATE RESORT PARK

1020 Jackson Hill Rd. (Take Highway 70 West to White Bluff)

Burns 37029

❏   Phone: (615) 797-9052 or (615) 797-3101

Web: www.state.tn.us/environment/parks/montbell/

❏   Hours: Daily 6:00am-10:00pm.

❏   Admission: $3.00 per vehicle, per day.

The treasure was iron ore, and it lured men by the hundreds to this area of Middle Tennessee. This is the site of the first Cumberland Presbyterian Church. They also offer an arcade, ball courts, golf course, campsites, modern cabins, lake swimming, fishing, hiking, and paddleboat and rowboat rentals. Nearby, at the Narrows of the Harpeth park, are canoeing and an Indian ceremonial art center. The Inn and restaurant feature modern lodging and dining. Amenities include cable television, indoor year-round pool, jacuzzi, and outdoor pool (seasonal), exercise room and laundry facilities. Every room has a view of the lake. Ranger programs offered in Cultural Heritage and Discovering Nature.

HISTORIC CRAGFONT

200 Cragfont Road (off Hwy 25)

Castalian Springs 37031

❑ Phone: (615) 452-7070. **Web: www.srlab.net/cragfont**
❑ Hours: Tuesday-Friday 10:00am-5:00pm, Sunday 1:00-5:00pm
(Mid-April thru October). By appt. rest of year.
❑ Admission: $5.00 adult, $4.00 senior (55+), $3.00 child (6-12).

When completed in 1802, it was the finest mansion house on the Tennessee frontier. Built by General James Winchester - a frontiersman, politician, soldier and one of the founders of Memphis. A visit to Cragfont is a step into the past combining cultural and architectural history. Summertime brings Day Camps and Pioneer Days involving crafts, games, storytellers, and daily refreshments (camp fee).

WYNNEWOOD

210 Old Hwy 25

Castalian Springs 37031

❑ Phone: (615) 452-5463
Web: www.srlab.net/bledsoe/wynnewood.html
❑ Hours: Monday-Saturday 10:00am-4:00pm, Sunday 1:00-5:00pm. Closed Sundays from November-March. Closed all holidays.
❑ Admission: $4.00 adult, $0.50 child (12 & under), $1.50 teens.

This two-story tall and 142-foot long large log structure (1828) served as a stagecoach inn and later as a mineral springs resort. By the 1840s the Wynnes had built a row of cottages on the lawn east of the inn and set up a race course in the bottom near Lick Creek. Most guests were attracted by the medicinal qualities of the mineral waters but one frequent visitor, Andrew Jackson, liked the race course best and he usually brought a favorite thoroughbred to run against one of Wynne's horses when he visited.

BLEDSOE'S FORT HISTORIC PARK

State Hwy 25 (SR 25 & SR 49)

Castalian Springs 37031

❑   Phone: (615) 452-5463. **Web: www.srlab.net/bledsoe**
❑   Hours: Daily daylight to dusk.
❑   Admission: FREE

The self-guided walking tour of Bledsoe Fort Historical Park is a one mile walk through the shaded hills retracing the pioneer footprints along the Avery Trace, the first road leading from eastern Tennessee into middle Tennessee. The tour continues past the 1890's Parker Cabin, the Hugh Rogan house, a 200 year old stone cottage from the Indian War period, the pioneer cemetery including the markers of brothers Isaac and Anthony Bledsoe, and the Cavern of Skulls. The tour is interpreted by signs providing historical information relating to the sites.

HENRY HORTON STATE PARK RESORT

4358 Nashville Highway (I-65 to exit 46 east on Hwy 412 to 431S, turn right, then left on Hwy 99 to Hwy 31A)

Chapel Hill 37034

❑   Phone: (931) 364-2222 or (800) 250-8612
     Web: www.state.tn.us/environment/parks/henry/
❑   Hours: Public area gate closes at 10:00p.m.

The park is located on the former estate of the late Henry H. Horton, 36th governor of Tennessee. This park, located on the shores of the historic Duck River, provides hours of recreational enjoyment. The Resort Inn with restaurant (Southern cuisine at popular prices) is open weekends with continental breakfast provided for inn/cabin guests. The seasonal swimming pool is open summers.

CUSTOMS HOUSE MUSEUM & CULTURAL CENTER

200 South Second Street (downtown at the corner of Second St. & Madison St), **Clarksville** 37040

- ❑ Phone: (931) 648-5780. **Web: www.customshousemuseum.org**
- ❑ Hours: Tuesday-Saturday 10:00am-5:00pm, Sunday 1:00-5:00pm.
- ❑ Admission: $4.00 adult, $3.00 senior (55+), $2.00 college students, $1.00 student (age 6-18). FREE on Sundays.
- ❑ Miscellaneous: Suggested lodging at Country Inn & Suites, I-24, exit 4 (931-645-1400 or www.countryinns.com/clarksvilletn). Indoor/outdoor pool, full deluxe hot continental breakfast, refrigerator and microwave in every room.

Built in 1898 as a US Post Office and Customs House for trade, this site is now a regional history museum. Memory Lane/Main Street has many actual artifacts with a great walk-in log cabin. The Explorer's Floor is a special area for the entire family to solve puzzles and play games. Learn in fantasy in Aunt Alice's Attic, the Kroger Jr. grocery store, optical illusions and a Bubble Room. What is a Fantasmagraph? Make your own Zoetrope. Model trains run every Sunday afternoon. Otherwise, there are push buttons to start different trains in motion. "Neat!" was the kids' reaction.

CLARKSVILLE SPEEDWAY

1600 Needmore Road

Clarksville 37041

- ❑ Phone: (931) 645-2523
- ❑ Hours: Saturday nights (April-November).
- ❑ Admission: $12-$25.00.

1/8 mile Drag Races for street cars and motorcycles. 1/4 mile high bank clay oval track for mini, street, prostreet, UMP openwheel & late model cars. Go-cart race track for all ages. Fences park area for children.

CUMBERLAND RIVERWALK & "AS THE RIVER FLOWS" EXHIBIT

McGregor Park, Riverside Drive

Clarksville 37041

❑   Phone: (931) 645-7476

❑   Hours: Daylight hours for park. Daily 8:00am-5:00pm (Center).
Extended hours (April-October) until 8:00pm.

❑   Admission: FREE

The riverfront promenade includes an amphitheater, overlooks, a playground, picnic areas, a boating ramp, etc. The RiverCenter has a permanent exhibit featuring a chronological display with mural map showing the settlement of the town (1780-1784) and 12 display panels showing the history of the Cumberland River from 15,000 BC to present day. What crop did they send along the river (called Black Patch)? Most families like to walk the Riverwalk & picnic on nice days, enjoying the modern amenities the river offers.

DUNBAR CAVE STATE NATURAL AREA

401 Old Dunbar Cave Road

Clarksville 37041

❑   Phone: (931) 648-5526

❑   Hours: Daily 8:00am-Dark. Visitors Center 8:00am-4:30pm.

This 110-acre park has a cave and surrounding mineral springs (once a resort in the early 1900s). In the 1930s and 40s, the huge cave served as a naturally air-conditioned venue for Big Bands and was once owned by country music legend, Roy Acuff. Picnic areas, hiking and fishing are popular as are occasional guided cave tours along with a historical slide show.

L & N TRAIN STATION

Commerce & 10th Streets

Clarksville 37041

❑   Phone: (931) 553-2486

❑   Hours: Tuesday, Thursday & Saturday 9:00am-1:00pm.

❑   Admission: $1.00

HISTORIC COLLINSVILLE

4711 Weakley Road (SR 13S to Rte. 48S, east of Southside Rd, follow signs)

Clarksville (Southside) 37171

❑ Phone: (931) 648-9141. **Web: www.historiccollinsville.com**
❑ Hours: Thursday - Sunday 1:00-5:00pm (mid-May to mid-October).
❑ Admission: $4.00 general (age 5+), $5.00-$10.00 special events.
❑ Miscellaneous: Picnic areas and walking trails. Seasonal events like old-fashioned jubilees and Pioneer Days Open House and food each quarter.

A self-guided tour of a living-history museum featuring 16 restored log homes and outbuildings on 40 acres. The structures date from 1830 to 1870 with authentic furnishings. Indians once traveled this land, soldiers of the North and South once met here, and, cotton and sheep were raised by the early settlers and then transported down the Cumberland River. Stop by the Judge's home to see a Black Hawk Corn Sheller invented by Mr. Patch of Clarksville. Kids will gravitate to the Wildwood School and Church structure. See a Teacher's portable Library and try some lessons. In the Dogtrot House, look for an early baby walker and a bench that's also a cradle and table. A new Wildlife center displays historic animals of Tennessee and the world. See a mountain lion, elk, river otters and beaver in surroundings similar to the 1800s. Living history weekends really bring the village to life.

JAMES K POLK HOME

301-305 W. Seventh Street (I-65 exit 46, US 412 to US 31south. One block west of US 31)

Columbia 38401

❑ Phone: (931) 388-2354. **Web: www.jameskpolk.com**
❑ Hours: Monday-Saturday 9:00am-4:00pm, Sunday 1:00-5:00pm. Open until 5:00pm (April-October).
❑ Admission: $5.00 adult, $4.00 senior, $2.00 child (6-college age).

The James K. Polk Ancestral Home is the only surviving residence of the eleventh U.S. President (excluding the White House). Samuel Polk, a prosperous farmer and surveyor, built the brick house in 1816 while his oldest son James was attending the University of North Carolina. When the future President graduated in 1818, he returned to Tennessee and stayed with his parents until his marriage in 1824. While living in his family's Columbia home, James practiced law and began his political career by successfully running for the State Legislature. Today, the Home displays original items from James K. Polk's years in Tennessee and Washington, D.C. including furniture, paintings, and White House china. Polk's Sisters Homes and detached kitchen building are part of the tour (including intro video). Visitors to the kitchen see period cooking implements and household accessories. Demonstrations of early 19th century crafts and chores are presented here occasionally.

RENAISSANCE CENTER

855 Hwy 46S

Dickson 37055

❑   Phone: (615) 446-4450. **Web: www.rcenter.org**
❑   Hours: Monday-Saturday 9:00am-9:00pm.

Multi-faceted center with a planetarium & laser light shows, educational theater, science theater and hands-on classes. Training/shows in 3D multi-media is their specialty.

CROSS CREEKS NATIONAL WILDLIFE REFUGE

Route 1, Box 556 (3 miles east of town off Hwy 49)

Dover 37058

❑   Phone: (615) 232-7477
     http://gorp.away.com/gorp/resource/us_nwr/tn_cross.htm
❑   Hours: Refuge: Monday-Friday 7:00am-5:00pm, Saturday 9:00am-
     5:00pm (March-October). Visitors Center open year round.

Recreational opportunities on the refuge include public fishing, a limited hunting season, wildlife observation, photography, nature study, boating, and mushroom, berry and grape picking. Bicycling and horseback riding are also permitted on established roads during open periods. During the winter months, a foot trail and nature drive are available and the visitors center always offers wildlife exhibits and audio-visual programs.

FORT DONELSON NATIONAL MILITARY PARK

(I-24 north, then US 79 west - off Hwy 79), **Dover** 37058

❑   Phone: (931) 232-5706. **Web: www.nps.gov/fodo/**
❑   Hours: Daily 8:00am-4:30pm. Closed Christmas. Dover Hotel only open Noon-4:00pm in the summer.
❑   Admission: FREE

Fort Donelson interprets a crucial Civil War battle in which General U.S. Grant first gained fame. This is the site of the first major Union victory during the War. Accessible by a six-mile self-guided tour, you can see the earthen fort, river batteries, outer earthworks, the Dover Hotel (Surrender House) and the National Cemetery. Use the brochure as a guide and consider an optional cassette tour tape. Attend park programs and presentations. Hike the park trails. Stand at the cannon emplacements on the Cumberland River Bluff and imagine the bombardment of gunboats below. Find out why the Federals threw away their coats and blankets when a snowstorm was coming.

LAND BETWEEN THE LAKES NATIONAL RECREATION AREA

(north of US 79 between Dover & the Tennessee River)

Dover 37058

❑   Phone: (270) 924-2000 or (270) 924-2020. **Web: www.lbl.org**
❑   Hours: Central Time. Specific hours vary depending on facility.
❑   Admission: FREE, except for specific sites with admission fees.

Rediscover the simple pleasures of playing in the outdoors. Located in Western Kentucky and Tennessee, LBL offers 170,000 acres of wildlife, history, and outdoor recreation opportunities, wrapped by 300 miles of undeveloped shoreline. In Tennessee, there are opportunities to boat, fish, camp and hike or bike trails. Also, near the Kentucky border, THE HOMEPLACE serves as a living history farm of 1850. The farm re-creates daily activities of a typical rural family living near the river. Interpreters are dressed in period clothing and talk to guests while doing chores. The complex is formed of 16 buildings (many original), an interpretive center with exhibits/video, and many seasonal festivals. (Daily, April-October; closed Monday & Tuesday, November and March. Hours: Monday-Saturday 9:00am-5:00pm, Sunday 10:00am-5:00pm. Admission: $2.00-$3.50).

UNCLE CHARLIE'S OLD AMISH VILLAGE

1016 Brewer Road (US 43 & Brewer Road - just north of Lawrenceburg), **Ethridge** 38456

❑   Phone: (931) 829-4060. **Web: www.tennesseeamish.com**
❑   Hours: Daily except Sunday 9:00am-5:00pm.
❑   Admission: Amish Farm $5.00 adult, $4.00 child (4-12).
❑   Tours: Wagon or buggy rides last 1-1 1/2 hours (daily, except Sunday, 10:00am-4:00pm). $10.00 adult, $5.00 child (4-12).
Reservations please. Be sure to ask about rules regarding cameras.

Uncle Charlie's Old Amish Village showcases the history and lifestyle of the largest old order Amish settlement in the South. The first original settlement in the county began in 1944. Today, there are over 160 Amish families actively involved in farming. Visitors can take a seven-mile wagon ride and farm tour on a fleet of Belgian Draft Horses. See farming done the "old fashioned" way, with horse-drawn farm equipment, wagons and buggies. It's amazing to watch them gather hay out in the fields - mile high. What is the most unique & wonderful part is that you stop at several farms and "park" the wagon to visit on their front porches! Look over and purchase the homemade wares they have for sale. You will get to know what these "plain-folk" and their "simple" ways are all about. Find out why they allow no autos or tractors, have no electricity or telephones, and shun modern conveniences. Back at the homestead are a dozen original buildings on the "Old Amish Farm" with farm animals that you can see close-up. It's set up as if an Amish family just left. Must see!

CARNTON PLANTATION

1345 Carnton Lane (I-65 S exit 65, turn right, go to Mack Hatcher Pkwy, left, turn right on Hwy 431)

Franklin 37064

- ❑ Phone: (615) 794-0903. **Web: www.carnton.org**
- ❑ Hours: Monday - Saturday 9:00am-5:00pm, Sunday 1:00-5:00pm. Last tour one hour before closing.
- ❑ Admission: $8.00 adult, $7.00 senior, $3.00 child (under 12).

Late in the afternoon on November 30, 1864, the plantation was at the center of one of the largest and deadliest battles of the War Between the States. Over 20,000 members of the Confederate Army of Tennessee repeatedly charged the entrenched Union troops in a battle to take Franklin. The McGovack plantation house soon came into service as a hospital and when the house was filled, the dead and wounded were tended to in the surrounding yard. Numerous blood stains are still visible, especially on the porch.

CARTER HOUSE & FRANKLIN CIVIL WAR MUSEUM

1140 Columbia Avenue (I-65 exit 65, Hwy 96 west)

Franklin 37064

- ❑ Phone: (615) 791-1861. **Web: www.carter-house.org**
- ❑ Hours: Monday-Saturday 9:00am-4:00pm.
- ❑ Admission: $8.00 adult, $6.00 senior (65+), $3.00 child (7-13).
- ❑ Miscellaneous: Military Summer Camps, Girls 1800s Summer Camp.

During the November 1864 Battle of Franklin, it was used as a Federal Command Post by General Jacob D. Cox. During the battle, the Carter family hid in the cellar, avoiding the crossfire from the Union and Confederate forces that heavily damaged the house and surrounding buildings. You actually walk down into the cellar/family room to see where they fearfully hid. One of the Carter boys, however, Captain Tod Carter, was killed during the battle, along with over 2,000 Federal and 6,000 Confederate forces. Evidence of the battle is still noticeable today, as innumerable bullet holes still scar the house and other structures. Feel the bullet hole in the porch and hear the story about the soldier it nearly hit. Then go inside and see the blood stains in the corner. Why is the spindle in the upper staircase upside down? Your guided tour includes a video presentation, the house and the Franklin Civil War Museum.

BLEDSOE CREEK STATE PARK

400 Ziegler's Fort Road (Hwy. 25 East at the intersection of 31-E and 25 East), **Gallatin** 37066

❑   Phone: (615) 452-3706
     Web: www.state.tn.us/environment/parks/bledsoe/
❑   Hours: 7:00am-sunset.

Situated on the Bledsoe Creek embankment, the park provides hiking trails and boating, skiing and fishing on Old Hickory Lake. Many historical sites are nearby.

MANSKER'S STATION, HISTORIC FRONTIER LIFE CENTER

705 Caldwell Lane, Moss Wright Park (I-65 to exit 97, Goodlettsville/Longhollow Pike, east)

Goodlettsville 37072

❑   Phone: (615) 859-3678
     Web: www.southernrangers.org/manskers
❑   Hours: Monday-Saturday 9:00am-5:00pm, Sunday 1:00-5:00pm.
❑   Admission: $5.00 adult, $3.00 student. Includes Bowen
     Plantation tour. Last tour (6-12) departs at 4:00pm.
❑   Miscellaneous: The first weekend in May the fort site comes
     alive with the 18th Century Colonial Fair.

An authentic reconstruction of the 1779 frontier forted station typical of Kasper Mansker's first fort. Masker's Fort allows you to experience the lifestyle of early settlers in the 18th century. The Life Center tour includes a video (starts with a screaming Indian) to set the mood - could you survive? Through "living history" demonstrations (mostly in first person), you can touch the hand-hewn timbers, hear the steady click of the spinning wheel, see the blacksmith work, and smell the smoke of the cook fires. Help make a fire (borrow a tinderbox) or pretend your family is staying in one of the family cabins. The <u>BOWEN PLANTATION HOUSE</u> - area's earliest residence and region's oldest brick structure, help make shortbread (yummy, try some) or beaten biscuits (kids can beat the dough 500 times!) or pretend you're having tea in the parlor.

MUSIC CITY RACEWAY

3302 Ivy Point Road (track: Music City Raceway)

Goodlettsville 37072

❑   Phone: (615) 264-0375. **Web: www.musiccityraceway.com**

Long-time NHRA championship drag racing with their season running March-November on Tuesday, Friday and Saturday nights. Admission varies but children 12 and under are FREE.

OLD HICKORY LAKE VISITOR CENTER

Rockland Road, 5 Power Plant Road (I-65N exit 96, Rte. 386E, right on Conference Dr, left on 31E to Rockland Rec Area)

Hendersonville 37075

❑   Phone: (615) 822-4846
❑   Hours: Most days, 10:00am-4:00pm.

Old Hickory Lake Visitor Center offers an interactive history of the lake and the navigational lock and dam system, operated by the US Army Corps of Engineers. Museum-style displays, playground, beach (Rte. 2) and picnic sites are also available.

ROCK CASTLE

139 Rock Castle Lane (south of Gallatin Road, Rte. 31 on Indian Lake Road, turn right)

Hendersonville 37075

❑   Phone: (615) 824-0502. **Web: www.historicrockcastle.cjb.net**
❑   Hours: Tuesday-Saturday (March-December)
❑   Admission: $5.00 adult, $4.00 senior, $3.00 child (6-12).

General Daniel and Sarah Smith's 1794 home is built of limestone (first rock structure in Tennessee) and furnished with period antiques and walnut woodwork. The Family Bible, private letters, and Daniel Smith's library of over two hundred books, are in the collection here. The general acted as surveyor for this frontier, produced the state's first map and is credited with naming the state of Tennessee. Summer Kid Day Camps.

TRINITY MUSIC CITY USA

One Music Village Blvd. (I-65N to SR 386 exit, then to exit 8, take 2 rights), **Hendersonville** 37075

❑   Phone: (615) 826-9191. **Web: www.tbn.org**
❑   Hours: Monday-Saturday, 10:00am-6:00pm. Summer holidays & Sundays 1:00-6:00pm. Closed Thanksgiving, Christmas & New Years.
❑   Admission: FREE
❑   Tours: 11:45am & 2:45pm Monday -Saturday. Sunday at 2:45pm.
❑   Miscellaneous: Mention to the gift shop staff that you read about this site in <u>Kids Love Tennessee</u>, and receive a "HAPPY PACK" FREE fun pack.

Start with a grounds tour or the Virtual Reality Theatre, but, be sure to do both! In the theatre, you'll first see a short intro video about the complex and Conway Twitty's origins here (before it became Trinity). Then, walk down the recreated streets of Jerusalem to the Virtual Reality Theatre where you'll view a 1 hour motion picture production of "The Revolutionary" (walk the streets with Jesus) or "The Emissary" (exciting events from the book of Acts). At times, you'll hear sound from all directions and even feel your seats rumble. It's very engaging! Twice daily, tours include the original estate of Conway Twitty of country music fame (love all the royal blue velvet). Then, walk through a recording studio used by many famous Christian artists. See the large mixing boards and separate rooms for vocals and each instrument played. Now, check out the WPGD TV studios and theatre. See the various sets and stages used for regular programming like "Praise the Lord" or "Swan's Place". Look out for the boom cameras lurking about.

What fun to see a motion picture, a recording studio and a TV station…all for FREE!

LEWIS COUNTY MUSEUM OF NATURAL & LOCAL HISTORY

108 East Main Street

Hohenwald 38462

❑   Phone: (931) 796-1550
❑   Hours: Monday-Saturday 10:00am-4:00pm, Sunday 1:00-4:00pm.
❑   Admission: $2.00 adult, $0.50 child.

There are over 120 specimens of rare and exotic animal trophy mounts at the Lewis County Museum of Natural and Local History. One of the largest collections of wild animal mounts in the Western Hemisphere. You can admire tiny dik-diks and giant elands, the smallest and largest of the antelope family. You can see an elephant's tail used as a fly swatter, and you can walk through a doorway framed with a pair of seven feet long ivory tusks. You can wander down aisles and gaze upon hartebeest, gazelle, oryx, nyala, gnu, bushbusk, kudu, the elusive bongo, and water and cape buffalo. The museum also contains displays on Lewis County's history beginning with early Indian artifacts and Meriwether Lewis' untimely death on the Natchez Trace in 1809. You can enter a log cabin replica and see how early country folk lived. Other displays recall the Swiss and German settlements of the 1890's, iron ore and phosphate mining ventures, Civil War relics, and 125 bird and snake eggs from around the world.

NATCHEZ TRACE PARKWAY HISTORIC SITES

(stretching from SW Nashville to the TN/AL border & further into MS)

Hohenwald 38462

❑   Phone: (800) 305-7417 Information, (931) 796-7264 Farmstead
     Web: www.nps.gov/natr/

The 444-mile Natchez Trace Parkway commemorates an ancient trail that connected southern portions of the Mississippi River to salt licks in today's central Tennessee. Over the centuries, the Choctaw, Chickasaw and other American Indians have left their mark on the Trace. Today, visitors can experience this All-American Road through hiking, biking, horseback riding and camping. BLACKBURN FARMSTEAD & PIONEER MUSEUM - US Hwy 412, Mile Marker 391. Open most weekends April-November. Circa 1810 log buildings. The first Lewis County Court met in this historic house until the first courthouse was built. The grand jury is said to have convened in the log corn crib still standing behind the house. Both buildings are listed on the National Register of Historic Places. Various artifacts from the pioneer days and Native American artifacts found nearby are on display. MERIWETHER LEWIS NATIONAL MONUMENT - Pkwy and Hwy 20. Site of the mysterious death and grave of American explorer Merimether Lewis, one of the leaders of the Lewis & Clark Expedition along the Missouri River. The surrounding park contains a display on Lewis. Also hiking trails, picnic areas and a campground. FREE. BAKER'S BLUFF - near Shady Grove (931) 729-5774. Scenic view overlooking the Duck River and farmlands. THE GORDON HOUSE - near Shady Grove built around 1817 by Capt. John Gordon, a prominent early settler who was also acclaimed as a fearless spy. JACKSON FALLS - Shady Grove historic rest stop with large spring and waterfalls that made for a good camping site for troops (even Andrew Jackson, for whom the falls were named).

LORETTA LYNN'S RANCH MUSEUM & CAMPGROUND

44 Hurricane Mills Road (I-40 exit 143, Hwy 13 North)

Hurricane Mills 37078

❑   Phone: (931) 296-1840. **Web: www.lorettalynn.com**
❑   Hours: Daily 9:00am-5:00pm (April-October).
❑   Admission: $10.00 adult, $5.00 child.

The ranch offers tours of Loretta's plantation home and Coal Miner's Daughter Museum, as well as horseback riding, swimming and canoeing. Visiting this complex, you'll see a complete history of her life, including displays honoring her family, home life, ranch life and musical career. Walk through her tour bus and see the 1977 Cadillac she loved to write hit songs in while driving on tour. See some of her original song sheets on notebook paper or her first homemade dress to perform in. Glimpse inside detailed replicas of her first Nashville home with original furnishings and the little one-room schoolhouse she attended in the hills of Kentucky. She has even scattered hand-written notes in many displays putting the artifact descriptions in "her own words". Loretta Lynn's Family Campground features Boone Hill Cabins and Stagecoach Hill Log Cabins, plus tent and RV camping sites. Westerntown has shops and snacks. Tours of the Plantation home, Butcher Holler House and Coal Mine are a neat glimpse into Loretta's life before and after fame.

DAVID CROCKETT STATE PARK

1400 West Gaines (west of the city on US 64)

Lawrenceburg 38464

❑   Phone: (931) 762-9408

   Web: www.state.tn.us/environment/parks/davidsp/

❑   Hours: Daily 7:00am-Dark (park). Museum: 10:00am-5:00pm
      (Memorial Day-Labor Day).

In 1817, the infamous Davy Crockett moved to Lawrence County and served as a justice of the peace, a colonel of the militia, and as state representative. Along the banks of Shoal Creek, he established a diversified industry consisting of a powdermill, a gristmill and a distillery. Financial difficulties from a flood in 1821 caused Crockett to move to West Tennessee where he was elected to Congress. Crockett died at the Alamo Mission while aiding the Texans in their fight for independence from Mexico. The park museum exhibits depict the life and times of Crockett as a pioneer, soldier, politician and industrialist. A park naturalist and recreation director are on duty throughout the summer months. Both provide a variety of planned activities and programs including guided tours, organized games, arts and crafts, historical demonstrations and presentations, campfires, movies, slide shows, hayrides and the

Tennessee Valley Jamboree every summer Friday night. The restaurant overlooks 40-acre scenic Lake Lindsey and features home-style cooking served up buffet style. Other activities: camping, fishing, boating, biking & hiking. An olympic-sized swimming pool with a bathhouse and concession stand and lifeguards on duty is open from Memorial Day until late summer.

VAUGHAN MEMORIAL MUSEUM, JAMES D.

2nd Floor, Sun Trust Bank, Public Square

Lawrenceburg 38464

❑ Phone: (931) 762-8991

James D. Vaughan was the founder of Southern Gospel music, owner of Tennessee's first radio station, music publisher, and taught the South how to sing with the renowned Vaughan School of Music. Beginning in 1911, Vaughan began holding a regular music "normal" school in Lawrenceburg to train "shape-note-singing" school instructors. The United States Congress has declared and recognized Lawrenceburg, Tennessee as the Birthplace of Southern Gospel Music. This museum highlights Vaughan and his contemporaries. FREE. Open during building business hours.

CRACKER BARREL HEADQUARTERS

305 Hartman Drive (I-40 , Exit# 238, US 231 to W. Main St, north on Hartman), **Lebanon** 37087

❑ Phone: (615) 444-5533 (ext Décor Warehouse)
   Web: www.crackerbarrel.com
❑ Admission: FREE
❑ Tours: Tuesday & Thursday, group tours (6 or more people). Ask to be part of another tour if your family has less than 6 people.

Original site for the old-time restaurant chain established in 1969. Cracker Barrel combines country home-cooking with antique shopping in the country store. Tour the antiques warehouse...the place they put together the design of the store furnishings (unique antiques, signs, etc). All items are real antiques! No reproductions. What theme is best for an area? They figure out what the town's known for and work around that (ex. Famous people, music, craft or industry). Parents love the organization in here! Kids will search for old-fashioned toys. Everything gets a bath and then clear coat or refinished/restored when it is brought to the warehouse. Look for the Cracker Barrel Barbie and old, valuable Coca-Cola signs.

FIDDLERS GROVE HISTORIC VILLAGE

945 Baddour Pkwy, James E. Ward Agricultural Center (I-40 east to the 239B exit)

Lebanon 37087

❑   Phone: (615) 443-2626

   Web: www.wilsoncountytn.com/ag_center.htm

❑   Hours: Daily 10:00am-3:00pm (May-October)

❑   Admission: Guided tours, $5.00 adult, $3.00 senior and child.

❑   Tours: Highly recommend taking the guided tours - so many stories to hear. Maybe during the Wilson County Fair (mid-August).

❑   Miscellaneous: May we recommend the Country Inn & Suites (I-40 & US 231) at 615-470-1001. Full continental breakfast, warm indoor pool & jacuzzi, reasonable rates, and a refrigerator and microwave in every room.

Village of more than 40 structures, original and replicated, with local historical significance. Witness what life was like in the 1800's for a resident of Wilson County. Sit in a chair in the schoolhouse, peak in the sheriff's office and old jail. See Sam Houston's house or a slave family's first home. Self guided and guided tours available.

LEBANON MUSEUM AND HISTORY CENTER

200 Castle Heights Avenue N. (lower entrance of the City of Lebanon Administration Building) (off I-40, US 231N, left on Main St., right into Castle Heights)

Lebanon 37087

❑   Phone: (615) 443-2839. **Web: www.lebanontn.org**

❑   Hours: Monday-Friday 8:00am-4:00pm.

For updates visit our website: www.kidslovepublications.com

Walk through the history of Lebanon from prehistoric to modern times. Audio descriptions by famous residents introduce visitors to the periods on display and take advantage of the touch-screen computers for your own research. Start with fossils from town - can you guess what the bones come from? Learn about slaves during and after the war. Look for kids items like the Tank Bank. General Patton trained maneuvers here. You can arrange a tour of Sellars Mound from this site. As you round the square, on your way to the museum, take note of the 1800 Neddy Jacobs log cabin.

CEDARS OF LEBANON STATE PARK

328 Cedar Forest Road (6 miles south of I-40 on U.S. Highway 231/SR 10)

Lebanon 37090

❑   Phone: (615) 443-2769 or (800) 713-5180 cabins
     Web: www.state.tn.us/environment/parks/cedars/
❑   Hours: Summer 8:00am-10:00pm, Winter 8:00am-8:00pm.
❑   Admission: $3.00 per vehicle, per day rate.

Cedars of Lebanon State Park is named for the dense cedar forest that existed in the Biblical lands of Lebanon. 831 acres are open to the public with a variety of recreational activities such as hiking, an Olympic-plus size swimming pool, playground, horseshoe pits, softball field, volleyball courts, and tennis courts. Cedars of Lebanon has nine modern, two-bedroom cabins that can sleep up to six people. In April, look for over 20 native wildflowers, which can be seen in the cedar glades during the annual wildflower tours.

NASHVILLE SUPERSPEEDWAY

4874-F McCrary Road

Lebanon 37090

❑   Phone: (615) 726-1818
     Web: www.nashvillesuperspeedway.com

The 1.33- mile "D" oval hosts major NASCAR and Indy events. A special alcohol & tobacco free grandstand area is perfect for making race day a real family outing. Events sell out early, so be prepared.

MOUSETAIL LANDING STATE PARK

Rte. 3, box 280B (I-40 west to exit 143, Hwy 13S for 9 miles. Right on Hwy 438 for 25 miles)

Linden 37096

❑ Phone: (731) 847-0841

Web: www.state.tn.us/environment/parks/mouse/

❑ Hours: Park, 7:00am-10:00pm. Office/Center, 8:00am-4:30pm.

❑ Admission: FREE

Located on the east banks of the Tennessee River, the park office serves as a museum/interpretive center. Exhibits include a snake skin, stuffed beaver, owl, hawk, turkey, duck and a goose. There is an Indian artifact collection and other area artifacts. The scenic Buffalo River flows nearby, providing opportunity for family canoe float trips. A swimming beach and a small stream at the entrance of the park are enjoyable for small children and adults to wade in with its cold, clear water. Also picnic areas, playgrounds, fishing and boating.

LYNNVILLE RAILROAD MUSEUM

1722 Main Street (I-65 exit 27, Rte. 129 or Rte. 31N, turn right on Rte. 129), **Lynnville** 38472

❑ Phone: (931) 527-3700

Web: www.lynnvillerailroad.com/museum.php

❑ Hours: Wednesday-Saturday 10:00am-4:00pm (May-October).

Inside, a telegrapher sits at his post, keying a message to the station down the line. The conductor stands at the window, watch in hand, mindful of his schedule. An operating HO scale model railroad depicts Lynnville as it was in the 1930's. Enjoy the comforts of a vintage passenger coach, in the original seats, and watch a video on present day operating steam & diesel tourist railroads. The Milky Way Farms Museum, contained in a vintage passenger coach of a restored steam locomotive, details some memories of the candy giant and his enormous farm nearby. Sit in the engineer's seat, grab the levers, blow the whistle and clang the bell. Stop by the restored Lynnville Pharmacy, Soda Pop Junction, built in 1860, and order a soft drink from the circa 1940 soda fountain.

CANNONSBURGH VILLAGE

312 South Front Street (I-24 exit 78B, turn right on Broad Street)

Murfreesboro 37130

❑   Phone: (615) 890-0355

   Web: www.johnsonfolks.com/cburg.htm

❑   Hours: Tuesday-Saturday 10:00am-5:00pm, Sunday 1:00-5:00pm (May-November).

❑   Tours: Free admission for self-guided tours. Fee charged for guided tours. Open Year-round with seasonal change in times.

Since Murfreesboro's original name was Cannonsburgh, it seems appropriate that this collection of buildings in downtown Murfreesboro should again pay tribute to Minos Cannon, a prominent early settler. Particularly notable, is the 2000 gallon red cedar bucket which was made in Murfreesboro in 1887, where it represents the industrial past of the area. There's also a one-room schoolhouse, chapel, gristmill, blacksmith and doctor's office (back when they made house calls). The most interesting buildings are the old Leeman house (check out the Newspaper insulation/wallpaper) and the General Store (look for the original cash register). Best to visit during seasonal festivals when there is activity in the village.

DISCOVERY CENTER AT MURFREE SPRING

502 Southeast Broad Street (I-24 exit 81B)

Murfreesboro 37130

❑   Phone: (615) 890-2300. **Web: www.discoverycenteronline.org**

❑   Hours: Monday-Saturday 10:00am-5:00pm. Closed major holidays.

❑   Admission: $5.00 adult, $4.00 child (18 & under).

The new facility has 15 permanent, indoor exhibit areas plus 20 acres of wetland habitat (our favorite area). Accessible by boardwalks, the habitat has interpretive signs with weekly guided walks and studies. Look for the giant carp and large beaver dams. Inside, play with simple machines, fly an airplane or climb on a real firetruck, visit an International Bazaar, or relive history. The Family Playspace (age 5 & under w/ care-givers) includes a giant "climb-in-and-around" tree, a country cottage for family role play, a farmer's market place, and an infant PlayPond. Neat, unique exhibits included Body Sculpture and Simple Machines (move the heavy bowling ball with teamwork and simple gizmos).

STONES RIVER NATIONAL BATTLEFIELD/ FORTRESS ROSECRANS

3501 Old Nashville Hwy. (Hwy 41/70 north to Thompson Lane)

Murfreesboro 37133

- ❑   Phone: (615) 893-9501. **Web: www.nps.gov/stri/**
- ❑   Hours: Daily 8:00am-5:00pm. Closed Christmas.
- ❑   Admission: FREE
- ❑   Miscellaneous: From late May through mid-November ranger walks and talks are presented daily. On summer, and occasional spring and fall weekends, living history programs are presented. A spur connector to the Greenway System bike/hike trail is open during daylight hours.

A fierce battle took place at Stones River between December 31, 1862 and January 2, 1863. General Bragg's Confederates withdrew after the battle, allowing General Rosecrans and the Union army to control middle Tennessee. This was the bloodiest Civil War battle in the state. Portions of Fortress Rosecrans, a large earthen Union fort constructed after the battle, still stand. A Visitor center contains a small museum and very detailed video program about the battle. The battlefield may be toured by car or foot along a loop tour road. Best for students interested in battle strategies.

DOWNTOWN NASHVILLE ON BROADWAY
Nashville 37201

❑   Phone: (615) 256-2805

Some sites of interest include:

❑   HATCH SHOW PRINT: The Hatch Brothers started in 1870
        and still continues to use the same techniques employed in the
        15th century. Hatch has always been a leading poster printer for
        circuses and best known for posters of Grand Ole Opry stars.
        Visit the shop, watch them prepare a typical poster and, if you
        like what you've seen, pick out your own piece of Hatch Show
        tradition.

❑   TENNESSEE FOX TROT CAROUSEL: (end of Broadway @
        Riverfront Park), $2.00/ride, weather permitting. This whimsical
        carousel was designed so that each sculpture represents someone
        or something of local fame. For example, Chet Atkins, President
        Andrew Jackson, Davy Crockett or Olympian Wilma Rudolph.

❑   ERNEST TUBBS RECORD SHOP: famous posters and
        pictures of many who performed here and were discovered (ex.
        Loretta Lynn, Alan Jackson).

❑   COUNTRY MUSIC CLUBS: many open in the daytime and
        evenings where you can hear acts and grab a bite to eat.

PARTHENON, THE
2600 West End Avenue (Centennial Park)

Nashville 37201

❑   Phone: (615) 862-8431. **Web: www.parthenon.org**
❑   Hours: Tuesday-Saturday 9:00am-4:30pm. Sundays 12:30-
        4:30pm (April-September only).
❑   Admission: $2.00-$3.50 (age 4+).

Completely gold-plated in 2002, the grey-eyed goddess Athena
Parthenos stands 42 feet tall in the Parthenon. The goddess' floor-
length robe, helmet, shield, spear and the statue perched in her hand
are dressed with gold touches. The process of applying little sheets
of gold leaf paper (after Athena was iced down) is interesting to
learn. This is the tallest indoor sculpture in the Western world.

WILDHORSE SALOON

120 Second Avenue North (I-40 Broadway exit east, left on
Second), **Nashville** 37201

❑   Phone: (615) 902-8200. **Web: www.wildhorsesaloon.com**

The Wildhorse is Nashville's premiere country music dance and
dining club. The Wildhorse opens daily at 11:00am, serves a full menu
until midnight, and offers live entertainment beginning at 7:00pm.
Often, stars or, "soon-to-be" stars perform (check their website for
show schedules) while you enjoy dessert. After a satisfying meal, step
onto the dance floor and work it off! Free dance lessons are offered
daily (7:00-9:00pm weekdays, 2:00-9:00pm weekends). That's why
anyone who visits the Wildhorse can't help but join in the dancing.
Entrees range from around $16.00, ($4.00/kids menu). We
recommend the steak!

ADVENTURE SCIENCE CENTER

800 Fort Negley Blvd. (I-40 exit 210C or I-65 exit 81, follow signs
toward stadium), **Nashville** 37203

❑   Phone: (615) 862-5160. **Web: www.adventuresci.com**
❑   Hours: Monday-Saturday 10:00am-5:00pm. Sunday 12:30-
       5:30pm. Closed Monday from Labor Day to Memorial Day.
       Closed on Easter, Thanksgiving, Christmas Day & New Years Day
❑   Admission: $8.75 adult, $6.75 senior (60+) & child (3-12).
       Planetarium, extra $2.00.
❑   Miscellaneous: Planetarium shows throughout the day.

Climb the Adventure Tower - all seven levels! Power an elevator
by bicycling, lift a car off the ground using a fulcrum, then climb
through the roof inside the Adventure Tower's giant glass pyramid.
Here, they're not just learning science concepts; they're applying
them and having fun. Design parachutes and launch air rockets. In
Mission Possible, enable a disabled person in a wheelchair by
trying to use a wheelchair yourself to do simple tasks. Be a
construction worker building a city. Stand inside the body of a
giant guitar, pluck the strings and FEEL the vibration. Where else
but Music City, USA, could you do this and get the best view of
town…all, in one tower?

COUNTRY MUSIC HALL OF FAME AND MUSEUM

222 5th Avenue S (I-65 exit 209B, Broadway), **Nashville** 37203

❑   Phone: (615) 416-2096 or (800) 852-6437
     Web: www.countrymusichalloffame.com
❑   Hours: Daily 9:00am-5:00pm. Closed Thanksgiving, Christmas
     and New Years. Closed Tuesday (January-March)
❑   Admission: $12.95 adult, $7.95 child (6-17).
❑   Tours: Tours of RCA's Studio B are available thru packages that
     include a bus tour of Music Row. Tours depart from the Country
     Music Hall of Fame and Museum, 10:00am - 2:30pm. (additional
     $10-12.00 per person for package). We highly recommend this
     add-on!
❑   Miscellaneous: SoBro Grill - southern style lunch menu. Music
     Store, Demonstration Gallery and live performances most days.

Hear and see how country music has evolved. Once inside, an enormous two-story Wall of Gold Records is cased so that you can listen to the words and tunes that have earned these recording artists' fame. See rare costumes (Dale Evans & Roy Rogers original boots), instruments (Elvis' gold piano or Mother Maybelle Carter's Gibson guitar) and artifacts (like Elvis' solid gold Cadillac or Minnie Pearl's straw hat (w/ price tag of $1.98). Kids love the cowboy convertible. Nearby, sit down and laugh a spell watching old Hee Haw shows. Through video, you hear Garth Brooks talk about George Jones or Tim McGraw talk about life on the road. Favorite country songs are played everywhere. With touch-screen computer stations, visitors can design costumes, ask songwriters and stars programmed questions, learn country dancing, select and view a video clip, visit a star's web site or create you own CD of country music classics to take home. Kids absolutely love Styles on Stage for Kids. Imagine designing and modeling Alan Jackson for a concert! RCA'S STUDIO B - the museum has returned the interior and exterior to their look during the glory days when Chet Atkins ran the studio. The oldest recording studio in Nashville, it helped form the "Nashville Sound" in the 1960's. Some of the famous hits recorded: Elvis' "It's Now or Never" and "Are You

Lonesome Tonight?"; Roy Orbison's "Only the Lonely", the Everly Brothers "All I Have to Do is Dream" and Dolly Parton's "Jolene". You actually see, touch and hear the instruments and microphones used by the stars! The studio tour includes a detailed commentary of Music Row sites you pass en route.

FRIST CENTER FOR THE VISUAL ARTS

919 Broadway (I-40W or I-65N exit 209B, turn right on Demonbreun Street, traveling toward downtown)

Nashville 37203

- ❑ Phone: (615) 244-3340 **Web: www.fristcenter.org**
- ❑ Hours: Monday-Saturday 10:00am-5:30pm, Thursday until 8:00pm, Sunday 1:00-5:00pm. Closed major winter holidays.
- ❑ Admission: $8.50 adult, $7.50 senior (65+) and college students. Children FREE (18 & under).
- ❑ Tours: Docent-led tours of featured exhibitions are offered at 1:30pm, Monday – Thursday, and 2:00pm Saturdays and Sundays. There are additional guided tours offered at 6:30pm Thursday evenings and 11:00am Saturday mornings.

The old downtown post office was converted into this art deco of rotating exhibits from around the world. Fun for kids is located in the second-floor ArtQuest Gallery, featuring 30 art stations where visitors can design their own exhibit, make art or play with visual concepts after they've been inspired by the works currently on exhibit…and, items in everyday life and culture. Then, they can take their artwork home. (best for students 4th grade and up, who have been exposed to some artistic concepts)

NASHVILLE PREDATORS HOCKEY

501 Broadway (Gaylord Entertainment Center)

Nashville 37203

- ❑ Phone: (615) 770-2300 or (615) 770-PUCK tickets
  Web: www.nashvillepredators.com

Hard-hitting, fast-action NHL Hockey with their regular season running October-April. Evening games begin at 7:00pm, home afternoon games begin at 2:00pm.

For updates visit our website: www.kidslovepublications.com

NASHVILLE SOUNDS BASEBALL

534 Chestnut Street (Home Field: Greer Stadium)

Nashville 37203

❑   Phone: (615) 242-4371. **Web: www.nashvillesounds.com**

A pro team operating as a AAA affiliate of the Pittsburgh Pirates and a member of the Pacific Coast League. 72 games played early April-early September. Admission: $6.00-$10.00.

TENNESSEE SPORTS HALL OF FAME

501 Broadway (Gaylord Entertainment Center)

Nashville 37203

❑   Phone: (615) 242-4750 or (888) 846-8384
     Web: www.TSHF.net
❑   Hours: Monday-Saturday 10:00am-5:00pm.
❑   Admission: $2.00-$3.00 (age 4+).

This site focuses on everything from team to extreme sports with a continuous video stream of Tennessee sports images. The Museum also features interactive games such as a virtual reality, one-on-one basketball game, a strength training apparatus used by Olympic swimmers, college football and basketball exhibits, NASCAR video games, two 30-seat theaters with sports videos, and more.

AGRICULTURAL MUSEUM

Ellington Agricultural Center (I-65: Take Exit #78-A east on Harding Place)

Nashville 37204

❑   Phone: (615) 837-5197
     Web: www.picktnproducts.org/agmuseum
❑   Hours: Daily 9:00am-4:00pm except state holidays.
❑   Admission: FREE
❑   Tours: Guided tours require reservations with a small fee for demonstrations and educational programs.

The museum has an extensive collection of home and farm artifacts from the 19th and early 20th centuries along with rural Tennessee prints and folk art sculptures. Textiles, a woodworking collection, buggies, wagons and large items like the McCormick reaper and Jumbo steam engine are exhibited in a renovated plantation barn. Log cabins, a small farm house, kitchen/herb garden, perennial garden and nature trail are also part of the museum tour.

SPEEDWAY AT NASHVILLE FAIRGROUNDS

(track at Tennessee State Fairgrounds)

Nashville 37204

❑　　Phone: (615) 726-1818. **Web: www.fairgroundsspeedway.net**

Rated by NASCAR as the "#1 Short Track in America", there is Nascar sanctioned racing on Saturday nights weekly from April-September. Late Model Stock Cars, SuperTrucks, Street Modifieds and Pure Stocks. Motor home parking with free hookups. Check website for schedule and details.

BELLE MEADE PLANTATION

5025 Harding Road

Nashville 37205

❑　　Phone: (615) 356-0501 or (800) 270-3991
　　　　Web: www.bellemeadeplantation.com
❑　　Hours: Monday-Saturday 9:00am-5:00pm, Sunday 11:00am-
　　　　5:00pm. (Closed Thanksgiving, Christmas, and New Year's).
❑　　Admission: $10.00 adult, $8.50 senior, $4.00 child (6-12).
❑　　Miscellaneous: On-site restaurant.

This "Queen of Tennessee Plantations", 1853 Greek Revival mansion was once a major thoroughbred stud farm and nursery. Tours are given by lavishly costumed interpreters around the grounds, log cabin, huge Carriage House and especially the mansion. During the Battle of Nashville, Union and rebel forces skirmished in the front yard, and the mansion's massive stone columns were riddled with bullets, the evidence still visible today.

CHEEKWOOD BOTANICAL GARDEN &
MUSEUM OF ART

1200 Forrest Park Drive (Harding Place to Belle Meade Blvd to
Page Road to Forrest Park Dr)

Nashville 37205

❑   Phone: (615) 356-8000. **Web: www.cheekwood.org**
❑   Hours: Tuesday-Saturday 9:30am-4:30pm, Sunday 11:00am-
    4:30pm. Closed most of January & Mondays (except Summer).
❑   Admission: $10.00 adult, $8.00 senior, $5.00 youth (6-17) and
    college, $25.00 family. After 3:00pm, half price.
❑   Miscellaneous: Especially on Saturdays from 10:00am - noon,
    everyone and anyone can find their creative interest. Drop in any
    time between 10:00am - noon, no reservations required. Every
    week there is a different project that highlights the collections and
    exhibits at Cheekwood. The Class is Free, Only a $1.00 donation is
    requested for materials. (Gate fee applies to Non-Members)

The estate, turned art museum and botanical gardens, has
interactive learning centers, the Wildflower Garden's pond full of
frogs, and the 16-foot rabbit made out of balls of wire on the
Woodland Sculpture Trail.

NASHVILLE BALLET

Tennessee Performing Arts Center (3630 Redmon Street)

Nashville 37209

❑   Phone: (615) 297-2966 or (615) 255-ARTS tickets
    Web: www.nashvilleballet.com
❑   Admission: $19.00-$45.00.

Noted for its versatility, the season includes performances of
classical (Romeo and Juliet) and contemporary works with
weekend, matinee and evening performances. The Nutcracker
performed mid-December weekends every year. Children's off-site
ballets performed at a well-known public site (ex. Library) several
times per year.

NASHVILLE CHILDREN'S THEATRE

724 Second Avenue South

Nashville 37210

❑   Phone: (615) 254-9103. **Web: www.nct-dragonsite.org**
❑   Hours: Monday-Friday 10:00am and 11:30am. Select Saturday
     and Sunday 2:30pm.
❑   Admission: $7.50-$9.50.

A non-profit, long-standing pro theatre that brings magical productions of classic children's literature and folk tales each season (ex. Three Little Pigs, Treasure Island). Performed at different theatres throughout town (ex. Hill Theatre).

TENNESSEE CENTRAL RAILWAY MUSEUM

220 Willow Street

Nashville 37210

❑   Phone: (615) 244-9001. **Web: www.tcry.org**
❑   Hours: Tuesday, Thursday, Saturday 9:00am-3:00pm (Museum).
❑   Admission: Varies with each type of excursion. Best to visit
     website for details. Generally, $17-$29.00.
❑   Tours: Selected Saturday Excursions Depart usually at 9:00am
     and always include some type of storytelling or re-enactment.

Tour the museum full of timetables, locks, switch keys, menus, bells, headlights, cabooses, camp cars, passenger cars and locomotives on display. Excursion Train Rides visit Watertown or Lebanon for a stop and a chance to visit shops and enjoy a meal. Trips include re-enactments of a train robbery or fairyland with Mother Goose style characters or a Civil War re-enactment with Morgan's Raiders. All of the cars are climate-controlled and every seat provides a great view of the countryside. Seating from coach to first class with a dining car, dome car and gift shop car.

NASHVILLE ZOO AT GRASSMERE

3777 Nolensville Road (I-24 exit 56 or I-65 exit 78, follow signs)

Nashville 37211

❑ Phone: (615) 833-1534. **Web: www.nashvillezoo.org**

❑ Hours: Daily 9:00am-6:00pm (April-October), 9:00-4:00pm (rest of year). Closed major winter holidays.

❑ Admission: $8.00 adult, $7.00 senior, $6.00 child (3-12). $2.00 parking.

Visitors get up close to the animals at Critter Encounters (monkeys, lemurs, goats, sheep and baby camels). Near the entry, look for two Manchurian Cranes and a pair of saddle-billed storks, alligators and flamingos. You can also tour the historic home and working farm to experience life in the 19th century…with animals. Allow time to play at the country's largest community-built playground (66,000 sq. feet of Jungle Gym) and cool off at the nearby Terrace rain room or under shadowing vines. The newer Bamboo Trail features animals found in bamboo forests around the globe. Walk a trail through a thick bamboo tree forest and discover red pandas, clouded leopards, primates, birds and a tranquil Koi pond.

GAYLORD OPRYLAND HOTEL

2800 Opryland Drive (I-40 to Briley Pkwy, exit 12)

Nashville 37214

❑ Phone: (615) 889-1000 or (877) 234-OPRY reservations
Web: www.gaylordopryland.com

The kids enter the lobby and never stop the "oohs and aahs". They couldn't believe everywhere we walked was under one roof! Pretty cool to go on a long nature trail (Garden Conservatory) and never leave the building. It's always a comfortable 72 degrees under the glass atriums that encompass acres and acres of lush indoor gardens, winding pathways, and sparkling waterfalls. Step aboard one of the Delta River Flatboats ($5.00/person, age 5+, depart every 15-20 minutes) and take a scenic cruise down a winding indoor river where you'll pass gardens and majestic waterfalls. The tour includes interesting little-known facts about the Hotel, and if you're lucky you may catch a glimpse of Donny, the eighty-pound catfish. Choose from several restaurants including a grand Antebellum-style restaurant, Old Hickory Steakhouse, any of island eateries (Pizza, barbeque, grill, deli, ice cream, etc), Cascades Atrium or Magnolia's Rachels. There are four outdoor swimming pools and a fitness center on the premises. Kids Station is a drop-in childcare "resort within a resort," where kids ages three to twelve years old can stay for an hour or play for a day. Your children will be entertained as they explore the 2,500-square-foot Kids Station where they can happily do crafts, perform or watch videos. Rooms rates: Guestrooms (average $140-$180 per night) & numerous suites higher. Family Fun packages (w/nearby attraction tickets) are around $300 for 3 days.

GENERAL JACKSON SHOWBOAT

2812 Opryland Drive (I-40 exit Briley Pkwy to exit 12, Opryland, follow signs)

Nashville 37214

❑   Phone: (615) 871-6100. **Web: www.generaljackson.com**
❑   Hours: Cruises depart daily late February - mid November. Midday Cruise is 2 1/2 hours departing at Noon. Meal cruises board at 11:30am.
❑   Admission: Midday $21.00-$38.00 per person (age 4+). Without a meal option, less expensive ($8.00-$10.00) midday party cruises occasionally available spring-fall (good weather seasons). Additional food is available for purchase.
❑   Miscellaneous: Holiday Cruises and Evening Cruises for special "dinner & dancing" style fine cruising.

Styled in the grand tradition of the paddlewheel riverboats that cruised the great Southern waterways in the 1800s, the General Jackson was named after the first steamboat to operate on the Cumberland River in 1817. We recommend the midday cruise for families titled: "Now That's Country". This casual, country-themed cruise includes a delicious lunch buffet (chicken & pulled pork BBQ w/ fixins) and a show, featuring Tim Watson (full of laughs and great songs...and he does a "mid-air split" at the end!). Children's activities are scheduled on midday cruises from May-mid September. General admission tickets include outer deck seating (with snacks and beverages served inside), live band entertainment and a kids tour. Children can take a walking tour of the boat with Miss Sarah and hear tall tales about life on the river. Plus, each child will receive a custom coloring page. Historical points of interest you'll hear about are locks, dams, riverfront parks, navigational lights and a cave. Well worth the time while in Nashville!

GIBSON BLUEGRASS SHOWCASE

161 Opry Mills Drive (across from the Grand Ole Opry)

Nashville 37214

❑   Phone: (615) 514-2200. Web: **www.gibsonshowcase.com**
❑   Hours: Monday-Saturday 10:00am-9:30pm, Sunday 11:00am-
        7:00pm (Opry Mills shopping complex)

Watch the Gibson Original Instrument luthiers hand craft each mandolin, banjo and Dobro. Learn about Gibson's 100-plus years of history as you get an up-close view of skilled artisans as they design, carve, paint, polish and ship one-of-a-kind instruments around the world. You won't believe how they can shape and carve wood into those smooth guitar lines. Every station is well-lit with precise instruments handling the specialty products. Usually, the family is treated to a brief solo by an employee testing a guitar. Then you all get to strum some instruments in the Playing Area. The 35,000 square foot facility (the only manufacturing center in a retail store) also houses a retail shop where you can purchase one of these world class instruments or mementos of your Bluegrass Showcase experience.

GRAND OLE OPRY

2804 Opryland Drive (Briley Pkwy to exit 11, Opry Mills Drive)

Nashville 37214

❑ Phone: (615) 871-OPRY. **Web: www.opry.com**
❑ Hours: Friday, Saturday 6:30pm and 9:30pm. Tuesday 7:00pm (Memorial Day-mid December only). Winter shows @ Ryman Auditorium. Generally 2 1/2 hours.
❑ Admission: $27.00-$32.00 adult, $17.00-$32.00 child (ages 4-11), under 3 FREE if sit on lap.

From Nashville to all points within reach, the Opry has been broadcast live over WSM AM 650 since 1925 (world's longest-running live radio show). Aspiring performers will share the stage with legends in country, bluegrass, and comedy. One of the Opry's priceless qualities continues to be the uniqueness of each show-guests never know who might strike up a rare duet or who might stop by for a surprise appearance! We saw famous stars like Whispering Bill Anderson, T. Bubba (comic), Little Jimmy Dickens and Steve Wariner ("Holes in the Floor of Heaven" fame). You'll see a two hour program full of 6-8 artists…mostly singing old-time, knee-slapping country. Special memory note – *cameras are allowed*!

GRAND OLE OPRY MUSEUM

2802 Opryland Drive (Briley Pkwy to exit 11, across from Opry House in the Opry Plaza)

Nashville 37214

❑ Phone: (615) 889-3060. **Web: www.opry.com**
❑ Hours: Open daily at 10:00am, closing times vary depending on Opry performances. Closed January & February.
❑ Admission: FREE

The museum features interactive exhibits as well as memorabilia from past and present members including: Roy Acuff, Minnie Pearl, Vince Gill & Marty Stuart. Kids can play on a mock-up of the stage of the real Opry, then gaze at stars' costumes (crazy &

bright, aren't they?). The Opry began on a floor of an insurance company's offices, eventually gaining popularity and moving into Ryman. The Opry said goodbye to the Ryman Auditorium as its venue in 1974. The Grand Ole Opry House maintains a connection to the traditions of the Ryman through an eight-foot circle of wood that was removed from the Ryman stage and placed center stage at the Opry House. Great walk down Country Memory Lane.

MUSIC VALLEY WAX MUSEUM

2515 McGavock Pike (near Opryland Complex)

Nashville 37214

❑ Phone: (615) 883-3612
❑ Hours: Daily 9:00am-9:00pm (summer), closes at 5:00pm rest of year. Closed Thanksgiving and Christmas.
❑ Admission: $3.50 adult, $3.00 senior (65+), $1.50 child (6-12).

The Wax Museum features more than 50 wax figures of old-time country music's stars. Many look like the famous folks and they are dressed in original costumes, in original surroundings. Look for the "Sidewalk of the Stars" where 250+ entertainers have placed their footprints, handprints and signatures in concrete.

NASHVILLE TROLLEY TOURS

Second Avenue & Broadway (tickets at Gray Line Visitor Center)

Nashville 37214

❑ Phone: (615) 248-4437
❑ Admission: $10.00 adult, $5.00 child (5-11)
❑ Tours: Depart every 90 minutes beginning at 11:00am until 3:30pm (extended hours on weekends).

One hour downtown and Music Row narrated tour aboard an old-fashioned trolley.

RAINFOREST CAFÉ EDUCATIONAL TOURS

Opry Mills

Nashville 37214

❑   Phone: (615) 514-5000. **Web: www.rainforestcafe.com**
❑   Tours: Usually begin at 10:00am and include lunch. Must be
      scheduled in advance.

The theme restaurant and wildlife preserve is filled with live and mechanical animals: ongoing rainstorms (even thunder and lightning); a talking rainforest tree; giant "walk-thru" aquarium; and hand-sculpted "cave like" rock everywhere. Preschoolers love the fish tank but may be uneasy with the motorized large gorillas and elephants. Did you know they give Educational Group Tours? What a light-hearted way to introduce your kids to the animals, plants and environs of the rainforest. The Adventure uncovers why elephants have big ears and why the Café's residents collect pennies for charity. What is your favorite fish in the coral reef? Include a group lunch afterwards in your plans (for around $8.00 per person). Nibble on Jurassic Tidbits or Paradise Pizza plus drink and dessert.

TEXAS TROUBADOUR THEATRE

2416 Music Valley Drive (Opryland area)

Nashville 37214

❑   Phone: (615) 885-0028
❑   Hours: Vary with show.
❑   Admission: FREE for Jamboree and Cowboy church. Fee for
      special shows.

The Ernest Tubb Midnight Jamboree, a live country music radio broadcast every Saturday night from the theatre on WSM AM, has followed the Grand Ole Opry for many years. Nashville Cowboy Church is here. The Music Valley Jubilee, a spectacular 2 hour musical and special Tribute shows (ex. Elvis) are here, too.

VALLEY PARK AMUSEMENT PARK

Music Valley, McGavock Pike (Opryland area complex)

Nashville 37214

❑   Phone: (615) 885-1515

A small amusement park with a ferris wheel, ten thrill rides and ten kiddie rides. Admission fee varies.

WAVE COUNTRY

2320 Two Rivers Parkway (near Opryland), **Nashville** 37214

❑   Phone: (615) 885-1052
     Web: http://nashville.gov/parks/wave_country.htm
❑   Hours: Daily 10:00am-5:00pm (Memorial Day weekend thru the
     first day of school). Weekends only after school starts thru Labor Day.
❑   Admission: $6.00 adult, $5.00 child (3-12), FREE for children 2
     and under. Wave Runner Special: Kids admitted for half price
     after 3:00 PM, Monday - Thursday.

The area's only wave-action swimming pool where you can ride the waves, or just let them lap at your feet. There are floats available for you to rent, and there are calm, "non-wave" periods as well. Or, have fun on the three water slides in the park, a children's playground, or sand volleyball pits. Extensive fast-food concessions available.

NASHVILLE SYMPHONY ORCHESTRA

Jackson Hall, TN Performing Arts Center,

Nashville 37215

❑   Phone: (615) 783-1200 office or (615) 783-1212 tickets
     Web: www.nashvillesymphony.org
❑   Admission: $10.00-$15.00 general for Pied Piper concerts.

The Symphony features a full schedule of classical, pops and special events concerts. Happy Holidays Concerts are brimming with holiday favorites, sing-alongs, and a visit from jolly Old Saint Nick. This interactive celebration is a wonderful way for your family to kick-off the holiday season (Thanksgiving weekend). Pied Piper concerts are shorter, more interactive concerts designed for children ages 3-8. Families are encouraged to join activities that relate to the concert beginning at 10:15am, before each performance.

RYMAN AUDITORIUM

116 Fifth Avenue North (downtown) (I-40 to Broadway east (towards downtown and Cumberland River), left on 5th Ave)

Nashville 37219

❏ Phone: (615) 889-3060 tickets or (615) 458-8700 general
Web: www.ryman.com
❏ Hours: Daily 9:00am-4:00pm. Closed New Years, Thanksgiving and Christmas.
❏ Admission: $8.00 adult, $4.00 child (4-11). Evening performance rates vary.

The Ryman Auditorium, a former home of the Grand Ole Opry (1943-1974), offers self-guided tours that showcase the legendary stars who have graced her stage, from country's biggest names to Mae West, Rudolf Valentino, and W.C. Fields. Have a seat in the original pews as you watch "If These Walls Could Talk", a short film featuring the people and events that have made the Ryman famous. Step onto the actual stage and get your picture taken holding the microphone and strumming a guitar. Then stroll past hallways of old photos and posters. In the evening, you can return to the performance hall for one of many shows and concerts scheduled year-round.

RADNOR LAKE STATE NATURAL AREA

1160 Otter Creek Road (6 miles southwest of downtown)

Nashville 37220

❏ Phone: (615) 373-3467
Web: www.state.tn.us/environment/parks/radnor/
❏ Admission: $3.00 per vehicle, per day.

Radnor Lake is a wildlife sanctuary which provides outstanding scenic beauty and nature observation. Popular among bird watchers and photographers, the park has hiking trails ranging from easy to strenuous, an interpretive program (like special hikes and canoe floats), and a museum and visitors center.

For updates visit our website: www.kidslovepublications.com

TRAVELLERS REST HISTORIC HOME

636 Farrell Parkway (I-65 exit 78B, Harding Place West to US31S,
follow signs)

Nashville 37220

❑   Phone: (615) 832-8197
    Web: www.travellersrestplantation.org
❑   Hours: Monday-Saturday 10:00am-4:00pm, Sunday 1:00-
    4:00pm, except Thanksgiving, Christmas Day, and New Years
    Day.
❑   Admission: $8.00 adult, $7.00 senior (65+), $3.00 child (6-12).
❑   Miscellaneous: Celebrate John Overton's birthday (reduced
    admission) on April 9th.

Discover "One Thousand Years of Tennessee History" at an 18th
century historic home where docents share stories on the 50 minute
tour. The site's history begins with its first inhabitants, pre-historic
Native Americans. Then, the exhibits take you through the early
national period, the Antebellum period and the tragedy of the Civil
War. The slaves cared for the kids almost completely. Why was
sugar locked up at night? Who were some of the travelers through
this house? Tours can have a lifestyle focus or a war battle focus.

CHAFFIN'S BARN DINNER THEATRE

8204 Highway 100

Nashville 37221

❑   Phone: (615) 646-9977 or (800) 282-BARN
    Web: www.dinnertheatre.com
❑   Admission: $28.00-$40.00 adult, $20.00 child.

Musicals, comedies and mysteries combine Nashville talent with
great Broadway style plays. Pre-parties and camps for kids before
new shows (mostly summertime). The Main and Backstage
theatres perform Tuesday through Saturday evenings with
occasional Sunday Matinees and Thursday Senior Matinees. Buffet
is served (adult price included in $40.00 ticket) if you want, before
the evening shows.

PURITY DAIRIES

360 Murfreesboro Road (I-40W exit 213, Spence Lane, turn right,
then left at Elm Hill Pike to end)

Nashville 37224

❑   Phone: (615) 244-1900. **Web: www.puritydairies.com**
❑   Admission: FREE
❑   Tours: Thursday & Friday at 10:00am, 11:00am, Noon &
1:00pm. Great background for tour on website. Reservations
please.

You pass the cute ice-cream parlor as you enter the tour room. In
here, the company shows a film about milk and dairy treat
production. An ice cream treat is served, complimentary, as the big
curtains are opened, revealing a huge window into the world of an
ice cream factory! Up close, you'll see them making Nutty Buddy
or Ice Cream sandwiches. Further away, you can see gobs of fresh
ice cream pouring out as it fills 1/2 gallon containers. The "show"
is mesmerizing as just one machine feeds chocolate, another part
squeezes in the vanilla ice cream, and another part wraps the treat.
The packaged treats are whisked off to the deep freeze. Do you
recognize the narrator of the video? Cute, isn't it?

TENNESSEE TITANS FOOTBALL

Baptist Sports Park, 460 Great Circle Road (Home Field: The
Coliseum)

Nashville 37228

❑   Phone: (615) 565-4000. **Web: www.titansonline.com**

NFL pro team plays at the Coliseum located on the east bank of the
Cumberland River, downtown. Hey kids, if you're a Titans fan and
14 years old or younger, you'll have a blast as a member of the
Titans Kids Club. An official membership card lets you into a
Special Titans Day at The Coliseum for members only (and your
parent(s)/guardian) where you can enjoy Titans games lunch, and a
chance to interact with Titans players.

BICENTENNIAL CAPITOL MALL
STATE PARK

598 James Robertson Parkway (Located at the foot of the State
Capitol between James Roberson Parkway, Jefferson Street, 6th
and 7th Avenues), **Nashville** 37243

❑   Phone: (615) 741-5800

     Web: www.state.tn.us/environment/parks/bicenmal/

❑   Hours: Daylight hours.

Opened in 1996 to celebrate Tennessee's 200th birthday, the park
pays tribute to the history, architecture and geography of the state.
It compliments the tour of the state Capitol building. Tour
Tennessee's History via a 200-foot granite map of the state. See 31
fountains designating major rivers. Marble columns divide the
history of the state into decades. The park also has a Wall of
History, WWII Memorial, Court of Three Stars and Walk of
Counties. Picnic tables, restrooms and vending machines are
located under the railroad trestle. A visitor center/gift shop is also
located under the trestle.

TENNESSEE STATE CAPITOL

(Charlotte Avenue between 6th & 7th Avenues)

Nashville 37243

❑   Phone: (615) 741-0830

❑   Hours: Monday-Friday 9:00am-4:00pm

❑   Admission: FREE

❑   Tours: Guided tours are available on Monday-Friday at 9:00am,
     10:00am, 11:00am, 1:00 pm, 2:00pm, and 3:00pm. and last from
     thirty minutes to one hour depending upon the size of group.

The Tennessee State Capitol stands today, much as it did in 1859.
The grounds of the State Capitol contain statues honoring Sam
Davis, Sgt. Alvin York, and Presidents Andrew Jackson and
Andrew Johnson. The tombs of President and Mrs. James K. Polk
are also located on the Capitol grounds.

TENNESSEE STATE MUSEUM

505 Deaderick, Polk Cultural Center (Fifth Avenue, between Union & Deaderick)

Nashville 37243

- ❑ Phone: (615) 741-2692. **Web: www.tnmuseum.org**
- ❑ Hours: Tuesday-Saturday 10:00am-5:00pm, Sunday 1:00-5:00pm. Closed all major holidays.
- ❑ Admission: FREE

Here you'll find the historical highlights of Tennessee from different periods of time. Trace the prehistoric Woodland Indians to Daniel Boone's & Davy Crockett's time, Civil War weapons and 18th and 19th century dioramas with stories. Look for Andrew Jackson's top hat, Andrew Johnson's piano, James Polk's walking cane, Daniel Boone's musket, Davy Crockett's powder horn, or Sam Davis' torn boot (cut by soldiers to try to find enemy papers). There are reproductions of an early 19th century grist mill and authentic settings of an 18th century print shop, frontier cabin, Antebellum parlor, and Victorian painting gallery. In addition, there are exhibits about African-American soldiers in the Civil War, a free black family living in Knoxville before and after that war, and the women's suffrage movement. The MILITARY MUSEUM is located in the War Memorial Building across the street. Exhibits cover America's overseas conflicts, beginning with the Spanish-American War and ending with World War II in 1945. On display, Sgt. Alvin York's uniform.

X *IMAGINARIUM CHILDREN'S MUSEUM*

CLOSED

7104 Crossroad Blvd.

Nashville (Brentwood) 37027

- ❑ Phone: (615) 373-9596
- ❑ Hours: vary
- ❑ Admission: $4.00 adult, $6.00 child (2+).

An interactive exploration experience of discovery exploring themed areas from prehistoric dinos to puppet shows.

HERMITAGE, HOME OF PRESIDENT ANDREW JACKSON

4580 Rachel's Lane (I-40 exit 221 onto Old Hickory Blvd.)

Nashville (Hermitage) 37076

- ❑ Phone: (615) 889-2941. **Web: www.thehermitage.com**
- ❑ Hours: Daily 9:00am-5:00pm. Closed Thanksgiving, Christmas, and third week in January.
- ❑ Admission: $12.00 adult, $11.00 senior (62+) and students (13-18), $5.00 child (6-12), $34.00 family.
- ❑ Tours: Guided Grounds Tours outside mansion (May-October).
- ❑ Miscellaneous: Summer: watch archaeologists uncover secrets of the plantation's past (maybe help discover the original kitchen or slave quarters). See the bone dominos and clay marbles already recovered from the slave cabins. When we were there, they were digging for slave graves.

President... General... "Old Hickory"... Hero. He so dominated his era that it is now known as the "Age of Jackson" - the transition from untamed wilderness to international power. Here is the place Jackson and his beloved wife, Rachel, called home for over 40 years and where he returned in 1837 after two turbulent terms as president. Historically costumed interpreters guide you through the 30-minute mansion tour, recounting objects and tales of his family life (original furniture, sword, glasses, Bible, etc). On the first floor are the master bedrooms (even the room where he died). In the library, what are the huge books on the floor? On the remainder of the plantation, gain insight into the daily lives of slaves working the property (growing cotton, raising livestock). See the first Hermitage Cabins & Church where the Jacksons lived in the early 1800s or the Tulip Grove Mansion - home to Jackson's nephew Donelson. The Visitors Center Museum features changing exhibits about Jackson's life and career (w/15-minute film presentation) and you can walk to the gardens where Andrew and Rachel Jackson are buried.

LONG HUNTER STATE PARK

2910 Hobson Pike (Hwy 71, I-40 exit 226A)

Nashville (Hermitage) 37076

❑   Phone: (615) 885-2422

Web: www.state.tn.us/environment/parks/longhunt/

❑   Hours: 7:00am to sunset.

❑   Admission: $3.00 per vehicle, per day.

Situated on J. Percy Priest Lake, the park features boating, sailing, fishing, hiking, picnicking, camping, swimming and wildlife observation. The visitors center offers exhibits and information on the park's unique flora and fauna (due to the unique cedar glade environment).

NASHVILLE SHORES OUTDOOR WATER PARK

4001 Bell Road (Take I-40 East from Nashville to Old Hickory Boulevard (Exit 221B) and go South. Turn Right on Bell Road)

Nashville (Hermitage) 37076

❑   Phone: (615) 889-7050. **Web: www.nashvilleshores.com**

❑   Hours: Summertime, usually 10:00am-7:00pm.

❑   Admission:$16.00-$19.00 (age 3+). $5.00 OFF after 3:00pm every day.

The park features the seven largest waterslides in Tennessee, as well as giant pools, beaches and mini-golf. Rafts and body slides, some open, some enclosed. Cabin, pontoon, parasailing and jet ski rentals also.

JOHNSONVILLE STATE HISTORIC PARK

Route 1, Box 374 (off US 70)

New Johnsonville 37134

❑   Phone: (931) 535-2789

Web: www.state.tn.us/environment/parks/johnson/

❑   Hours: Daily 8:00am-sundown.

❑   Admission: $3.00 per vehicle entrance fee.

For updates visit our website: www.kidslovepublications.com

This 600-acre park on the eastern side of Kentucky Lake overlooks the site of the Battle of Johnsonville. Cavalry forces under Lt. Gen. Nathan Bedford Forrest sank four Federal gunboats downstream and destroyed a Union Army supply depot at Johnsonville. Four of the original breastworks are beautifully preserved. Interpretive tours are available and the on-site museum exhibits the history of the battle. Fishing and hiking are available.

MERRY MEADE MEADOWS

1770 Poplar Hill Road

Prospect 38477

❏   Phone: (931) 363-8754. **Web: www.merrymeademeadows.com**
❏   Admission: $25.00 suggested donation per carload. Used to provide over 3000 bales of hay, 12 tons of grain, professional care, etc.
❏   Tours: Monday - Friday 10:00am-4:00pm. Weekends and Holidays by appointment.
❏   Miscellaneous: Old-fashioned food fun in town at Prospect Ice Cream Pizza Parlor or Prospect Station Grist Mill.

This unique haven for abused and neglected draft horses houses over thirty horses at one time. Many had been starved, beaten or were ill. All have recovered (horses and other rescued animals like chickens, goats, donkeys) and enjoy hearty feedings and care each day. Pet a Gentle Giant, offer the horses an apple treat, and meet some special ones that are favorites of the farm. Careful, you may want to adopt one to take home!

SAM DAVIS TRAIL

100 South Second Street, **Pulaski** 38478

❏   Phone: (931) 363-3789

Self-guided tour provides cassettes and brochure to follow stops at sites related to Sam Davis, Boy Hero of the Confederacy, who was captured by the Union army and executed as a spy. Sites include a monument, museum, cemetery and statue on the town square. Brochures available at the Chamber of Commerce Monday-Friday FREE admission.

SAM DAVIS HOME

1399 Sam Davis Road (I-24 exit 66B, Rte. 102N, follow signs)

Smyrna 37167

- ❏   Phone: (615) 459-2341. **Web: www.samdavishome.org**
- ❏   Hours: Monday-Saturday 10:00am-4:00pm, Sunday 1:00-
    4:00pm. Extended summer hours.
- ❏   Admission: $7.00 adult, $5.00 senior, $3.00 child.
- ❏   Miscellaneous: Start with the video and then guided tour at the
    new Visitors Center and museum.

Sam Davis was a 21-year-old Confederate Army courier soldier who was hanged as a spy when he refused to identify an informant after being captured by Union forces in 1863. His boyhood house museum situated on 168 acres is dedicated to the Confederate hero. His last words, now famous, were "If I had a thousand lives to live, I'd give them all rather than betray a friend". Read the last letter that Sam sent to his mother. Why was he really not a spy, just a courier for spies? See Sam's boyhood bedroom - look for the original laptop desk. Ask about Hush Puppies in the kitchen.

SATURN FACTORY TOURS

100 Saturn Parkway (I-65 S exit 53, 396 West to US 31S)

Spring Hill 37174

- ❏   Phone: (931) 486-5778 or (800) 326-3321.
    Web: www.saturn.com
- ❏   Admission: FREE
- ❏   Tours: Must be age 6+, 42" tall, no shorts. Monday, Tuesday,
    Thursday, Friday Public Tours at 8:30am, 10:00am, 1:00pm &
    2:30pm. Wednesday tours at 10:00am, 1:00pm, 2:30pm.
    Closed on national holidays and the first 2 weeks of July.
    Reservations required.

A horse barn has been renovated into the Welcome Center with interactive displays and exhibits on the Saturn story. The displays are arranged in eight horse stalls. You'll see historical mementos and videos on teamwork and the manufacturing story (even see the polymer beads that make up Saturn body panels).

This American manufacturing company makes power train, general assembly and body systems buildings. On tour, you'll get a close-up look at the stages of assembly.

RIPPAVILLA PLANTATION

5700 Main Street (on Hwy. 31, one quarter of a mile south of the Saturn Parkway exit off I-65)

Spring Hill 38402

❑   Phone: (931) 486-9037. **Web: www.rippavilla.org**
❑   Hours: Tuesday-Saturday 10:00am-5:00pm, Sunday 1:00-5:00pm.
❑   Admission: $8.00 adult, $6.00 senior (62+), $4.00 child (6-16). Additional small fee for Mule Museum.

The restored 1855 plantation home and gardens offer a guided tour. Around Rippavilla, the grounds contain several Historic structures from the past and an excellent view of a portion of the Battle of Spring Hill fought on November 29, 1864. Just behind the Plantation house is an original Freedman's Bureau school. Further back on the property, you'll find several foundations for slave cabins and one slave residence. This land is where, on the morning of November 30th, 1864, General John Bell Hood met with his Generals to have breakfast before the army of Tennessee marched north to engage in the battle of Franklin. The kids might be interested in the Mule Museum on the property to see farming machinery and artifacts from the late 19th and early 20th century.

Chapter 3
Area - Middle East (ME)

Our Favorites...

* Christus Gardens - Gatlinburg

* Ober Gatlinburg

* Ripley's Aquarium of the Smokies - Gatlinburg

* James White Fort & Volunteer Landing Area - Knoxville

* Women's Basketball Hall of Fame - Knoxville

* Sam Houston Schoolhouse - Maryville

* Museum of Appalachia - Norris

* Norris Dam State Park - Norris

* Sweetwater Valley Farm - Philadelphia

* Dollywood & Splash Country - Pigeon Forge

* Dixie Stampede - Pigeon Forge

* Cade's Cove - Townsend

"In the Huddle"
Women's Basketball
Hall of Fame

COVE LAKE STATE PARK

110 Cove Lake Lane (Hwy 25W)

Caryville 37714

- ❏ Phone: (423) 566-9701
  Web: www.state.tn.us/environment/parks/covelak/
- ❏ Hours: Daily 8:00am-sunset.
- ❏ Admission: $3.00 per vehicle park entrance.

Situated in a mountain valley setting on the eastern edge of the Cumberland Mountains, there are scenic nature trails and bike trails leading through the open grasslands and woodlands. In the winter, several hundred Canadian Geese make this lakeshore their feeding ground. Nearby is the Devil's Race Trace whose steep pinnacle rock affords a panoramic view. There is a 3.5 mile paved hiking trail that is also used for biking. Other activities: camping, swimming, recreation center, boating and fishing.

A WALK IN THE WOODS

4413 Scenic Drive East

Gatlinburg 37738

- ❏ Phone: (865) 436-8283. **Web: www.awalkinthewoods.com**
- ❏ Admission: $20.00-$25.00 per person (includes snacks). 20% discount for children (under 18) and seniors. Group discount 5+ people.

Come for A Walk in the Woods and explore meadows sparkling with wildflowers...the majesty of old-growth trees....the beauty of a waterfall. Or stand on top of a mountain, surrounded by a floating mist. Erik and Vesna Plakanis have hiked hundreds of miles through these mountains and they'll lead you to some of their favorite hidden spots. When you take a walk with them, you'll hear Cherokee lore and Appalachian tall tales. You'll also find out what people of this area did for food and medicine before the invention of the grocery store and pharmacy. You might even get to sample a tasty mountain treat. Every walk is geared towards enjoying the journey at a pleasant pace.

CHRISTUS GARDENS

510 River Road (one block from the center of town,
behind the aquarium), **Gatlinburg** 37738

- ❑   Phone: (865) 436-5155. **Web: www.christusgardens.com**
- ❑   Hours: Daily 8:00am-9:00pm (April-October). Daily 9:00am-
  5:00pm (November-March). Last tour 45 minutes before closing.
  Closed Christmas Day.
- ❑   Admission: $9.95 adult, $3.65 child (7-13).

The Greatest Story Ever Told. You will have the experience of
walking through a Biblical world of 2000 years ago, seeing life-
size, life-like representations of important scenes from the life of
Jesus Christ. Every scene has figures and costumes with
tremendous detail and includes short narratives. Look at the
"Carrara Face" sculpture - not only the eyes but the entire face
seems to follow your every movement (remember your parents
saying... "The Lord is always watching")! The Biblical Coin
Collection includes the Shekel of Tyre, possibly a part of Judas'
Thirty Pieces of Silver, and "widow's mite" and "tribute penny."
Looking for spiritual refreshment away from the hub-bub of the
busy tourist town?…this is the place.

COOTER'S GARAGE

157 Parkway

Gatlinburg 37738

- ❑   Phone: (865) 430-9909. **Web: www.cootersplace.com**
- ❑   Hours: Most days during daylight hours.
- ❑   Admission: FREE

If you love "the Dukes of Hazzard", you will love a visit to
Cooter's Garage... operated by none other than ol' "Cooter"
himself. Ben Jones, who played the Duke Boys sidekick, is your
host. It features pictures, props, costumes, and memorabilia from
the television show. On some weekend evenings, they convert the
garage into a theatre, and present the "Hazzard County Hoedown,"
a foot stomping, hand clapping show with the best in bluegrass and
classic country music. Cast members visit frequently and Cooter
will be in Gatlinburg almost every week.

GATLINBURG SKYLIFT
765 Parkway (traffic light #7)

Gatlinburg 37738

❑   Phone: (865) 436-4307. **Web: www.gatlinburgskylift.com**
❑   Hours: Daily 9:00am-5:00pm. Extended hours until 10:00pm
      (April-October).
❑   Admission: $8.99 adult, $5.99 child (3-11).
❑   Miscellaneous: Gift shop, snack bar. Digital photos taken at the
      top for a fee.

Sky lift up Crockett Mountain for a scenic view of the Smokies.

GATLINBURG THEATRES
Parkway

Gatlinburg 37738

BACK TO THE 50'S THEATER - March-May, June 50s rock
and Roll Show 3 nights per week. Bluegrass Show Monday night.
(865) 430-5777.

SWEET FANNY ADAMS THEATER - Each year two new
musical comedies open mid-April. (865) 436-4039.

GREAT SMOKY MOUNTAINS
NATIONAL PARK
US 441, Newfound Gap Road (I-40 to US 66 to US 441S to park
hdqtrs)

Gatlinburg 37738

❑   Phone: (865) 436-1200
      Web: www.americanparknetwork.com
❑   Miscellaneous: Molasses making and other pioneer activities are
      part of the park schedule each day.

Great Smoky Mountains National Park *(cont.)*

❑   **SUGARLANDS VISITOR CENTER** - located near the park's main, northern entrance. Park film shown in a state-of-the-art theater. Natural history exhibits include mounted specimens of park animals in re-creations of their habitats and reproductions of journals kept by the first park naturalists. Ranger talks and slide shows daily (spring & fall).

❑   **ALUM CAVE BLUFFS** - The 100 foot high Bluffs have been used to mine saltpeter and alum used in making gunpowder, medicines and munitions manufacturing. Day hikers begin at Newfound Gap Road near CHIMNEY TOPS pinnacles Overlook (strenuous). The trail goes 5 1/2 miles one-way and goes through Arch Rock.

❑   **CHEROKEE ORCHARD ROAD AND ROARING FORK MOTOR NATURE TRAIL** - Along these roads and trails are collections of historic sites including the remains of the Ogle Homestead, log cabins and a cemetery. Closed roads in winter. No large vehicle access.

❑   **CLINGMANS DOME** - Highest spot in the Smokies with forest and an observation platform rising above the evergreens. Drive to Clingmans Dome Road southwest off Newfound Gap. Reaching the platform requires a steep, half-mile walk from the parking lot. Closed in winter.

❑   **CADES COVE** - see separate listing

❑   **OCONALUFTEE VISITOR CENTER** - located near the main southern entrance of the park. MOUNTAIN FARM MUSEUM.

GUINNESS WORLD OF RECORDS MUSEUM

631 Parkway (between traffic light #6 & #7)

Gatlinburg 37738

❑   Phone: (865) 436-9100. **Web: www.gatlinburg.com/guinness/**
❑   Hours: Daily 9:00am-10:00pm
❑   Admission: $9.95 adult, $5.95 child (6-12).

See hundreds of exhibits from the best-selling Guinness Book of World Records. Featured are memorabilia of famous record-holders:

Elvis, Beatles and the Batmobile. Displays of the World's oldest man, the tallest man, or who receives the most fan mail? Also, Animal shows, Interactive record games and many areas to sit and watch Guinness News Network shows and specials. Very interesting place.

OBER GATLINBURG

1001 Parkway (stoplight #9)

Gatlinburg 37738

❑ Phone: (865) 436-5423 **Web: www.obergatlinburg.com**
❑ Hours: Tramway runs Daily mid-morning to mid-evening, depending on season. Amusements, restaurant, and snack bars open at 10:00am, close around 6:00-9:00pm.

Points of interest include:

❑ <u>AERIAL TRAMWAY</u> - Enjoy spectacular views of downtown, the mountains and the Black Bear Habitat year-round from aboard a 120 passenger Aerial Tramway. Departs regularly from downtown Gatlinburg to Ober Gatlinburg Ski Resort & Amusement Park. $9.00 adult, $6.00 child (7-11). Admission good all that day and the next. You can also drive up the hill.

❑ <u>ALPINE SLIDE</u> - Your ride combines a Scenic Chairlift ride up the mountain with a fun filled weaving, wandering dipping descent on one of two 1800' tracks through woods and ski trails. You can control your own speed with a braking device on each sled. Accelerate or slow down as you ride down the mountain through curves, straight-aways and hairpin turns into the valley. No special skills or clothing are needed. $5.00 per person. (Ages 6 and under are free but must ride with ticketed adult age 18 or older). *This ride is unique and the best ride of the park!*

❑ <u>BLACK BEAR HABITAT</u> - educational look at furry neighbors including our two yearlings. There's a curator on hand to answer any questions you might have. $ 2.00 per person (age 7+).

Ober Gatlinburg *(cont.)*

❑ WATER RIDES *(without getting too wet!)* - Lightnin' Raft Ride:
Come as you are - No swimwear necessary to enjoy Ober's
Lightnin' Raft Ride and covered Shoot-the-Chute Water Rides.
These "dry-ride" water rides have a 40 foot vertical drop. Blue
Cyclone Rapids: Get a good grip on the handles of your air-
inflated bob sled as you plunge from over 60 feet high into a dark
hole pushing "white water" waves as you race down a fully-
enclosed fiberglass chute.

❑ SKI TRAILS - offers 8 ski trails serviced by two quad and one
double chairlift which keeps you out of lift lines and on the
slopes.

❑ SCENIC CHAIRLIFT - for $5.00 per person, The Scenic
Chairlift offers one of the most awe-inspiring views of the Great
Smokies. On top, your photo is taken and available to you for a
small charge.

❑ OTHER FUN - Trampoline Thing, Bungee Run (not drop),
Arcade, Go Karts, Indoor Ice Skating, Kiddie Land play fort,
Miniature Golf ($2.50 per person), Velcro Wall Jump.

RIPLEY'S AQUARIUM OF THE SMOKIES

88 River Road (traffic light #5)

Gatlinburg 37738

❑ Phone: (888) 240-1358
Web: www.ripleysaquariumofthesmokies.com
❑ Hours: Daily 9:00am-9:00pm. Open later on weekends.
❑ Admission: $17.95 adult, $9.95 child (6-11), $3.95 preschooler (2-5).
❑ Miscellaneous: May we suggest lodging at the Holiday Inn
Sunspree Family Resort (800-435-9201, **www.4lodging.com**,
520 Historic Nature Trail). Refrigerator in every room, 3 pools (2
indoor) & whirlpool.

This must-see attraction is the place to see schools of fish, mean
piranha, an unbelievable frogfish (don't they look like coral?), or
baby-with-daddy seahorses. Walk by the top of the shark tube, then
go under the tube thru the world's longest shark tube. It will "freak

you out" when the first giant sawfish, shark or sting ray sneaks over your head! This is just amazing! Tropical Rain Forest, Coral Reef (meet loads of reef fish like Dory and Nemo), Discovery Center, Gallery of the Seas, and Touch-a-Bay Ray. Who! Aah! All over this place! Love the "mood" music they play, too! Be sure to catch a dive show into any one of the massive tanks at this wonderful aquarium (our favorite anywhere!).

RIPLEY'S BELIEVE IT OR NOT MUSEUM

800 Parkway (traffic light #7)

Gatlinburg 37738

❑   Phone: (865) 436-5096. **Web: www.ripleys.com**
❑   Hours: Daily 9:00am-9:00pm. Open later summers.
❑   Admission: $12.95 adult (12+), $11.95 senior, $6.95 child (6-11).

During his career, Ripley visited 198 countries, traveling a distance of 19 complete trips around the world. He began collecting unusual artifacts featured in his unique newspaper "Believe It or Not!". Meet the Giraffe-necked woman from Burmal, see a genuine shrunken head or the real Fiji Mermaid. Rolling your tongue in the trick mirror is probably the best exhibit. Seeing really is believing, or not? A little scary and bizarre for younger kids.

RIPLEY'S MOVING THEATER

(traffic light #8 on parkway), **Gatlinburg** 37738

❑   Phone: (865) 436-9763
❑   Hours: Daily 9:00am-Midnight.
❑   Miscellaneous: Must be 43" tall to ride. This is a worthwhile
        stop for any families with strong backs and stomachs! Movie
        admission prices charged.

Feel the rain, the wind, and the snow when you visit the Ripley's Moving Theater! See two 3D movies on our giant screen. Bump, dip, and turn with seats that move in eight different directions and experience the 6 channel digital surround sound audio...truly makes you feel like you're in the show. Both movies included in one low price.

SPACE NEEDLE

115 Historic Nature Trail-Airport Road (traffic light #8)

Gatlinburg 37738

❑   Phone: (865) 436-4629. **Web: www.gatlinburgspaceneedle.com**

Day or night, you can ride the elevator 342 Ft. to the observation tower. Free admission to Family Arcade. $2.00-$6.00 per person (age 6+).

STAR CARS MUSEUM

914 Parkway (near traffic light #8)

Gatlinburg 37738

❑   Phone: (865) 430-7900. **Web: www.starcarstn.com**
❑   Hours: Daily 9:00am-10:00pm
❑   Admission:$9.95 adult, $5.95 child (6-12).

From the Ghostbuster's ambulance, to the Beverly Hillbilly's Jalopy (look for Granny in the rocking chair), George Barris has created tons of famous Hollywood vehicles. See the Andy Griffith display, Jurassic Park, the talking Knight Rider car, Flintstones car and the original Batman studio and prop car. Three theaters show movie footage about the cars and Barris' extreme career. Even learn the trick to how ghost cars operate. Great visuals and many favorite photo-ops.

INDIAN MOUNTAIN STATE PARK

Indian Mountain Road (I-75 exit 160, go north on U.S. Hwy. 25 to State Hwy. 297, make a right on London and a left on Dairy Street)

Jellico 37762

❑   Phone: (423) 784-7958
     Web: www.state.tn.us/environment/parks/indian/
❑   Hours: Daily 7:00am-sunset.

Located at the base of the Cumberland Mountains, this park is popular with campers. Park visitors can enjoy fishing at the two small lakes, picnicking, camping, and two walking trails (one paved and one unpaved). The park has a 80' x 42' swimming pool that is open from Memorial Day through late summer.

FORT SOUTHWEST POINT

(near Hwy. 58, overlooking junction of TN, Clinch, and Emory Rivers)

Kingston 37763

❑   Phone: (865) 376-3641. **Web: www.southwestpoint.com**
❑   Hours: Mostly weekends (April-September)
❑   Admission: FREE, donations accepted.
❑   Miscellaneous: Best to visit during family weekend activities & reenactments.

Fort Southwest Point is the only fort in Tennessee being reconstructed on its original foundation. The completed sections of the fort include a barracks, a blockhouse and 250 feet of palisade walls. A separate building houses the welcome center and museum. The fort is owned, operated, and maintained by the City of Kingston. The fort was constructed in 1797 and remained a working fort through 1811 when it was deemed that soldiers were no longer needed. At its peak there were over 625 soldiers stationed here.

WATTS BAR LAKE AREA

(Hwy 58)

Kingston 37763

❑   Phone: (865) 376-4201

Watts Bar Lake provides 783 miles of shoreline for fishing, boating, swimming, camping, hiking, and skiing. There are numerous boat docks and launching ramps throughout Roane County. Watts Bar Lake's many coves and islands, with natural sand beaches, make it an ideal lake for all water sports. Bird watchers will enjoy spotting eagles, herons, egrets, woodpeckers and others along the reservoir. For breathtaking views on the valley, lake and mountains, hike through the Mount Roosevelt State Forest running thru the area (Rockwood).

EAST TENNESSEE HISTORY CENTER

600 Market Street (corner of Market & Clinch Avenue, downtown)

Knoxville 37901

❑   Phone: (865) 215-8824. **Web: www.east-tennessee-history.org**
❑   Hours: Monday-Saturday 10:00am-4:00pm, Sunday 1:00-
    5:00pm.
❑   Admission: FREE
❑   Miscellaneous: The new, enlarged center closes May 2004, with
    scheduled re-opening by December 2004.

A visit to the Center will bring you face to face with the region's history makers. Here you will find larger than life figures, such as David (Davy) Crockett, Nancy Ward, and Sgt. Alvin C. York. Visitors enter in the year 1750 and follow the road to statehood in 1796. The legacy of the Cherokee Indians' "Trail of Tears" is illustrated, as well as an overcoat made by President Andrew Johnson, an East Tennessee tailor by trade. The Children's area is called Davy's Attic with a small log cabin full of clothing like Davy Crockett wore, books and puppets. The Museum also has "hold-it" boxes stationed everywhere. The boxes contain items that children can pick up and examine that relate to the period. Find out why a Governor's battle was called the "War of the Roses" or why Oak Ridge is called the "Secret City".

KNOXVILLE SYMPHONY ORCHESTRA

406 Union Avenue (most concerts @ Tennessee Theatre or Civic Auditorium)

Knoxville 37901

❑   Phone: (865) 291-3310 tickets or (865) 523-1178 office
    Web: www.knoxvillesymphony.com

Artists, mascots and superstars join the Maestro and the musicians for Pops, Youth Orchestra, Family and Holiday concerts. The Family Concert pre-show has a fun "Instrument Petting Zoo" where kids touch and play real orchestra instruments and learn why and how they produce different sounds.

TENNESSEE CHILDREN'S DANCE ENSEMBLE

4216 Sutherland Avenue

Knoxville 37901

❑   Phone: (865) 588-8842. **Web: www.korrnet.org/tcde/**

A unique modern dance company of 24 dancers, ages 8-17 which serve as Goodwill Ambassadors for the State of Tennessee plus regional performances a few times/year.

BLOUNT MANSION

200 West Hill Avenue (downtown, corner of Gay St & Hill Ave, near Volunteer Landing)

Knoxville 37902

❑   Phone: (865) 525-2375 or (888) 654-0016
      Web: www.blountmansion.org
❑   Hours: Monday-Saturday 9:30am-5:00pm (April - mid December).
      Closed Saturdays (January-March) and major holidays.
❑   Admission: $4.95 adult, $2.50 child (6-17).

This National Historic Landmark is the 1792 home of Territorial Governor William Blount (and signer of the US Constitution), the first and only governor of the Territory Southwest of the River Ohio. It is also the birthplace of Tennessee statehood in 1796. The frontier capital still stands on the original site. Start with a short introduction video that focuses on his diplomacy with the Cherokee. Hear about the many changes to the house. Look for the elegant original Blount shoe buckles and the children's toys. See the room where the state Constitution was signed. Interesting details shared throughout the tour about Blount family life, too.

STAR OF KNOXVILLE, TENNESSEE RIVERBOAT COMPANY

300 Neyland Drive (Volunteer Landing)

Knoxville 37902

❏   Phone: (865) 525-7827 or (800) 509-BOAT
      Web: http://tnriverboat.com

The authentic, Mississippi-style paddlewheel boat offers a view of Knoxville from the water on a brunch, luncheon, dinner (includes food & entertainment) or sightseeing cruise ($7.00-$12.00 per person, departs 3:00pm, Thursday-Sunday, May-October). Join the sightseeing cruise for a look at original historic sights along the beautiful Tennessee River. During the history commentary, the Captain will show points of interest along the river. The Star of Knoxville is fully air-conditioned and heated.

THREE RIVERS RAMBLER

Neyland Drive (Volunteer Landing between Calhouns & the boathouse)

Knoxville 37902

❏   Phone: (865) 524-9411. **Web: www.threeriversrambler.com**
❏   Hours: Saturday & Sunday 2:00pm and 5:00pm (April-
      November) except football home game days.
❏   Admission: $16.95 adult, $14.95 senior (55+), $9.95 child (6-12).
      Pullman luxury car $19.95 (all ages).

This vintage steam engine train takes guests on a 90-minute excursion to the Forks of the River and back, through some historic and scenic countrysides. On the trip back, stop for a while on the trestle bridge to feel like the train is flying in mid-air. Learn a little of the history of the town and famous folks who helped build it. An open air rail car is available to ride and each car is supplied with a uniformed conductor who explains the sites and is available for questions. At the Asbury Quarry, the train makes a brief stop where the locomotive is switched to return back to the depot. If it's very hot (90° F.+)...pay the extra for the air-conditioned luxury car.

EAST TENNESSEE DISCOVERY CENTER

516 N. Beaman St. at Chilhowee Park (I-40 exit 392, follow signs)

Knoxville 37914

❑   Phone: (865) 594-1494. **Web: www.etdiscovery.org**
❑   Hours: Monday-Friday 9:00am-5:00pm, Saturday 10:00am-
    5:00pm.
❑   Admission: $2.00-$4.00 (age 3+).

Hands-on science exhibits, Planetarium, Kidspace area for younger kids, Lego Construction Junction, Simple Machines and Energy experiments, and live arthropod, marine and reptile exhibits. Current living "creatures" include Madagascar giant hissing cockroaches, a honey bee colony, a scorpion, tarantula, black widow spider, millipedes, a leopard gecko and a ball python. Enter the Discovery Space shuttle and explore the universe through interactive control panel switches, spacecraft dioramas, question and answer lightboxes, and a shuttle "monitor" from which you can view space-related videos. Then step into the "Moon Room", where you can imagine what it would be like on the moon.

KNOXVILLE ZOO

3500 Knoxville Zoo Drive (I-40, near Rutledge Pike exit #392)

Knoxville 37914

❑   Phone: (865) 637-5331. **Web: www.knoxville-zoo.org**
❑   Hours: Daily 9:30am-4:30pm every day except Christmas. Spring
    & Fall weekend hours extended. Summer hours extended every day.
    Winter hours begin at 10:00am.
❑   Admission: $10.95 adult, $8.95 senior (65+), $6.95 child (3-12).
    Parking $3.00
❑   Miscellaneous: Camel rides for $3.00. The new KIDS COVE will
    be like life in Cades Cove in the Smokies during the 1800s. There
    are theatrical cabins, veggie gardens, animals & play spaces
    where kids interact with animals & role-play as farmers & zookeepers.

Mamie, Jana, Ellie and Tonka would like you to visit them in their new African Elephant Preserve (barn, pools, mud hole and man-made trees). Another set of animals love visitors at Black Bear

Falls. The exhibit has been recreated from an actual setting in the Smoky Mountains and brings visitors as close as they should get to a black bear. A 40-foot long tunnel designed as a huge hollow log provides up close "cubby" views of the black bears. Chimp Ridge is a 1.5 acre, open-air exhibit housing chimpanzees...with two full viewing areas to allow children to observe the animals. The Meerkats exhibit includes the ever-present "lookout" meerkat on duty. The zoo also features many other natural environments including Prairie Dog Pass (kids can crawl under and get a "Prairie Dog view" of the world), Pridelands, Penguin Rock and Tortoise Territory. Love the nature trails!

GATEWAY REGIONAL VISITOR CENTER

Volunteer Landing,

Knoxville 37915

❑   Phone: (865) 971-4440 or (800) 727-8045
      Web: www.volunteer-landing.com
❑   Hours: Monday-Saturday 9:00am-5:00pm, Sunday 1:00-5:00pm.
      Closed New Years, Thanksgiving, Christmastime.
❑   Admission: FREE
❑   Miscellaneous: The Star of Knoxville Riverboat and the Three
      Rivers Rambler train have depots near here. Calhoun's barbeque
      restaurant (on the river, daily lunch and dinner, 865-673-3355 or
      www.calhouns.com) have wonderful ribs and chicken to try
      while at the Landing. The FREE Knoxville Trolley has 4
      different lines that take you to every possible site near or in
      downtown. Saves you the hassle of parking, especially weekdays
      and sport weekends.

The Center serves as the primary information center for Knoxville and the surrounding area. The Southern Highlands Natural Atrium has pull-out drawers at kid-level full of fascinating items from the National Park sites surrounding town including bugs, leaves, rocks, etc. In the Oak Ridge Tech Garden, kids can play tic-tac-toe against a robot or look at a child's room with points magnified with a scanning electron microscope. The rest of Volunteer Landing offers attractions and eateries on the Tennessee River. At the

Marina paddle, pontoon, and houseboats are available for rental (865-633-5004 or **www.volunteermarina.com**). There are numerous historical markers along the one-mile riverwalk, including interactive displays that tell of the historic significance of the river (waterfalls & fountains, too). This is the place to start your visit in town because you really get a handle on the historical and fun attractions around town and in East Tennessee.

JAMES WHITE FORT

205 East Hill Avenue (Volunteer Landing area)

Knoxville 37915

❑   Phone: (865) 525-6514
     Web: www.vic.com/tnchron/RESOURCE/WHITE.htm
❑   Hours: Monday-Friday 10:00am-4:00pm (January, February),
     Monday-Saturday 9:30am-4:30pm (March-December).
❑   Admission: $5.00 adult, $2.00 child (6-12).

Located on a bluff above the Tennessee River near downtown, the fort was built in 1786 by General James White, Knoxville's founder. General White brought his wife and children across the mountains from North Carolina to claim land given to him for his service in the American Revolution. Originally it consisted of his home, three cabins and the stockade wall used to protect the little community from Indian attacks and the threat of wild animals. What would the pioneers eat? They often used bread bowls instead of plates. How would you cook? What are your chores? The guides here really ask questions and engage the kids in what pioneer life was like.

KNOXVILLE ICE BEARS

500 Howard Baker, Jr Drive (games played at Civic Coliseum)

Knoxville 37915

❑   Phone: (865) 521-9991. **Web: www.knoxvilleicebears.com**

Between October and March, the new Ice Bears will play 29 home games (part of the Atlantic Coast Hockey League). $6.00-$15.00 per ticket.

WOMEN'S BASKETBALL HALL OF FAME

700 Hall of Fame Drive (I-40 exit 388, then Summitt Hill Dr. exit,
near Volunteer Landing)

Knoxville 37915

- ❑ Phone: (865) 633-9000. **Web: www.WBHOF.com**
- ❑ Hours: Monday-Saturday 10:00am-7:00pm, Sunday 1:00-
  6:00pm. Closed on Christmas Day, Thanksgiving Day and Easter
  with abbreviated hours on some holidays.
- ❑ Admission: $7.95 adult, $5.95 senior (62+) & child (6-15).
- ❑ Miscellaneous: May we suggest the Best Western Cedar Bluff
  exit 378A. (865) 539-0058 or (800) 348-2562. They have
  reasonable, clean, spacious rooms with an outdoor pool and
  continental breakfast. Located on the west side of town with
  loads of restaurants nearby.

The world's most interactive Hall of Fame brings college, Olympic
and Pro teams' history to life. The facility features three indoor
courts, an interactive locker room where visitors can hear a coach's
halftime talk or "In the Huddle" pep talk with the coach (great
photo ops). Put yourself in a Hall of Fame's induction pics or sit on
benches amongst players. See the world's largest basketball or try
your skills on the Ballgirl Athletic Playground. Dioramas feature
an early basketball scene and the Red Heads actual touring car.
Tip-Off Theater's inspirational film packs all the emotion of more
than 100 years of history of women's basketball into 15 minutes. A
very inspiring and exciting museum!

IJAMS NATURE CENTER

2915 Island Home Avenue (south of Fort Loudon Lake)

Knoxville 37920

- ❑ Phone: (865) 577-4717 **Web: www.ijams.org**
- ❑ Hours: Monday-Friday 9:00am-4:00pm, Saturday Noon-4:00pm,
  Sunday 1:00-5:00pm. Grounds open 8:00am until sunset.
- ❑ Admission: FREE

The regional environmental education center is surrounded by
more than 150 acres of beautiful forests, meadows, ponds and

gardens connected by 5 miles of trails. Special events include evening walks in the park, canoe trips, junior naturalist workshops, Bug Night, Invasive Species Movie Marathon and Music in the Park.

MARBLE SPRINGS STATE HISTORIC FARMSTEAD

1220 W. Gov. John Sevier Highway (at the corner of Gov. John Sevier Highway and Neubert Springs)

Knoxville 37920

❑   Phone: (865) 573-5508

   Web: www.korrnet.org/jsma/index.html

❑   Hours: Tuesday-Saturday 10:00am-5:00pm. Weekdays (Monday-Thursday) only in the spring and fall. Limited winter hours.

❑   Admission: Yes, varies with event.

John Sevier, Tennessee's first governor, built this house when he came to the state capital in 1796. Marble Springs continued to be his home during his six terms as governor and two terms as a US Rep. This working farmstead, log structures and farm animals are used to educate the public about the life and times of the Governor.

HISTORIC CANDY FACTORY AND WORLD'S FAIR PARK SITES

1060 World's Fair Park Drive

Knoxville 37996

❑   Phone: (865) 546-5707

A collection of shops and galleries featuring the works of local and regional artists. Also, home to a working chocolate factory (watch the ooey-gooey folks dipping chocolates by hand), near a children's playground called Fort Kid. Food cafes with light lunchtime snacks available. Also, the Art Museum Sunsphere and playful water fountains are in this square block area.

KNOXVILLE MUSEUM OF ART

1050 World's Fair Park Drive (near US 441 & US 11/70, I-40 exit 388, follow signs)

Knoxville 37996

❑ Phone: (865) 525-6101. **Web: www.knoxart.org**
❑ Hours: Tuesday-Friday Noon-8:00pm or 9:00pm, Saturday-Sunday 11:00am-5:00pm. Closed major holidays.
❑ Admission: $5.00 adult (age 18+). FREE child.
❑ Miscellaneous: In the World's Fair Park is the Sunsphere, the 266-foot tall steel tower with a golden globe that was built for the 1982 World's Fair. Across the street is Fort Kid playground.

Highlighted in the permanent collection are works of American art created during and after the 1960s. The museum also contains five galleries, a Sculpture Terrace, and an Exploratory Gallery. In Exploratory, "put your face on" or walk into portraits, work on paper, abstract paint and read art-related books and games. The space is designed for pre-kindergarten and elementary school groups during weekdays, and self-directed for parents and children on weekends and holidays.

UNIVERSITY OF TENNESSEE CAMPUS

(most off or near Volunteer Blvd running thru the heart of campus)

Knoxville 37996

Some sites you want to see include:

FOOTBALL HALL OF FAME: (865-974-5789). 1704 Johnny Majors Drive, Neyland Thompson Sports Center. Monday-Friday 8:00am-5:00pm. FREE. The museum stands as a tribute to the student athletes who shaped 100+ years of Volunteer Football.

MCCLUNG MUSEUM: (865-974-2144). 1327 Circle Park Drive, next to Visitors Info & Parking. **http://mcclungmuseum.utk.edu**. Monday-Saturday 9:00am-5:00pm, Sunday 1:00-5:00pm. Closed holidays. The Geology and Fossil History of Tennessee exhibition focuses on the many years of the state's geologic past and explores, thru graphics and animation, formations and drift. Special features are six life-size dioramas of life forms at various times with actual fossils of creatures, a replica of a giant dinosaur marine lizard or T-rex, and actual dino eggs. Also, Ancient Egypt and a Freshwater Mussels exhibit. Look for the many unusual fossils, both on display or under "walk-on windows" at your feet. A video portrays the journey of Cherokee through the ages.

GARDENS: (865) 974-7324). Neyland Drive at the Agriculture Campus. Daily sunrise to sunset. FREE. More than 1400 varieties of herbs and woody landscape plants, the All-America Flower Trials and TenneSelect program.

MCKENZIE SCULPTURE OF ATHLETES: (865-974-1250). 1801 Volunteer Blvd., Thornton Athletic Student Life Center. FREE. 8:00am-4:00pm, Monday-Friday. Over 100 sculptural works including statuettes, bas-reliefs, medals, portrait medallions and plaques, which celebrate athletic achievement.

UNIVERSITY OF TENNESSEE ATHLETICS: NCAA baseball, basketball, cross-country, golf, swimming, track, volleyball & football. (800) 332-VOLS.

SAM HOUSTON SCHOOLHOUSE

3650 Old Sam Houston School Road (Hwy 33 north of town, follow signs)

Maryville 37804

❑   Phone: (865) 983-1550
❑   Hours: Tuesday - Saturday 10:00am-5:00pm, Sunday 1:00-5:00pm.
❑   Admission: $1.00 adult, FREE child.

The oldest one-room log schoolhouse in the state (1794). Built two years before Tennessee became a state, the schoolhouse in Blount County is named for former Tennessee Gov. Sam Houston who opened the schoolhouse and served as one of its enthusiastic instructors. Students, ranging in age from 6 to 60, paid $8 to attend classes. Visitors will find benches for students, the teacher's desk (and 19th century readers) and a fireplace used to warm the room. Look for the unique window covers that also served as tables. Houston was attorney general and a two-term congressman while in Tennessee. In his younger years, he was adopted by the Cherokee and named "the Raven". Years later, after relocating to Texas, he became governor and president of the Republic of Texas, making him the only individual serving as governor of two states. He boldly fought for the rights of Indians in the West left after the Trail of Tears…trying to make an Indian state just for them. Be sure to ask for the audio self-guided tour. It's very well done and easy to follow for kids.

BIG RIDGE STATE PARK

1015 Big Ridge Road (From I-75 exit 122, take Hwy. 61 east approx. 12 miles)

Maynardville 37807

❑   Phone: (865) 992-5523
     Web: www.state.tn.us/environment/parks/bigridge/direct.htm
❑   Hours: Daily 8:00am-10:00pm. Nature Center closes at 4:30pm.
❑   Admission: FREE

The heavily forested, 3,687-acre park lies on the southern shore of TVA's Norris Lake. In the Nature Center natural, historical and cultural exhibits depict scenes in the Big Ridge area including a display of mounted fauna of the Big Ridge area. The cabins are rustic in style. Everything is located mainly in one big room. Cabins have hardwood floors, kitchen, linens, many w/ fireplaces/firewood, and screened in porches. There is no air conditioning, televisions or phones. Five cabins sit lakeside. Fourteen sit on the ridge. Other activities include: camping, boating, hiking, fishing and playground/sport field areas.

MUSEUM OF APPALACHIA

Highway 61 (I-75 exit 122)

Norris 37769

❑   Phone: (865) 494-7680 **Web: www.museumofappalachia.com**
❑   Hours: Year Round during daylight hours. Closed only on Christmas.

For updates visit our website: www.kidslovepublications.com

❑ Admission: $12.00 adult (13-54), $10.00 senior (55+), $5.00 child (6-12), $28.00 family rate.

Discover the pre-WWII heritage of the area at this 65-acre Appalachian history complex. John Rice Irwin's open-air museum is called "the most authentic and complete replica of pioneer Appalachian life in the world." The museum contains over 250,000 pioneer everyday relics including 30 log structures - a chapel, a schoolhouse, cabins and barns. There's even a restaurant and craft center. Of special interest to kids is the Mark Twain Family Cabin, Uncle John's dirt floor cabin (used as Daniel Boone's TV Home), and the Children's Corner in the Hall of Fame building. Look for a shoe carved from coal and a lot of whittlers and fiddlers who used their spare time to create famous works or just plain weird works of art? (i.e. A ukulele made from matchsticks or a "ukuweewee" – a "bed pan" banjo). A great, leisurely day trip...with lots to look see.

NORRIS DAM STATE PARK

125 Village Green Circle (From I-75, take exit 128 and go 2.5 miles south on Hwy. 441 to the entrance of the park),

Norris 37769

❑ Phone: (865) 426-7461

http://www.state.tn.us/environment/parks/parks/NorrisDam/

❑ Hours: Park Hours: Summer 8:00am - 10:00pm. Winter 8:00am - sundown. Lenoir Museum Hours: Wednesday-Sunday 9:00am-5:00pm.

The first dam built in the TVA system, this area provided part of the electricity for the now historic Manhattan Project. The park recreation center is located at the Village Green Complex. A fee paid outdoor pool (only open June - early August), badminton, volleyball, basketball and many other activities are available to park visitors. Norris Lake is a sportsman's paradise offering 800 miles of shore-line for camping, boating, fishing and more. The park has 19 rustic vacation cabins and 10 three-bedroom deluxe cabins. All are located in quiet, wooded settings and are completely equipped for housekeeping including electrical appliances, cooking and serving utensils, and linens. Guided activities include a nice morning lake cruise, wildlife tours, critter scavenger hunts and crafts or owl/bat walks. <u>18TH CENTURY RICE GRIST MILL</u> Originally constructed in 1798 along Lost Creek, this mill was operated by four generations of the Rice family. At times, the mill was also rigged to power a sawmill, a cotton gin, a trip hammer and even to operate a dynamo that supplied electrical lights for the Rice home in 1899. Clear Creek Trail runs along the stream feeding the mill…very scenic…look for trout. <u>LENOIR MUSEUM</u> - display of pre-industrial revolution equipment and products. When you visit the Museum, make sure and get a close look at the antique barrel organ. The organ plays ten different tunes with 110 wood pipes to make the music. In all, 44 figures are in action. These figures include dancers dancing, a clown clowning, foot soldiers marching, a woman churning and a blacksmith hard at work. Also, ask about the collection of antique mouse traps.

AMERICAN MUSEUM OF SCIENCE AND ENERGY

300 South Tulane Avenue (I-75S exit 122, Hwy 61 turns into Hwy 95, Oak Ridge Pkwy to traffic light #10. or I-40 exit 376, Rte. 162N)

Oak Ridge 37830

❑ Phone: (865) 576-3200. **Web: www.amse.org**
❑ Hours: Tuesday-Saturday 9:00am-5:00pm, Sunday 1:00-5:00pm. Closed Christmas, Thanksgiving and New Years.
❑ Admission: $3.00 adult, $2.00 senior (65+) and child (6-17).
❑ Miscellaneous: Best for kids nearing middle school age and older, mostly because they have studied some of the science behind atomic energy.

About one-third of the museum is devoted to the World War II Manhattan Project that created the secret city of Oak Ridge…enriching uranium that is used in nuclear bombs. One-third highlights basic science and technology and one-third is devoted to fossil fuels and alternative energy sources. There are live demonstrations for audience participation, hands-on activities, and models and devices to explore, experiment and discover more about how the world works through science. Key spots are the: Solar Energy Project, Cold War/Civil Defense - model of atomic plant, sample lab diorama, and try-on assembly lab equipment. Real Robots, Science & Tech Career Centers - modern uses for old technology facilities. Atoms and Atom Smashers - This is a regularly scheduled demonstration (2-3 times daily) that combines a discussion of basic atomic structure with a "hair raising" demonstration of static electricity. Volunteer to become a very positively charged person! Funny and fun!

CHILDREN'S MUSEUM OF OAK RIDGE

461 West Outer Drive (SR 95 to SR 62NW to Outer Drive, east)

Oak Ridge 37830

❑   Phone: (865) 482-1074

   Web: http://childrensmuseumofoakridge.org

❑   Hours: Monday-Friday 9:00am-5:00pm, Saturday-Sunday 1:30-
   4:30pm. Summer Saturdays open 11:00am.

❑   Admission: $6.00 adult, $5.00 senior, $4.00 child (3-18).

The motto of the museum is "please touch". Learn new ideas, develop useful skills - there is something for all ages. Tour the simulated Amazon rainforest, complete with sound effects, a waterfall, a railed walkway, beautiful murals, an observation deck high in the forest canopy-and many trees, flowers, and wild animals. Now, watch a large model train display, or visit The Homestead consisting of three re-constructed log houses furnished with artifacts from 1850 to 1880. Each cabin depicts life on the frontier. Students frequently participate by role playing here and at City Life / Country Life (two period rooms, circa 1910). It is not unusual to watch children walking around in wooden shoes and another group "making music" on an African Balafon in the International Hall. Waterworks or the Discovery Lab touch on science.

SECRET CITY SCENIC EXCURSION TRAIN
Hwy 58, East TN Technology Park, **Oak Ridge** 37830

❑   Phone: (865) 241-2140

   Web: www.techscribes.com/sarm/sarm.htm

❑   Hours: Spring, Summer and Fall season schedules. See Seasonal
   & Special Events. Regular Trips June - September depart on the
   1st & 3rd Saturday each month at 11:00am, 1:00pm, 3:00pm and
   5:30pm Dinner Train.

❑   Admission: $12.00 adult. $8.00 child (12 and under). Lap
   children are free.

Ride the Atomic Train on a 12-mile tour through the once secret
K-25 Manhattan Project site and enjoy the scenic beauty of the
Blair Community.

WWII MANHATTAN PROJECT SITES
302 S. Tulane Avenue

Oak Ridge 37830

❑   Phone: (865) 482-7821

The self-guided auto tour map and/or tape of World War II's Secret
City gives you the opportunity to experience the important sites
built by the government for the now historic Manhattan Project -
the government code name for the development of the Atomic
Bomb! When this small valley grew in 1942 it consumed 1/7th of
the electricity in the United States, had the 4th largest bus
transportation system and employed 75,000 workers. The
highlight is the **EAST TENNESSEE TECHNOLOGY PARK
OVERLOOK** *(Former K-25 WWII Manhattan Project Facility)*
Hwy. 58, Oak Ridge, (865) 574-9683. View the historic former
Manhattan Project Facility in this overlook that features pictures,
historic displays and video. Daily, 9:00pm-5:00pm FREE. Small
fee for tape/CD tour.

SWEETWATER VALLEY FARM

17988 West Lee Highway (I-75 exit 68, SR 323 east to Hwy 11, turn left)

Philadelphia 37846

❑   Phone: (865) 458-9192 or (877) 862-4332
     Web: www.sweetwatervalley.com
❑   Hours: Monday-Saturday 10:00am-4:00pm. Extended store hours seasonally.
❑   Tours: Monday-Saturday 9:00am (summer). Saturdays at 10:00am & 2:00pm (spring). Pre-arranged group tours include an activity pack for each child (sm. Fee).
❑   Miscellaneous: If you just stop in, you can watch a video and sample - 15 minutes.

Sweetwater Valley Farms boasts the best farmstead cheese in the state with names like Tennessee Aged Cheddar and Volunteer Jack. Their cows and what they eat are part of their secret. Stop in and see how cheese is made while tasting delicious samples. The phrase "curds and whey" turns into reality when visitors are able to observe cheesemaking thru a viewing window. "Cheddar" becomes a verb which describes the process of pasteurization, culturing (ugh!), slabbing, draining, milling, blocking and aging. If you opt for the farm tour, you'll get a close view of the Feed Shed. Cows have 4 stomachs and need lots of food (it takes 100 lbs of feed and 50 gallons of water to make just 10 gallons of milk). They serve them 8 different grain blends made from things like cottonseed and tofu! Very interesting agricultural tour!

DINOSAUR WALK MUSEUM

106 Showplace Blvd. (near stoplight 1, right on the parkway)

Pigeon Forge 37863

❑   Phone: (865) 428-4003. **Web: www.dinosaurwalkmuseum.com**
❑   Hours: 9:00am-8:00pm daily except Christmas.
❑   Admission: $9.95 adult, $6.95 child (6-18). Look for discount pricing coupons around town…otherwise the small, but tall, museum is pricey.

Dinosaur Walk Museum *(cont.)*

Walk among nature's largest creatures as you watch over 50 realistic life-size sculptures of dinosaurs and other giant creatures (killer shark, sea lizards, flocks of flying reptiles). The creatures, some standing two-stories tall, are displayed in natural settings complete with waterfalls and special sound effects. To add to the experience, parents like the informative text that accompanies each exhibit...telling the story of each life form. Guess what, Moms, there's also over 20 reptile exhibits featuring some of the world's most venomous snakes. Your kids will probably know more about these creatures than you...be prepared for "Wows". The largest replicas we've ever seen...some you even walk under!

DOLLY'S SPLASH COUNTRY

1020 Dollywood Lane (turn off parkway at stoplight #8)

Pigeon Forge 37863

- ❑   Phone: (865) 428-9488. **Web: www.dollyssplashcountry.com**
- ❑   Hours: Mid-May to early September. Daytime hours. See website for details.
- ❑   Admission: $24.00-$29.00 (age 4+). Combo packages with Dollywood at a discount available.
- ❑   Miscellaneous: Showers, changing rooms, lockers and concessions. Bring your own towels.

Located on 25 wooded acres, this waterpark provides life jackets and lifeguards for safety. There's a 25,000 sq. ft. Wave Pool, 13 Water Slides (from mild to wild), a Lazy River (the longest and most pleasant we've seen!), and two interactive Child's Play areas. Raintree Hollow is a large area of the complex with two slides for the water blasters. Mountain Twist is a 3-slide complex with twists, turns and a 42-foot drop. Some areas are shady, some in the sun. Lots of places to lounge near every ride make the park very manageable for families.

DOLLYWOOD

1020 Dollywood Lane (one mile off the parkway)

Pigeon Forge 37863

- ❑ Phone: (865) 428-9494 or –9488. **Web: www.dollywood.com**
- ❑ Hours: Daily 9:00am until dark (June - mid August). Otherwise open 3-5 days/week (April, May, late August, September-December). Best to view website for details.
- ❑ Admission:$29.00-$38.00 per person (age 4+). Second day is half price. Add about $20.00 per day if combined with Splash Country.
- ❑ Miscellaneous: There are 5 sit-down restaurants and over one dozen fast food spots throughout the park…most offer BBQ and southern buffet specialties. Festival of Nations runs April-mid May: sample entertainment, crafts, cultures and foods from around the globe (many exotic, ethnic dances and music). Harvest Celebration & Gospel Jubilee in October.

Dolly Parton grew up with the Smokies as her playground, so she decided to theme her entertainment park after a combination of her childhood and the Appalachian Mountains. 22 thrilling rides (from a 70 mph triple loop coaster to leaping over a mountain waterfall at 50 mph) and over 40 shows (from new country to the 50s to gospel acts) are the big draw here. Explore unique areas where kids run and soak each other at Dreamland Forest (US's largest treehouse). Adventures in Imagination includes an interactive museum of Dolly's life and a four-dimensional simulator ride on a journey through the Smoky Mountains (fun, but very jerky and bumpy). Browse thru dozens of Master Craftsmen's showcases where old-art like glassblowing, blacksmithing, wagonmaking, etc. are demonstrated. Each season brings a different theme but summertime brings popular icons of children's entertainment in a character show, extreme sports shows, street performers and many hands-on activities. Worried about hot summer days…most of the rides get you wet…or, at least windy! Also, most of the rides are for all school-aged kids…just check with someone exiting the ride if you have concerns about the "scare" factor.

FUN TIME TROLLEYS

Pigeon Forge 37863

❑   Phone: (865) 453-6444

Fun Time Trolleys takes you to more than 100 stops throughout the city…for only 25 cents per person.

NATIONAL FREEDOM MUSEUM

110 Showplace Blvd. (near Stoplight 1, right on the parkway)

Pigeon Forge 37863

❑   Phone: (865) 908-6003. **Web: www.veteransmemorialpf.com**
❑   Hours: Daily 9:00am - 8:00pm, except Christmas.
❑   Admission: $11.00 adult, $10.00 veteran, $6.95 teen (12-18), $4.95 child (6-11). Look for discount coupons around town.

Look for the full-size WWII P-51 Mustang and you've found the place. Thousands of exhibits here cover the American Revolution, Civil War, Indian Wars, Spanish-American War, World Wars, Korean War, Vietnam, Gulf War and even as recent as the War on Terror. Observe, or bring along a veteran who lived through these wars…you'll soon realize the sacrifices made by our veterans. Notable exhibits are one of the World's largest life-size Memorial Bronzes of men-in-action or the radio-controlled fighter plant - cool. The many famous death masks are notable and, the walls of names of those who died in war are very touching…as is this emotionally and beautifully displayed site of honor.

OLD MILL AND GENERAL STORE

160 Old Mill Avenue (traffic light #7, just off parkway)

Pigeon Forge 37863

❑   Phone: (865) 453-4628 or (888) 453-6455
     Web: www.old-mill.com
❑   Hours: Restaurant hours: Daily 7:30am-9:00pm.
❑   Tours: Guided tours

❑   Miscellaneous: The Old Mill Restaurant is noted for its southern cooking. Specialties include signature corn chowder, pot roast and gravy, homemade chicken and dumplings, southern fried chicken, and their delicious pecan pie. Biscuits made from scratch, homemade banana nut muffins, and stone ground grits are just a few items featuring products ground at the mill next door. All dinners are served with corn chowder, homemade fritters, salad, veggies and free dessert.

Step back in time at this scenic, water-powered Grist Mill. Browse through the General Store, where you can purchase fresh stone-ground products. In the same building, where for many years farmers dropped off wagons of kernel corn and picked up their bags of flour and grits, you can take a guided tour and see how the Old Mill grinds corn into meal using the same machinery that was considered antique a hundred years ago.

PIGEON FORGE THEATERS

Parkway

Pigeon Forge 37863

❑   Admission: Varies between $10.00-$30.00 per person.

BLACK BEAR JAMBOREE DINNER & SHOW - High-flying Country Dinner Revue, 5:00pm & 8:00pm, shows daily. (865) 908-7469 or (800) 985-5494

THE BLACKWOOD BROTHERS - Great gospel to classic country music. Breakfast show 8:30am. (865) 908-7469 or (800) 985-5494

CLASSIC COUNTRY THEATER - Best of the 50s, 60s, & 70s music. Showtime 8:00pm. Opens in March. (865) 774-7469 or (866) 430-8422.

COUNTRY TONITE THEATRE - the show's foundation is country music, from classics to contemporary. Award-winning cloggers. Opens in March. (865) 453-2003 or (800) 792-4308.

Pigeon Forge Theaters *(cont.)*

ELWOOD SMOOCH'S OLE SMOKY HOEDOWN - Musical comedy clown Elwood Smooch and his versatile family of singers and musicians present the "Happiest Show in the Smokies". Showtime 7:30pm (3-5 days/week). Patty Waszak - One Gal...30 Instruments also at theatre. (865) 428-5600.

GRAND ILLUSION - Illusionist Terry Evanswood dazzles and mystifies morning audiences at Country Tonite Theatre. A two-hour tour into the world of magic and mystery. Showtime 10:00am. (865) 453-2003 or (800) 792-4308.

LOUISE MANDRELL THEATER - Louise Mandrell has put her name on this theater and her many talents on stage featuring singing, dancing and playing numerous instruments. Musical variety, beautiful costumes and special effects. Mostly songs grandparents enjoy. Showtime 7:30pm (4-6 days per week, beginning in April). (865) 453-6263 or (800) 768-1170.

INTEGRITY - A strong southern gospel group performs weekdays at 10:00am and Sundays at 7:30pm at the Louise Mandrell Theater. (865) 453-6263 or (800) 768-1170

SMOKY MOUNTAIN JUBILEE - a production filled with classic and current country music, Appalachian clogging, traditional gospel tunes and comedy. Weekends January - April, varied schedule May-June. Showtime 8:30pm. (865) 428-1836.

COMEDY BARN THEATER - Clean comedians, magicians, jugglers, fire-eaters plus funny Country Bands and barnyard animals. Shows nightly (except January/February) @ 8:15pm, some matinees on weekends, (865) 428-5222 or (800) 29-Laugh or **www.comedybarn.com**.

SCENIC HELICOPTER TOURS

2491 Parkway, **Pigeon Forge** 37863

❑   Phone: (865) 453-6342 or (877) 428-6929
    Web: www.scenichelicopters.com
❑   Hours: Monday - Saturday 10:00am - Dark (weather permitting),
    Sunday Noon - Dark (weather permitting).

For updates visit our website: www.kidslovepublications.com

❏   Admission: Flights begin as low as $10.00 per person and go up
      in price.

Spectacular views of the mountain area. You can say you "Flew
over the Smokies"!

❏   INTRODUCTION RIDE - $10.00 per person - Nice sample ride.
      800 to 1000 feet high, this 4 mile trip gives you an idea what a
      helicopter ride is like with a beautiful view.

❏   RIVER ISLAND (8-9 miles) - $15.00 per person - This flight
      takes you over the French Broad river and rolling hills of Sevier
      County, from 1000 feet above where you can see the beautiful
      panorama of the area. With an air speed at over 100 mph, you
      will cover almost 8 miles.

❏   DOUGLAS LAKE (10-12 miles) $23.00 per person - This flight
      soars up over 1200 feet, above pretty Tennessee farm country, on
      the way to Douglas Dam with a beautiful lake view.

❏   BLUFF MOUNTAIN (14-16 miles) $30.00 per person - As you
      depart from the heliport toward the lower foothills of Bluff
      Mountain at 1500 feet you will be amazed at the view of the
      Smoky Mountains.

❏   FOOTHILLS (22-24 miles) $45.00 per person - This seems to be
      the most popular flight taken by couples and families who want
      to take advantage of the opportunity to fly over beautiful
      mountains as well as enjoy a little city view. You'll be snapping
      pictures the entire flight.

TRACK FAMILY RECREATION CENTER, (THE)

2575 Parkway (traffic light #3)

Pigeon Forge 37863

❏   Phone: (865) 453-4777. **Web: www.funatthetrack.com**
❏   Hours: Open 9:00am or 10:00am until dark.
❏   Admission: $2.25-$6.00 per ride per person

The action-packed family recreation center features the ultimate in
go-kart tracks, like the Wild Woody, a three-tiered go-kart/roller
coaster hybrid. Themed miniature golf, splash 'em on bumper
boats, or test your courage from the top of the bungee jumping

tower. Other features: The Rio Grande Train, The Carousel, The Red Baron Plane Ride, Spin Tops, Swings, Ferris Wheel, and Noah's Lark Giant Swinging Boat. Clean, safe environment...easy to manage all the rides as a family.

DIXIE STAMPEDE, DOLLY PARTON'S DINNER & SHOW

3849 Parkway (near stoplight #8 on the parkway)

Pigeon Forge 37868

❑ Phone: (865) 453-4400 or (800) 356-1676
Web: www.dixiestampede.com

❑ Hours: Year-round, almost daily at 6:00pm. Most Fridays, Saturdays and summer season also 8:30pm.

❑ Admission: $35.99 Adult, $18.99 Children(4-11yrs). Be sure to come hungry!

❑ Miscellaneous: Meet the horses in the show from 10:00am until showtime on display along the horsewalk outside. Farm animal allergies? Be prepared with your medications. May we suggest MainStay Suites, near traffic light #6 @ (888) 428-8350 or **www.mainstaypigeonforge.com**. Small kitchen, continental breakfast and fantastic indoor/outdoor pools plus a tube mini-lazy river!

The Smokies most fun place to eat! I guarantee it, says owner, Dolly Parton. The very action-packed dinner and show features 32 magnificent horses, beautiful costumes, gallant heroes, incredible horsemanship, and a stand to-your-feet patriotic finale...all in the massive indoor arena. All this excitement while enjoying a fabulous four-course feast that you have to eat with your hands! The soup and chicken are wonderful and while you're finishing your main course, you may be asked (kids and parents) to participate in several races - don't worry, everyone laughs with you and cheers you on. Kick back with live bluegrass music and comedy in the Carriage Room (snacks served there beforehand). You'll love the dancing horses and the pig and giant ostrich races! The comic, Skeeter, is the best!

MEMORIES THEATRE

2141 Parkway (between stoplights #0 & #1)

Pigeon Forge 37868

❏ Phone: (865) 428-7852 or (800) 325-3078
Web: www.memoriestheatre.com

❏ Hours: Monday-Saturday 8:00pm. Closed in January. Friday and
Saturday only in February and March.

❏ Admission: $24.50 adult, $19.00 teen, $5.00 child (7-12).

Tributes to legendary music artists are featured in Memories'
Salute to Elvis & Friends. "Elvis" and Charlie Hodge, Elvis' long-
time friend & band member, star in a "Tribute to Elvis" and are
joined by other entertainers who pay honor and perform as Kenny
Rogers, Roy Orbison, Buddy Holly, the Blues Brothers, Tom
Jones, Neil Diamond, Cher and Rod Stewart. Elvis cuts up and
engages Charlie in dialog about living and working with Elvis (get
the scoop). The "Friends" begin the show. Their amazing look-
alikeness, mannerisms and vocal talent really impressed us! Great
show to take kids to after they've visited Graceland or are fans of
some of the famous performers that started back in the 70s and
80s.

RAINFOREST ADVENTURES

109 Nascar Drive (off Parkway, north at Walmart, west at Nascar
Dr), **Sevierville** 37862

❏ Phone: (865) 428-4091. **Web: www.rfadventures.com**

❏ Hours: Daily 9:00am-6:00pm except Christmas day.

❏ Admission: $11.99 adult, $9.99 senior (55+), $6.99 child (3-12).

One of the largest tropical zoos in the world is home to tropical
birds, pythons and anacondas, tree frogs and giant tortoises…all
indoors. Your Jungle Expedition begins once you pass through the
recreated ancient ruins, past a 25 foot tall jungle waterfall, and
enter the Rainforest. Favorites may be the animated parrots,
cockatoos or Zabu, the Madagascan ring-tailed lemur. Live shows
are conducted daily on each of the odd hours of the day.

TENNESSEE MUSEUM OF AVIATION

135 Air Museum Way (I-40 exit 407, US 66 southwest, then North on US 441)

Sevierville 37864

❑   Phone: (866) AV-MUSEUM **Web: www.tnairmuseum.com**
❑   Hours: Monday-Saturday 10:00am-6:00pm, Sunday 1:00-6:00pm.
❑   Admission: $12.75 adult, $9.75 senior (60+), $6.75 child (6-12).

Experience warbirds in this ever-changing exhibit space. You might even witness a demonstration war plane fly-by. Dioramas with videos help explain the progress of flight and how planes were used in wartime. The flight simulator on combat missions is probably the most fun for kids. Worth it for big wartime aviation buffs...otherwise, somewhat pricey for the amount of family interest. Their special events (listed on their website) are the best time to visit.

FORBIDDEN CAVERNS

455 Blowing Cave Road (I-40 exit 432A, Hwy 411S OR I-40 exit 407, Hwy 66S to US 411N)

Sevierville 37876

❑   Phone: (865) 453-5972. **Web: www.forbiddencavern.com**
❑   Hours: Daily 10:00am-6:00pm (April-November).
❑   Admission: $10.00 adult, $9.00 senior, $5.00 child (5-12).

The one hour walking tour past shimmering formations, towering natural chimneys, numerous grottos and a crystal-clear stream is added to with special lighting effects, a sound presentation and information from tour guides. Look for the largest wall of rare cave onyx known to exist and remnants of moonshining apparatus.

MUSCLE CAR MUSEUM, FLOYD GARRETT'S

320 Winfield Dunn Parkway (I-40 exit 407, southwest on US 66, 9 miles)

Sevierville 37876

❑ Phone: (865) 908-0882. Web: www.musclecarmuseum.com
❑ Hours: Daily 9:00am-6:00pm. Closed Thanksgiving and Christmas.
❑ Admission: $8.95 adult, $3.00 child (8-12). FREE (age 7 and under).

Large, newer collection of American Muscle Cars (90+) including factory lightweights, rare engines, superstock cars and NASCAR items. Begin with Elvis' limo and Cadillac. Even see the famous TNN "Shadetree Mechanic" T-Bucket! Fun stop for racing fans on your way to the Smoky Mountains.

SMOKY MOUNTAIN DEER FARM & EXOTIC PETTING ZOO

478 Happy Hollow Lane

Sevierville 37876

❑ Phone: (865) 428-DEER. Web: www.deerfarmzoo.com
❑ Hours: Daily 10:00am-5:30pm. Closed Thanksgiving and Christmastime.
❑ Admission: $7.50 adult, $4.00 child (3-12). Feed cups $1.50-$3.50.
❑ Miscellaneous: Pony rides and horseback riding ($4.00-$20.00 extra).

Start or end your Smoky Mountain vacation at the Smoky Mountain Deer Farm & Exotic Petting Zoo. You can do more than just look at the deer at the Deer Farm. You're offered a rare opportunity to walk among, pet and feed over 100 hand-tamed deer as well as being able to interact with many other animals from around the world. See and pet ...zebra, zonkeys, camels, reindeer, kangaroos, wallabies, prairie dogs, miniature goats, exotic cattle, miniature horses and donkeys, and emu. The mini-mini horses are adorable. Fawns are born in June and July - the Bucks' antlers growing April through August; in full rack September through March.

TENNESSEE SMOKIES BASEBALL

3540 Line Drive (Smokies Park, I-40 East to Hwy. 66, Exit 407)

Sevierville (Kodak) 37764

❑   Phone: (865) 286-2300 or (888) 978-2288

Web: www.smokiesbaseball.com

Take your family out to the ballgame in a new stadium for AA affiliate for the St. Louis Cardinals, the Tennessee Smokies. Concessions and Double Play Café restaurant.

CADES COVE

10042 Campground Drive (just off Hwy 321, head south out of Townsend)

Townsend 37882

❑   Phone: (865) 448-4108 Park or (865) 448-6286 Hayrides

Web: www.smokymountains.org

❑   Hours: Basically, sunrise to sunset.

❑   Miscellaneous: Visitors Center. Many cabin resort rentals are nearby. Orientation Center has $1.00 book that explains every marker and stop. Plan to spend hours exploring here.

Cades Cove's 11-mile loop road takes visitors back to the late 19th century (pass by many historic structures). The Primitive Baptist Church is made of wood and has wonderful acoustics. Mike Clemmer (**www.clemmerdulcimer.com**) recorded his dulcimer CD there (great traveling music thru the cove!). There are many campgrounds, canoeing, horseback riding, hiking, biking and tubing opportunities thru various outfitters. You'll want to photograph the scenery and wildlife (1,500 kinds of flowering plants and more than 500 black bears). The best time for wildlife viewing is in the early morning or late afternoon. Cable Mill is a water-powered grist mill which demonstrates the grinding of corn into meal. There is a Visitors Center at the site with restrooms and a gift shop. Hayrides are a unique and fun way to see Cades Cove from April-October (fee of $6.00-8.00). There is also a "naturalist" hayride daily, June-October. Many of our readers have their favorite spots they go back to every year. *Be sure to take a picnic lunch – food service is not available.*

TUCKALEECHEE CAVERNS

(follow signs off US 321)

Townsend 37882

❑   Phone: (423) 448-2274. **Web: www.smokymountains.org**
❑   Hours: 9:00am-6:00pm (April-October). 10:00am-5:00pm (last half of March and first half of November).
❑   Admission: $11.00 adult, Half Price child (5-11).

Indians initially discovered these caverns and used them as a hidcout. Later two boys played around the area and re-discovered the cave. Later, walkways were build of concrete and lighting added. Tours of the stream passage, Fairyland and many formations are conducted approximately every 30 minutes by a guide.

WOOD N STRINGS DULCIMER SHOP

7645 East Lamar Alexander Parkway (Hwy 321)

Townsend 37882

❑   Phone: (865) 448-6647. **Web: www.clemmerdulcimer.com**
❑   Hours: Monday-Saturday 10:00am-5:00pm.
❑   Miscellaneous: Just west of Mike's place is the Little River Railroad & Lumber Co. Museum (open daily summer and October, weekends rest of spring and fall). The museum has a locomotive out front and is filled with FREE viewing of how the town was formed and the industry behind it.

Home of the "Clemmer Dulcimer" and "Ban-Jammer" (Mike Clemmer's inventions). The dulcimer is a wire-stringed, fretted musical instrument with its origin in the Appalachian Mountains. It means "sweet song" and Mike likes to make each instrument from specially chosen wood blends to continuously create that special sound. He'll show you the materials he uses and demonstrate many instruments with different sounds. If you're there on a Saturday (around 7:00pm), seasonally, they host a Pickin' Porch out front where locals can jam and spectators can enjoy. What a sweet sounding treat! *(Be sure to purchase Mike's CD before you head over to Cades Cove, down the road)*.

FROZEN HEAD STATE PARK

964 Flat Fork Road (US 27 north to SR 62 east to CR 116 north)

Wartburg 37887

❑   Phone: (423) 346-3318

      Web: www.state.tn.us/environment/parks/frzhead/

❑   Admission: $3.00 per vehicle, per day.

This large wilderness, forest area is named for a 3,324 foot peak which is often covered in ice or snow. 50 miles of backpacking and day-hiking trails provide wildlife and wildflower-viewing. Other activities: camping, horseback riding and fishing.

Chapter 4
Area - North East (NE)

Our Favorites...

* Andrew Johnson National Historic Site - Greeneville

* Hands On! Regional Museum - Johnson City

* Netherland Inn - Kingsport

* Exchange Place - Kingsport

* Davy Crockett Birthplace State Park - Limestone

* Rocky Mount - Piney Flats (near Johnson City)

"Pioneer Toy Fun"
Kids liked to play...even 200 years ago!

BRISTOL CAVERNS

1157 Bristol Caverns Highway (just off US 421S on Hwy 435)

Bristol 37620

❏   Phone: (423) 878-2011. **Web: www.bristolcaverns.com**

❏   Hours: Monday-Saturday 9:00am-5:00pm, Sunday 12:30-5:00pm
      (mid March - October). Slightly reduced hours rest of year.
      Closed winter holidays.

❏   Admission: $9.00 adult, $8.00 senior (60+), $4.50 child (5-12).

Once used by Indians as an attack and escape route, the
underground river that carved the chambers years ago remains an
intriguing feature of this cavern. A guided tour (departs about
every 20 minutes) of the caverns includes a walk along the banks
of an underground river. Visitors can take the lighted asphalt trail
that goes through several levels of the caverns.

BRISTOL MOTOR SPEEDWAY & DRAGWAY

2801 Bristol Highway 11E

Bristol 37620

❏   Phone: (423) 764-1161 tickets
      Web: www.bristolmotorspeedway.com

A motorsports and entertainment facility, esp. for NASCAR and
Winston Cup events. BMS boasts 147,000 grandstand seats plus
luxury skyboxes. June-August with special events like Music in the
Meadow concerts.

THEATRE BRISTOL

512 State Street (I-81N exit 3)

Bristol 37620

❏   Phone: (423) 968-4977. **Web: www.theatrebristol.org**

❏   Miscellaneous: Enjoy a look at the "Birthplace of Country
      Music" Mural (along State Street) and Museum (in the Mall).

The region's oldest children's theatre, The Discovery Series for
children consists of five musicals (Ex. Wizard of Oz, Scrooge).
Many selections are taken from required reading curriculum for
Elementary students. Some of the performances take place in the

ARTspace, a multi-purpose, black box theatre which seats up to 100. Most of the performances take place in The Paramount Center for the Arts, a restored 756-seat movie palace which has been converted to use as a performing arts theatre.

CHRISTY MISSION

1425 Chapel Hollow Road

Del Rio 37727

❑   Phone: (423) 487-2648

   www.discovercockecounty.com/_delrio/drattrac/drchrmis.htm

❑   Admission: FREE, donations accepted.

This is the actual location (Cutter Gap) where the book, plays and Broadway music, movie and television series "Christy" (by Catherine Marshall) was based on! A Story about a girl from North Carolina who came here to educate mountain children approximately one hundred years ago. Visit the original mission property (building is gone) anytime, or pick up a map of other sites along the road. The O'Teale Cabin is still available for touring.

SYCAMORE SHOALS STATE HISTORIC AREA

1651 West Elk Avenue (I-181 exit 31, take Rte. 321/67 to town)

Elizabethton 37643

❑   Phone: (423) 543-5808

   Web: www.state.tn.us/environment/parks/sycamore/

❑   Hours: Monday-Saturday 8:00am-4:30pm, Sunday 1:00-4:30pm.

❑   Miscellaneous: Visitors Center houses a museum, theater, and
       gift shop. Picnic area and 2-mile walking trail. Summer activities
       include Colonial Days & critter projects.

Step back in time to the turn of the 18th century with a visit to a Reconstruction of Fort Watauga as it stood in 1776. The original fort was excavated about a mile away on the shores of the Watauga River. The Overmountain Men mustered here in September 1780 before their march to fight the battle of King's Mountain. Here was established the first permanent American settlement outside the original 13 colonies and the Watauga Association - the first majority-rule system of American democratic government was formed in 1772. Playing in a fort is pretty fun.

❑ CARTER MANSION - 1013 Broad Street (in downtown on Rte. 67/321), 543-6140. The oldest frame house in Tennessee, was the home of John and Landon Carter. Built (1775-1780) on lands bought from the Cherokee, the structure is open for tours mid-May - mid-August, Wednesday-Sunday and by appointment. Built on the Woodland burial mound, it's affiliated with the first government, the Wataugans. The oldest know paintings in Tennessee were uncovered here…probably done by a child or amateur.

ERWIN NATIONAL FISH HATCHERY & UNICOI COUNTY HERITAGE MUSEUM

1715 Old Johnson City Hwy./ 520 Federal Hatchery Rd. (Hwy. 107, Just off I-181)

Erwin 37692

❑ Phone: (423) 743-4712 hatchery or (423) 743-9449 museum
   Web: http://southeast.fws.gov/erwin/index.html
❑ Hours: Hatchery Weekdays 7:00am-3:30pm. Museum: Daily 1:00-5:00pm (May-September), Weekends only (October).
❑ Admission: Donations

The hatchery produces rainbow trout in order to provide up to 15 million trout eggs to federal and state hatcheries for their trout stocking programs. Free hatchery group tours available by request. On the grounds of the hatchery, is a turn-of-the-century frame home of the former superintendent of the hatchery housing a Main Street representation, Indian artifacts, railroading, and Blue Ridge Pottery exhibits about the area.

ANDREW JOHNSON NATIONAL HISTORIC SITE

101 North College Street (I-81N take exit 23 to Rt. 11E north to College & Depot Sts., downtown)

Greeneville 37743

- ❑   Phone: (423) 638-3551. **Web: www.nps.gov/anjo**
- ❑   Hours: Visitors Center Open 9:00am-5:00pm daily. Closed New Years Day, Thanksgiving and Christmas.
- ❑   Admission: FREE
- ❑   Tours: Tours of Homestead every hour from 9:30am-11:30am and 1:30pm - 4:30pm.

Home of the nation's 17th President, the Andrew Johnson National Historic Site honors the life and work of the President and preserves his homes, tailor shop, and grave site. He worked his way from tailor to President. His presidency, from 1865 - 1869, illustrates the United States Constitution at work following Lincoln's assassination and during attempts to reunify a nation that had been torn by civil war. The museum displays a 14 minute video at the Visitors Center (which is where you should begin...find out how dearly he cherished the Constitution). Children have the opportunity to try on period clothing and then view Andrew Johnson's original Tailor Shop and his tools. Try lifting an iron from those days. If you listen closely, you can hear Johnson cutting fabric. Also, each visitor is given a replica of an 1868 impeachment ticket upon entering the Visitor Center. Visitors are encouraged to discover more about Andrew Johnson and the events leading up to his impeachment. What is the definition of impeachment? You can cast your vote to acquit or to find the president guilty at the "One Vote Counts" exhibit. Great intro to the political process and the enduring-ness of the Constitution.

ABRAHAM LINCOLN MUSEUM

Lincoln Memorial University (US 25E near the Cumberland Gap National Historic Park)

Harrogate 37752

❏   Phone: (423) 869-6235. **Web: www.lmunet.edu/museum/**

❏   Hours: Monday-Friday 9:00am-4:00pm, Saturday 11:00am-4:00pm, Sunday 1:00-4:00pm.

❏   Admission: $3.00 adult, $2.50 senior, $1.50 child (6-12).

At the main entrance to the University stands the magnificent Abraham Lincoln Museum exhibiting many rare items - the silver-topped cane Lincoln carried the night of his assassination, a lock of his hair clipped as he lay on his death bed and two life masks made of Lincoln. The founding of this University by Union General Oliver Otis Howard fulfilled President Lincoln's desire to help the people of East Tennessee who had remained loyal during the Civil War. Even see the bed Lincoln slept in on his birthday in 1861.

HANDS ON! REGIONAL MUSEUM

315 East Main Street (I-181 exit 32 west, between Market & Main, downtown),

Johnson City 37601

❏   Phone: (423) 434-HAND. **Web: www.handsonmuseum.org**

❏   Hours: Tuesday-Friday 9:00am-5:00pm, Saturday 10:00am-5:00pm, Sunday 1:00-5:00pm. Closed most major holidays.

❏   Admission: $6.00 (age 3+). Inquire about memberships & group discounts. Affiliated with 200+ museums around the US. Increased fees for special exhibits.

❏   Miscellaneous: Programs are offered throughout the day.

Some favorite exhibits: Outer Realm! The exhibit will have the look and feel of the International Space Station, a Space Shuttle, and an astronaut training area (control a Robot arm just like the astronauts!); Closet! This delightful exhibit is full of great dress-up clothes, boas, hats, costumes (open weekdays from 2:00-4:30pm - Weekend times vary); Raceways help visitors learn about the simple physics of moving objects- Golf balls loop, spin, roll, collide, and race down roller coaster ramps to demonstrate gravity, friction, acceleration, and momentum; The Discovery Room is a creative, hands-on exhibit allowing children to explore their creativity while learning about recycling; WKID-TV allows children to look at the "behind the scenes" workings of a TV station; The TVA/Water Play Dam - teaching about water power and electricity; Get Moving! features a Saturn automobile for children to explore both inside and out (including under the hood); The Ark focuses on exotic animals and touching the pelts provided. The amazingly large stuffed animals peeking out from windows of the Ark is so cleverly displayed!; The Katie Ellen Coal Mine has tunnels for exploring that shows the impact of mining of the local areas; Alive & Well features live animals such as turtles, fresh water fish, lizards, and snakes - even touch a Chocolate Chip starfish!; Wings Airplane/Flight Simulator exhibit; and Kids Bank - A working kid's ATM and money trivia round out this educational exhibit. The volunteer ideas and work here make it very unique.

TIPTON-HAYNES HISTORIC SITE

2620 South Roan Street (I-181 exit 31, left on University, left on South Roan)

Johnson City 37605

❑   Phone: (423) 926-3631

     www.tennessee.gov/environment/hist/stateown/tiptonha.php

❑   Hours: Monday-Saturday 9:00am-4:00pm (April-mid November). Weekdays only until 3:00pm (winters). Closed Thanksgiving and day after.

❑   Admission: Yes

Home of Col. John Tipton, John Tipton, Jr. and Confederate Senator Landon C. Haynes whose lives represent the history of Tennessee from pre-colonial times to Reconstruction. The site's first white resident was Colonel John Tipton, who built a substantial log house in 1784. Tipton was a signer and a framer of the first Tennessee Constitution. In an area including this site, the Battle of Franklin was fought in 1788, the only armed skirmish between supporters of the proposed state of Franklin and their opponents, who were loyal to North Carolina. John Tipton, Jr. served in the Tennessee General Assembly from 1803 to 1819. In 1839, the estate was given as a wedding present to Landon Carter Haynes, who had the home enlarged and renovated. He also had built a free-standing office building, where he practiced law. Haynes is chiefly remembered for his sponsorship of railroad-building and for his brilliant oratorical skills. Ten original and restored buildings and a newer museum are housed here. Often called Tennessee's most historic site because so much government-related activity occurred here.

WETLANDS WATER PARK

1523 Persimmon Ridge Road

Jonesborough 37659

❑   Phone: (423) 753-1553 or (888) 622-1885
❑   Hours: Summers Monday-Saturday 10:00am-6:00pm, Sunday Noon-6:00pm.
❑   Admission: $10.00 adult, $8.00 senior (55+) & child (12 & under). Half price after 3:00pm.

A rampage down the 200 foot giant flume or a boardwalk stroll thru the natural wetlands combines fun and nature. There are also otter slides, a Lazy River, pool, children's play area, volleyball courts, concessions and picnic areas.

BAYS MOUNTAIN PARK & PLANETARIUM

853 Bays Mountain Park Road (I-181, Kingsport exit, follow signs)

Kingsport 37660

❑   Phone: (423) 229-9447. **Web: www.baysmountain.com**
❑   Hours: Weekdays 8:30am-5:00pm, Weekends 1:00-8:00pm. Extended summer hours, reduced winter hours. Closed Thanksgiving, Christmas Eve and day, and New Years.
❑   Admission: $3.00 per carload. $1.50 fee per person for programs, barge ride.

A 3,000 acre nature preserve with more than 25 miles of hiking trails, barge rides on the 44 acre lake, wildlife habitats & programs (Wolf CAM & Howlings), saltwater tidal pool and marine aquariums, Planetarium theater and special sky-watching at the observatory - Saturday & Sunday & daily during the summer. Park hours: 8:30am-5:00pm. Extended hours during the summer. MOUNTAIN HERITAGE FARMSTEAD MUSEUM - Houses a collection of artifacts depicting farm & home life from the 1800's through the early 1900's. Learn the hardships of mountain life. Open weekends 2:00-5:00pm; daily in summer, small admission.

NETHERLAND INN

2144 Netherland Inn Road (I-181 exit 55 eastbound, turn right on Fairview, again right on Center)

Kingsport 37660

❑ Phone: (423) 246-6262. **Web: www.netherlandinn.com**
❑ Hours: Saturday-Sunday 2:00-4:00pm (May-October). Guided tours to the public. Group tours arranged the rest of the year.
❑ Admission: $3.00 adult, $2.00 senior, $1.00 student (age 6+).
❑ Miscellaneous: Suggested lodging: Comfort Inn, I-181 exit 57B, Hwy 93N to US11, (423) 378-4418.

The restored Inn faces the Old Stage Road and Holston River, which served as a migratory spot for settlers to build boats for their westward trip during the mid-1700's. The two rooms on the first floor accommodated the travelers on the 18 weekly scheduled stagecoach runs. There were some "wild times" in the tavern demonstrated by the bullet-riddled mantel. Many period pieces, flat boat cargo manifests and even graffiti of the age can be found here. The Netherland Inn hosted many famous persons including Presidents Andrew Jackson, Andrew Johnson and James Polk. On the property is The 1773 Daniel Boone House (from Virginia). The popular features of this cabin are the games and toys used by children during the 1700 and 1800s. Look for the 200 year old rocking horse and the mechanical paddle…for the young and young at heart - really cute stuff! Also, you'll find a ¼ scale replica of a flatboat built here. Loads of interesting artifacts and stories here!

EXCHANGE PLACE

4812 Orebank Road (SR 93 to Orebank Rd. exit)

Kingsport 37662

❑   Phone: (423) 288-6071. **Web: www.exchangeplace.info**
❑   Hours: Thursday-Friday 10:00am-2:00pm, Saturday-Sunday
     2:00-4:30pm. (May-October). This schedule by appointment only.
❑   Admission: FREE. Fee for special events...a good time to visit.

This mid-1800s living farmstead derived its name from the exchange of currency and of horses when it served as a stagecoach stop. Visit with the animals (meet Billy or Oreo), feed the sheep or chickens, or put up hay. Visit the Spring - the very reason the farm was built here (original buttermilk paint, look out for precious water spiders); Gathering Room - Mammy's bench (allowed mothers to work & rock their babies), the log piece displayed in here has a carving where Daniel Boone shot a bear on the property! Why did he always catch them near a beech tree?; Slave Cabin - where the family's favorite slave family lived; Or, the School Room - put on your apron or handkerchief and grab your slate! Once you cross the threshold doorway, be quiet and mind your manners! The volunteers here are passionate about this place!

WARRIORS' PATH STATE PARK

490 Hemlock Road (I-81 exit 59, Rte. 36 north)

Kingsport 37663

❑   Phone: (423) 239-8531
     Web: www.state.tn.us/environment/parks/warrior/
❑   Hours: 7:00am to 2 hours past dark.
❑   Admission: FREE

Once the pathway for the Cherokee and pioneers, now with hiking, picnicking, horseback riding, fishing, swimming, and a pool. 134 campsites, RV, and primitive sites. It is situated on the shores of TVA's Patrick Henry Reservoir on the Holston River.

DAVY CROCKETT BIRTHPLACE STATE PARK

1245 Davy Crockett Park Road (I-81N exit 23, then 3 miles off Hwy. 11E, follow signs)

Limestone 37681

❑ Phone: (423) 257-2167

www.state.tn.us/environment/parks/parks/DavyCrockettSHP/

❑ Hours: Park: 8:00am-dark. Museum: Wednesday-Friday 8:00am-4:30pm.

❑ Admission: $3.00 per vehicle park entrance.

❑ Miscellaneous: A short video about Davy Crockett can be viewed in the museum. August 17 is Davy Crockett Day. On premises is a swimming pool, picnic areas, fishing, hiking and many campsites.

The site of Davy Crockett's birth is now part of a state park. A replica of the log cabin where Crockett (celebrated frontiersman, warrior and backwoods statesman) was born (1786) is here on 105 partially wooded acres of land along the Nolichucky River. The cabin presents a typical frontier home much like the one in which Davy was born. The Visitor center's museum exhibits tell of different aspects of Davy's life. The real Mr. Crockett was probably never called Davy, nor was he just a frontiersman. Actually, he was more refined and less of a giant (he was only 5'9"). Davy was a survivor, comical and a big talker. Check out the memorabilia from the 50s - King of the Wild Frontier. Upset with the American government, he said (i.e. "forget you all…"), "I'm going to Texas". You'll find he was actually "Nature's Noblesman", not quite as wild as the tales…or was he? Come here to begin your discovery!

CROCKETT TAVERN AND PIONEER MUSEUM

2002 Morningside Drive (US 11E south, near US 25E, follow signs)

Morristown 37814

❑ Phone: (423) 587-9900

❑   Hours: Tuesday-Saturday 9:00am-5:00pm (May-October).

❑   Admission: $5.00 adult, $1.00 child (5-18).

The reconstructed log building is located on the site where Davy Crockett's parents built a home for their nine children. The home also served as a wayside inn for early travelers. Crockett, known for his hunting skills, tall tales and courageous volunteer spirit, spent his boyhood here. This is where he learned to hunt. Visitors will explore the kitchen, the loom room, which features a loom and the necessary spinning equipment; the big room, which can be equated to the living room of the present day; and the loft, where the family slept. Travellers renting slept one family to a bed.

PANTHER CREEK STATE PARK

2010 Panther Creek Park Road (I-40 exit 394, Hwy 11E north)

Morristown 37814

❑   Phone: (423) 587-7046

www.state.tn.us/environment/parks/parks/PantherCreek/

❑   Hours: Daily 6:00am-dark.

Legend has it that both Panther Creek and Panther Springs received their names from the claim of a Colonel Bradley of Virginia who, while exploring the area, shot a panther that fell into the spring. Near Point Lookout, the highest place in the park, the elevation reaches 1,460 feet above sea level. Other activities: camping, fishing, boating and horseback riding.

ROCKY MOUNT LIVING HISTORY MUSEUM

200 Hyder Hill Road (I-181/23 S exit 36, I-381 N, follow US 11E toward Bristol)

Piney Flats (near Johnson City) 37686

❑   Phone: (423) 538-7396 or (888) 538-1791

Web: www.rockymountmuseum.com

❑   Hours: Tuesday-Saturday 11:00am-5:00pm (March - mid December). Closed MLK Jr. Day, Labor Day, Thanksgiving Day, and weekends in December.

Rocky Mount Living History Museum *(cont.)*

❑   Admission: $6.00 adult, $5.00 senior (60+), $4.00 child (6-17), $20.00 family.

❑   Miscellaneous: Suggested lodging nearby @ Comfort Suites, Johnson City, exit 36, (423) 610-0010. Outdoor pool, large suite rooms w/refrigerator & microwave & large continental breakfast.

From October 1790 until March 1792, Rocky Mount served as the Territorial Capital of this region. Today this restored building, the only Territorial Capital on its original site in the United States, is a living history site. View the orientation video. Mrs. Cobb and her grandson, Frederick do a wonderful job taking you back to 1791 (in 1st person character!). They engage the children with questions. Hear stories about the Cobb family, Governor Blount, Indian affairs, and the latest gossip of the territory. Some even get to taste dishes such as gingerbread or sausage muffins cooked over an open fire.   Leaving the kitchen be sure to visit the garden (medicinal, culinary, and dye pot plants) and weaving room or sheep barn. On tour, check out the secret drawer, the "necessary", the reversible cradle, a snake gourd, a shoefly chair, or a beehive oven.

ROAN MOUNTAIN STATE PARK

1015 Hwy 143

Roan Mountain 37687

❑   Phone: (423) 772-0190 or (800) 250-8620
       Web: www.state.tn.us/environment/parks/parks/RoanMtn/
❑   Hours: 8:00am-4:30pm.

Park guests have opportunities to hike along creeks and ridges, fish for trout, play tennis, swim, cross-country ski, horseback ride, join rangers and naturalists for educational programs, and enjoy mountain music concerts. Guests who wish to stay overnight have a choice of RV and tent camping or 30 fully equipped cabins. The 6285 foot peak offers breathtaking views of the Appalachian Mountains. The Appalachian Trail and famous (best display of blossoms in the world, mid-June) Rhododendron Gardens of Roan Mountain can be accessed at Carver's Gap, an 8 mile drive from the park. <u>MILLER HOMESTEAD</u> - a century old farmhouse, open summers, with tours, mountain music, storytelling, and traditional skills demonstrated.

TENNESSEE NEWSPAPER AND PRINTING MUSEUM

415 South Depot Street

Rogersville 37857

❑   Phone: (423) 272-1961. **Web: www.rogersvilleheritage.org**
❑   Hours: Tuesday-Friday 10:00am-4:00pm, other times by appt.
❑   Miscellaneous: Grand Ole Opry star, Archie Campbell Complex, is on S. Main Street (423-235-5216) in town. Structures include the Ole Country Store, Gilleys Hotel and the Archie Campbell Museum.

A quaint 1890 Southern Railway Depot contains the state's only newspaper and printing museum. This town was where Tennessee's first newspaper was printed November, 1791 and you can see printing presses dating from then until the time when newspapers went online. Also on exhibit are early newspapers of interest.

Chapter 5
Area - South East (SE)

Our Favorites...

* Mayfield Dairy Farms Tours - Athens
* Lookout Mountain Incline - Chattanooga
* Rock City - Chattanooga
* Ruby Falls - Chattanooga
* Chattanooga Choo Choo Resort & Shuttle
* Chattanooga Ducks Tour
* Creative Discovery Museum - Chattanooga
* Museum Center at 5IVE Points - Cleveland
* Cherokee National Forest - Hiwassee & Ocoee Rivers
(Cleveland to Ducktown up to Fort Loudoun)
* Horsin' Around Carving School - Soddy Daisy
* Lost Sea - Sweetwater
* Sequoyah Birthplace Museum - Vonore

"...it's the Chattanooga Choo Choo..."

MAYFIELD DAIRY FARMS TOURS

4 Mayfield Lane (I-75 exit 52, Mt. Verd.
Turn east on Hwy 305 4.3 miles)

Athens 37303

❑   Phone: (423) 745-2151 or (800) MAYFIELD
     Web: www.mayfielddairy.com
❑   Hours: Monday-Saturday 9:00am-5:00pm (March-August).
     Monday-Friday 9:00am-4:00pm, Saturday 9:00am-2:00pm
     (September-February).
❑   Admission: FREE
❑   Tours: Tours begin every 30 minutes, last about 40 minutes.
     Last tour is one hour before closing. No milk production on
     Wednesday. No ice cream production on Saturday. Wear
     comfortable, non-slip shoes. Some stairs on tour.
❑   Miscellaneous: Gift shop and ice cream parlor.

Get the "scoop" on the history of this dairy through a film
presentation followed by a plant tour that includes how ice cream
treats are made and how milk is bottled. Begin by donning a hair
net and watch all the swirling and twirling and spinning and
turning and churning of jugs and cartons of milk and ice cream.
This fun tour includes a great look at how they make plastic milk
jugs, home-made, from a handful of tiny pellets...melted and
molded. It's amazing to see ice cream sandwiches made by one
machine! After this excellent guided visual tour - taste some of
their ice cream creations for sale (*one scoop is only $1.00!*). Try
unique Yellow Brick Road or Turtle Tracks. This is a must-see,
easy to understand, colorful factory tour!

MCMINN COUNTY LIVING HERITAGE
MUSEUM

522 West Madison Avenue (I-75 exit SR 30 east)

Athens 37371

❑   Phone: (423) 745-0329. **Web: www.usit.com/livher**
❑   Hours: Monday-Friday 10:00am-5:00pm. Saturday & Sunday
     2:00-5:00pm. Closed holidays.

McMinn County Living Heritage Museum *(cont.)*

A legacy of long ago as 30 exhibit rooms frame collections of old glassware, quilts, a dining room, a parlor, a church, a school room and artifacts from the Indian, Farming, and Industry lifestyles. Its been described as "rummaging through the attic of an entire community...".

LOOKOUT MOUNTAIN INCLINE RAILWAY

827 E. Brow Road/3917 St. Elmo Ave. (Lower Station) (near I-24, 3 blocks south of Hwy. 11, 41, 64 or 72 on Hwy. 58 – Bottom of Lookout Mountain), **Chattanooga** 37350

- ❑ Phone: (423) 821-4224. **Web: www.lookoutmtnattractions.com**
- ❑ Hours: Daily: 8:30am - 9:30pm (summer - last round trip leaves at 9:10pm; last one way leaves at 9:20pm). 9:00am - 6:00pm (April, May, September & October - last round trip leaves at 5:20pm.; last one way leaves at 5:40pm). 10:00am - 6:00pm (November-March - last round trip leaves at 5:20pm; last one way leaves at 5:40pm). Closed Christmas Day only.
- ❑ Admission: Tickets may be purchased at either the Lower or Upper Station and at the Chattanooga Visitors Center. Round trip $9.00 adult, Half price child (3-12). $1.00 discount for one way fares. Senior pricing is child pricing (December-February only). Combo prices with other Lookout Mountain attractions offered.
- ❑ Tours: Approximately 10 minutes, one way.
- ❑ Miscellaneous: Candy Connection, Snack Shoppe at Upper Station. Seasonal gift shop at Lower Station.

"America's Most Amazing Mile" delights guests as the Incline climbs historic Lookout Mountain. Chattanooga's surrounding mountains and valleys come in full view as the trolley-style railcars carry you high. The 72.7% grade of the track near the top gives the Incline the unique distinction of being the steepest passenger railway in the world. The free observation deck at the Upper Station is the highest overlook on Lookout Mountain. While at the upper station, be sure to visit the Incline's machine room where the giant gears and cables are put into motion. Be sure to check out the Incline Centennial Exhibits, too. And while you are traveling on the Incline, you will pass another Incline car on the single track. At the halfway point of the track, the two Incline cars pass along side each other. The "switch" allows the two cars to travel on a single track system. Make sure you wave to the folks in the other car. At 600 steep feet per minute, this is really cool!

COOLIDGE PARK AND WALNUT STREET BRIDGE

Tennessee Riverpark (across the river from the Tenn. Aquarium)

Chattanooga 37401

❑   Phone: (423) 757-2142
    Web: www.chattanooga.gov/cpr/parks/CoolidgePark.htm
❑   Hours: Park: sunrise to midnight. Carousel: Monday-Thursday
    11:00am-6:00pm, Friday & Saturday 11:00am-7:00pm, Sunday
    1:00-6:00pm. Fountains: Daily 8:00am-10:00pm (April-October).
❑   Admission: Carousel rides: $1.00 adult, $0.50 senior and child
    (13 & under).

Stroll across the world's longest pedestrian bridge, play in the Park's interactive water fountain and on the Walnut Wall Climbing Facility, or ride on the antique carousel (locally-made). Water spurts from both ground-level jets and to the surprise and delight of their targets, the mouths and snouts of stone animals (lions, tigers & bears). The park hosts open-air performances and has a Chattanooga Theatre Centre presenting regular plays.

TENNESSEE AQUARIUM

One Broad Street (I-24 to downtown, follow I-27 N to exit 1C, turn left at 2nd light)

Chattanooga 37401

❑   Phone: (423) 267-FISH or (800) 262-0695
    Web: www.tnaqua.org
❑   Hours: Daily 10:00am-7:30pm (ET). Last admittance time is
    6:00pm. IMAX shows begin at 11:00am. Closed Thanksgiving
    and Christmas.
❑   Admission: $14.00 adult, $7.50 child (3-12). Advance tickets can
    be purchased by phone or online. IMAX tickets extra.

Tennessee Aquarium *(cont.)*

❑   Tours: Have you ever wondered what it's like to fix meals for 9,000 animals every day? Have you ever thought about what it takes to clean a fish "bowl" containing 450,000 gallons of water? Call (423) 265-0698 to book your tour held at 3:00pm daily. Behind-the-scenes tour tickets may be purchased with an Aquarium admission ticket (additional $5.00-$7.00 per person). Children must be at least 10 years old and accompanied by an adult.

The Tennessee Aquarium tells the story of fresh water ecosystems. You follow the Tennessee River from its Appalachian beginnings through the swamp waters of the Mississippi River and into the Gulf of Mexico (lots of colorful fish), making side trips to some of the world's other great rivers. Our favorite area was Discovery Hall - pet a fish!-what does it feel like? Look for baby alligators in the nursery. Along the way, visitors travel through a 60-foot canyon and two living forests. In the rivers, you'll see the only mammals on-site...river otters and their playful antics. A look at the creepy alligator snapping turtle (prehistoric) or side-necked turtles is a highlight, too.

CHATTANOOGA CHOO CHOO *HOLIDAY INN RESORT*

1400 Market Street

Chattanooga 37402

❑   Phone: (423) 266-5000 or (800) TRACK-29
     Web: www.choochoo.com
❑   Admission: Rooms and great family packages from $99.00 - $229.00, depending on time of year and type of room, plus amount of perks included.
❑   Miscellaneous: The FREE shuttle bus to downtown is right next door and highly recommended for any downtown site visits.

"It's a train. It's a song. It's a hotel." This is the hotel made famous in the Glenn Miller song (hear it on their website). The 30-acre vacation family complex includes a 1900's train station (now a lobby and restaurant), three pools (one indoors) with waterfalls and slides, casual restaurants (like the Silver Diner car) and snackeries, shops, an arcade and overnight lodging in regular rooms, suites or actual Victorian parlor cars on the property. They have a trolley ride ($0.50) you can take thru the complex and the kids will like the largest model railroad museum in the South display (very small admission). The water garden is filled with more than 400 fish. Try the Station House Restaurant where your server is taking your order one minute, on stage singing the next. Maybe make it more special by ordering a Shirley Temple for the kids with dinner. Their pools and train station environment make this the perfect family stay in Chattanooga!

CHATTANOOGA DUCKS TOURS

201 West 5th Street (Corner of Broad St. & 5th Street)

Chattanooga 37402

- ❑ Phone: (423) 756-DUCK. **Web: www.chattanoogaducks.com**
- ❑ Admission: $12.00 adult, $10.00 senior, $8.00 child (3-12).
  Tickets are available at the Visitors Center or on board.
- ❑ Tours: Best to call for reservations first. 45 minute tours. Ducks
  leave hourly from 10:00am-dusk. Sundays Noon-8:00pm. (May-
  October). Generally, weekends only, 1:00-5:00pm, weather
  pending (March, April).

The Chattanooga Duck's are unique ex-military amphibious vehicles made for the US Army to land troops on beaches during wartime. The Ducks are equally at home on land as well as water. Begin downtown with a "quacky" tour of famous sites. Then, hit the water as they tell you about Maclellan Island, the Tennessee River and places of natural and historical interest...most only accessible by boat. Hopefully, you'll observe a Great Blue Heron or migrating Warblers. The birds live among squirrels, rabbits, raccoons, beaver, fox, ducks, geese and other waterfowl. Good tour to do before you explore the city...they point out many sites along the way that might interest you. Buy a "Duck Quacker" whistle before you tour so you can "quack all the day"!

CHATTANOOGA LOOKOUTS

BellSouth Park, 201 Power Alley (I-24 east to exit 178 on US 27 N, downtown. Take exit 1C onto 4th St, first left on Chestnut)

Chattanooga 37402

❑   Phone: (423) 267-2208 or (800) 852-7572
    Web: www.lookouts.com

Double A Professional Baseball Team. Cincinnati Reds Affiliate since 1988. Join the Little Lookouts club. Tickets are $2.00-$8.00.

CHATTANOOGA REGIONAL HISTORY MUSEUM

400 Chestnut Street (across from Creative Discovery Museum)

Chattanooga 37402

❑   Phone: (423) 265-3247. **Web: www.chattanoogahistory.com**
❑   Hours: Monday-Friday 10:00am-4:30pm, Saturday & Sunday 11:00am-4:30pm. Closed major holidays.
❑   Admission: $4.00 adult, $3.50 senior, $3.00 child (5-18).

The Chattanooga Regional History Museum is the place you'll meet the region's peoples. Events are illustrated in five historical periods: Early Land, Early People; The Cherokee Nation; Growth & Conflict; The New South; and The Dynamo of Dixie. View the Marks On The Land orientation video about the history of Chattanooga. The Discover History Hallway makes the past accessible through hands-on interactive learning stations. Did you know Coca-Cola's bottling franchise, Moon Pies and Little Debbie's were first made here?

CHATTANOOGA RIVERBOAT CO. SOUTHERN BELLE

201 Riverfront Pkwy, Pier 2 (Ross's Landing across from Aquarium)

Chattanooga 37402

❑   Phone: (423) 266-4488 or (800) 766-2784
    Web: www.chattanoogariverboat.com

❑   Admission: (see brochure or online schedule) Sightseeing Cruises
        run $6.00-$12.00, Breakfast and Lunch Cruises run $9.00-
        $17.00. Family Nite Dinner Cruise and Monday nite Pizza
        Cruises are more.

❑   Tours: Boarding 30 minutes before departure (April-December).
        Basically 1-3 departures in the afternoon, one in the evening for
        dinner.

Enjoy the informative commentary on the city's history as you
float down the beautiful Tennessee River. Familiar sights like
Lookout Mountain and Chattanooga's skyline are leisurely viewed
as you snack or eat a meal. Entertainment on many evening dinner
cruises includes magicians and dance bands. Look in Seasonal &
Special Events for "themed" special events.

CREATIVE DISCOVERY MUSEUM

321 Chestnut Street (Riverfront District) (I-24 to downtown, then US
27 N to exit 1-C, 4th Street to Chestnut)

Chattanooga 37402

❑   Phone: (423) 756-2738. **Web: www.cdmfun.org**

❑   Hours: Daily 10:00am-6:00pm (summer). Monday-Saturday
        10:00am-5:00pm, Sunday Noon-5:00pm (September-May).
        Closed Wednesdays (September-February). Last ticket sold one
        hour prior to closing. Closed Thanksgiving and Christmastime.

❑   Admission: $7.95 adult, $5.95 child (2-12).

❑   Miscellaneous: Great gift shop for educational toys.

Specially designed for children ages 2-12, this museum is full of
hands-on discoveries in art (where you can sculpt, print and
puppet). See your face as a Dali or a Warhol painting. Let your
kids' imaginations run wild digging for dino bones or making
music. Play giant instruments. Sing in a canyon, a shower or a
concert hall! This place has the widest variety of musical
instruments to try. And, with each sound, a simple description of
the people behind the music (this is our favorite part of the site and
the best we've ever seen)! In the Inventors Workshop learn about
local inventors, then appear on ZOOM as you make your own
inventions. "RiverPlay" has a two story climbing structure

consisting of nets, slides, a spiral staircase, and even a lift to provide access for visitors who use wheelchairs. A multi-level riverboat is nearby - a pilot's cabin and crane lift are there. Underneath the climbing structure is a watercourse where kids can sail boats, learn about dams and locks, create river currents, and use water pressure to spin wheels and tip buckets. Can you climb all the way to the crows nest and raise the mast…it's high!

INTERNATIONAL TOWING & RECOVERY HALL OF FAME MUSEUM

3315 Broad Street

Chattanooga 37402

❏ Phone: (423) 267-3132

   Web: www.internationaltowingmuseum.org

❏ Hours: Monday-Friday 10:00am-4:30pm, Weekends 11:00am-
   5:00pm. Call for an appointment if you'd like to visit on a
   Tuesday, Wednesday, or Thursday (December-March). *As a rule
   of thumb - always call before you visit to make sure the museum
   is open.* Closed major holidays.

❏ Admission: $8.00 adult, $7.00 senior (55+), $4.00 child (6-18).

Enjoy restored antique wreckers and equipment, industry-related displays of tools, unique equipment, and pictorial histories of manufacturers who pioneered a worldwide industry. Model T's & Model A's with cranes and wreckers are fun to see. Chattanooga was chosen as the museum's home because the industry's first wrecker was fabricated a few blocks away from the museum at the Ernest Holmes Company. Understand the engineering behind a wrecker with exhibits like the drapery rod example. Tons of toy & collectible tow trucks are on display and available to purchase - a little boy's dream.

BLUFF VIEW ART DISTRICT

Corner of High & East 2nd Street (I-24, take Hwy 27 N, exit 1C to 4th St. to Art District)

Chattanooga 37403

❑   Phone: (423) 265-5033. **Web:www.bluffviewartdistrict.com**

Peer through the windows of The Chocolate Kitchen, the Courtyard & Pastry Kitchen, or the Bakery and Pasta Kitchen to get a sneak peek at the delicious concoctions being served at the District's fine restaurants. Now, grab a snack, dessert or meal at a café or restaurant in the area. If you still want more art...head over to the Hunter Museum of Art to view changing and permanent exhibits of regional fame (along the Tennessee River Walk, 423-267-0968 or www.huntermuseum.org, Open daily, Admission). The "Big Julie" and the "Fundraiser" sculptures are of interest (one is a life-like in the main lobby...amazing). Much of the modern glassworks are colorful with unusual shapes.

CHATTANOOGA AFRICAN-AMERICAN HISTORY MUSEUM/ BESSIE SMITH HALL

200 East Martin Luther King Jr. Blvd,

Chattanooga 37403

❑   Phone: (423) 266-8658. **Web: www.caamhistory.com**

❑   Hours: Monday-Friday 10:00am-5:00pm, Sunday Noon-dusk.

❑   Admission: $5.00 adult, $3.00 senior/student, $2.00 child (6-12).

The exhibits begin with a "Wall of Respect", dedicated to African-Americans who have achieved first in their professional endeavors. After passing the "Wall", the visitor travels through an authentic African dwelling and a section with a variety of statues, tools and artifacts depicting the life, work, art and worship of Africans before they came to America. There are other displays of Chattanooga African-American Civil War involvement, their achievements in sports and performing arts, portrayals of family and professional life and even a focus on the Civil Rights movement. The achievements of Bessie Smith are remembered at the annual Riverbend Festival and throughout the museum.

CHATTANOOGA ZOO AT WARNER PARK

1254 E. 3rd Street (I-24 exit 4th Ave., turn right, then left on 23rd
St.; turn right on Holtzclaw; left on McCallie Ave.; right into Warner
Park), **Chattanooga** 37404

- ❑   Phone: (423) 697-1322. **Web: http://zoo.chattanooga.org/**
- ❑   Hours: 9:00am-5:00pm (April-October). 10:00am-5:00pm
  (November-March). Closed: Christmas Day, New Year's Day,
  Martin Luther King Day, Thanksgiving Day.
- ❑   Admission: $4.00 adult, $3.00 senior (65+), $2.00 child (3-15).

A 5-acre zoo offering exotic animals and an animal contact area.
Newer exhibits feature lively chimps, a spider monkey habitat, and
an African Aviary home to Crowned Cranes and Pygmy Goats kids
can pet.

LAKE WINNEPESAUKAH AMUSEMENT PARK

Lakeview Drive (I-24 East to the Moore Road (exit 184) and go
straight to the 2nd traffic light and turn right onto McBrien Road)

Chattanooga 37412

- ❑   Phone: (877) LAKEWIN. **Web: www.lakewinnie.com**
- ❑   Hours: Weekends 10:00am- 8:00 or 10:00pm (April-mid-
  September). Open Thursday-Friday (May-early August).
- ❑   Admission: $3.00 (age 3+). $18.00 unlimited rides wristband.
  Individual Ride Tickets are available for .75¢ each. (rides range
  from 2-5 tickets). Children 21 and under must purchase gate
  admission with unlimited rides, or $9.50 value strip (14 ride tickets).

Free concerts featuring Christian, Country or Rock music artists
are regular items on the Lake Winnie calendar of events. Thirty
rides with exciting rides like the Cannon Ball Roller Coaster and
the Pipeline Plunge, an intense water ride featuring a five-story
maze of pipes that lead to a wet and wild final splash. Kiddie Land
at Lake Winnie has dozens of attractions designed for the youngest
of your family members.

BOOKER T. WASHINGTON STATE PARK

5801 Champion Road (I-75 exit 4, Hwy 153. Take exit Hwy 58, go 5 miles)

Chattanooga 37416

❑ Phone: (423) 894-4955

Web: www.state.tn.us/environment/parks/bookert

❑ Hours: 7:00am-dark.

❑ Admission: A $3.00 per vehicle, per day access fee is charged at this park.

Named for famous educator, Booker T. Washington, this 352-acre park is located on the shores of TVA's Chickamauga Reservoir. They have a year-round lodge and seasonal boat-launching ramp. The park has a large olympic size pool with diving board and a childrens' wading pool. The pool is open from early summer through Labor Day. Park recreation activities include hiking, field games, playgrounds, basketball, badminton, horseshoes, volleyball and board games.

CHATTANOOGA NATURE CENTER & REFLECTION RIDING

400 Garden Road (I-24W to exit 175, turn left onto Brown's Ferry, go to Cunnings Hwy, turn left; follow signs)

Chattanooga 37419

❑ Phone: (423) 821-1160

Web: www.chattanature.org & www.reflectionriding.org

❑ Hours: Monday-Saturday 9:00am-5:00pm. Sunday, 1:00-5:00pm.

❑ Admission: $6.00 adult, $3.00 senior (65+) and child (4-12).

❑ Miscellaneous: While visiting the Center, children can learn what it's like to be a real naturalist by checking out one of the Discovery Forest Backpacks (rental $3.50). Packed with study and field guides, binoculars, a microscope, and more...your child's next visit will become much more than a walk through the woods. We'd recommend attending during special events.

Chattanooga Nature Center & Reflection Riding *(cont.)*

DISCOVERY FOREST TREEHOUSE is a structure built among the arms of a 100-year-old Overcup Oak in the heart of the Nature Center's lowland forest wetlands. Stained glass works and many more pieces make it one of the most unique treehouses in the world. WILDLIFE WANDERLAND exhibit area: The centerpiece of this area is the Red Wolf exhibit where daily programming educates visitors. Unlike a zoo, the Wanderland holds only native birds and animals that are unable to be released because of their injuries and/or extensive human contact. If you have time, enter the REFLECTION RIDING Garden area (by car, bike or walking). The three-mile driving road (which gives the Riding its name) invites visitors to "ride" through the changes each season. Labels and signs tell of the horticulture, geology, history and geography of the area.

RACCOON MOUNTAIN CAVERNS

319 West Hills Drive (1.3 miles off Interstate 24. Exit Lookout Valley (Tiftonia), #174, Scenic US 41)

Chattanooga 37419

- ❑   Phone: (423) 821-CAVE or (800) 823-2267
  Web: www.raccoonmountain.com or www.wildcave.com
- ❑   Hours: Vary by season. Call first.
- ❑   Admission: Crystal Caverns Tour: $9.95 adult, $8.95 senior (65+), $5.50 child (5-12). Wild Cave tours vary by amount of activity.
- ❑   Tours: Crystal Caverns is 45 minutes, walking. Wild Cave is 2 to 6 hours (even overnight).
- ❑   Miscellaneous: Hiking trails, campground, swimming pool, playground, batting cages, and Go-Carts. They even have panning for gems with specialty Gold or Fossil Panning bags for purchase that almost guarantees a find.

Walk into the majestic Crystal Palace Room - one of the largest cave formation chambers in the Southeast. You will stroll along a smooth, circular walkway with gentle slopes and just a few steps as you view an assortment of stalactites, stalagmites, rim stone pools, fossils, and even evidence of past earthquakes. Wild Cave expeditions are tours with trained cavers guiding you through the vast underground network of chambers, canyons, tunnels, small streams, and large waterfalls that are beneath Raccoon Mountain. Strap on your elbow and knee pads and shimmy through dark crevices.

RACCOON MOUNTAIN PUMPED STORAGE FACILITY

Raccoon Mountain (TVA facility- I-24 exit 174, Hwy. 41, follow up mountain)

Chattanooga 37419

- ❏   Phone: (423) 825-3100. **Web: www.tva.gov**
- ❏   Hours: Year-round. Call for details to be sure they're open to the public for your visit. High security area.
- ❏   Admission: FREE

A 520 acre mountain top lake features scenic views of the Tennessee River Gorge. From the lake, visitors descend 1,100 feet (you go down a 19 story elevator in less than one minute!) into the mountain to a pump turbine room. After you stagger out of the elevator and regain your footing, observe how water from the lake is used to generate hydro-electric power. Nearly 2.3 miles of tunnels and shafts were excavated through shale, sandstone, and limestone for the project. The largest tunnel is about 36 feet in diameter. Do you know how they work? It's similar to a giant storage battery. There must be two water reservoirs, one located at a much higher level than the other.

TENNESSEE VALLEY RAILROAD

4119 Cromwell Road (Grand Junction Depot - near the Jersey Pike Exit off Highway 153 (past airport); 1 mile from I-75)

Chattanooga 37421

- ❏   Phone: (423) 894-8028 or (800) 397-5544
  Web: www.tvrail.com
- ❏   Admission: $12.50 adult, $6.50 child (age 3-12).

Tennessee Valley Railroad *(cont.)*

❑   Tours: Trains run everyday, April through October; Weekends
    through Thanksgiving. Departures 2 to 5 times daily. Approx.
    one hour trip. Special longer Dixie Land Excursions posted
    throughout the year (see Seasonal & Special Events).

❑   Miscellaneous: Hey Kids -- Bring your parents to a Day Out
    With Thomas™ (usually 1st two weekends in May). Activities
    pay tribute to everyone's favorite #1 engine with coloring pages,
    storytelling, Thomas & Friends™ videos, performances by
    clowns, appearances by Sir Topham Hatt™ , and the highlight is
    a 25-minute ride on a full-sized, vintage train pulled by Thomas
    the Tank Engine™!

"Missionary Ridge Local Service" is a six-mile, 50-minute
roundtrip from Grand Junction Station to East Chattanooga Depot,
crossing Chickamauga Creek, CSX mainline (ex-W&A), Tunnel
Boulevard and Awtry Street bridges and passing through pre-Civil
War Missionary Ridge Tunnel (over 950 ft. long built in 1858). If
you ride the last car, you can stand out on the porch when going
thru the tunnel for the best view. Passengers detrain in East
Chattanooga for a layover which includes viewing the locomotive
rotate on a turntable and a tour through the railyard and into the
restoration shop to see work in progress before reboarding the train
for the return trip. This stop looks just like a giant Thomas depot
on the Island of Sodor! In the depot, a conductor may help you
send a message.

AUDUBON ACRES

900 Sanctuary Road (From I-75, take Exit 3A to E. Brainerd
Road – East)

Chattanooga (East Brainerd) 37421

❑   Phone: (423) 892-1499. **Web: www.audubonchattanooga.org**
❑   Hours: Monday-Saturday 9:00am - dusk, Sunday 1:00pm -dusk.
❑   Admission: $2.00 adult, $1.00 child (5-12).

Over 100 acres of wildlife sanctuary with 4 miles of trails, a
pedestrian suspension bridge over the South Chickamauga Creek
and a reconstructed Cherokee cabin (dates back to the 1700s and is

For updates visit our website: www.kidslovepublications.com

said to be the birth place of Cherokee naturalist, Spring Frog). Little Owl Village is the location of a Mississippian Era Native American village in the 1400's and 1500's. This village is believed to be the location of the first contact between local Native Americans and Spanish explorers. It is being slowly restored as records indicate it was burned to the ground when the explorers invaded in the 1500's.

ROCK CITY

1400 Patten Road (I-24 exit 178 south, follow signs to Lookout)

Chattanooga (Lookout Mountain) 30750

- ❑ Phone: (706) 820-2531 or (877) 820-0759
  Web: www.seerockcity.com
- ❑ Hours: 8:30am - 5:00pm (early January to early April, late October to mid-November); 8:30am to 6:00pm (early April to Memorial Day weekend., Labor Day to end of October); 8:30am to 8:00pm (Memorial Day-Labor Day); 8:30am - 4:00pm (late November-just after New Years).
- ❑ Admission: $12.95 adult, $6.95 child (3-12). Combo prices with other Lookout Mountain Attractions offered.
- ❑ Tours: Self-guided tours take 60-90 minutes. The trail includes Fairyland Caverns and Mother Goose Village for kids.
- ❑ Miscellaneous: Mother Goose (summer) visits in her VILLAGE. Big Rock Café (built around a giant rock-sit by the big rock as you eat) or Cornerstone Station soda fountain.

The Grand Corridor welcomes you to unusual rock formations carved by nature. Look for the quiet, enchanted gnomes and elves around many corners...There's a wonderful outdoor family adventure ahead! Start at the Needles Eye - narrow passage. Deer Park - observe rare white Fallow deer in the wild – descendants of species transported here from Europe in the 1930s (our family thought they looked right out of a storybook!). Swing-A-Long Bridge - provides visitors with both a challenge and a breathtaking view. This engineering marvel stretches a full 180 feet through the blue sky. Lover's Leap - do you believe the stories of Indian braves and maidens thrown from this cliff? Seven States Flag Court -

from the time of the Civil War, people noted you could see 7 states from this lookout - Alabama, Georgia, Kentucky, North Carolina, South Carolina, Tennessee, and Virginia. Fat Man's Squeeze - think thin! And, the 1,000 Ton Balanced Rock - how does it stay up? Finally, enter the enchanted Fairyland Caverns where gnomes work & play in fairy tale settings in cave rooms. Garnet Carter and his wife first developed this land and, because of some construction delays, ended up inventing miniature golf and creating a "rock" park!

RUBY FALLS

1720 S. Scenic Hwy. (I-24 exit 178 or 174, follow signs)

Chattanooga (Lookout Mountain) 37409

- ❑   Phone: (423) 821-2544. **Web: www.rubyfalls.com**
- ❑   Hours: Daily 8:00am-8:00pm. Closed Christmas Day.
- ❑   Admission: $12.95 adult, $5.95 child (3-12). Combo prices with other Lookout Mountain Attractions offered.
- ❑   Tour: Minimum time for caverns tour is 1-1/2 hours. Guided tours take you on a one mile hike.
- ❑   Miscellaneous: Lookout Mountain Tower (stairs), the Fun Forest Playground, and gift shops/snack bar. Be sure to have the kids use the restroom before touring - only one way in and out.

The thundering 145 foot waterfall inside historic Lookout Mountain is the world's highest underground waterfall. A powerful earthquake, or more likely a series of them, caused the layers of rock in the Mountain to bend or fold upwards... cracks or crevices then occurred. Take a descending elevator tour that opens to cave paths of the Lookout Mountain Caverns. Look for rock formations that resemble steak and potatoes, an elephant's foot or an angel's wing. These caves were once used by Native Americans and Civil War troops for living space and as a hideout for the outlaws. The 1/2 hour wait is worth it as you enter the Falls room! The "light & sound" show that magically, spiritually occurs once you're by the Falls is awesome! Lots of oohs and aahs here...

BATTLES FOR CHATTANOOGA ELECTRIC MAP & MUSEUM

1110 E. Brow Road (I-24 W exit 178, Lookout Mtn., to Broad St. S (Hwy. 41), follow signs)

Chattanooga (Lookout Mtn) 37350

❑ Phone: (423) 821-2812 or (423) 821-7786 (Point Park)
Web: www.battlesforchattanooga.com

❑ Hours: Daily 9:00am-6:30pm (summer). 10:00am-5:00pm (rest of year).

❑ Admission: $5.95 adult, $3.95 child (3-12).

The kids' favorite feature will be the three-dimensional electronic battle map presentation of Chattanooga's Civil War history featuring 5,000 miniature soldiers, 650 lights, sound effects and exceptional details of the major battles which were fought here in November of 1863.   Hear and see about Chattanooga's Battle Above the Clouds and Sherman's assault on Missionary ridge before his historic March To the Sea. This is just long enough to help you visually see the battle from afar and understand the strategies involved without getting boring.

CHICKAMAUGA AND CHATTANOOGA NATIONAL MILITARY PARK

East Brow Road (atop Lookout Mountain)

Chattanooga (Lookout Mtn.) 37350

❑ Phone: (706) 866-9241Ranger or (423) 821-7786 Visitor Center
Web: www.nps.gov/chch

❑ Hours: Daily 8:00am-5:00pm except Christmas.

❑ Admission: $3.00 per each adult (age 17+) for Point Park and again for Cravens House. Pay by the honor system.

❑ Miscellaneous: Hiking and horse trails. Ranger guided talks and Civil War era demonstrations are conducted during the summer season.

In the fall of 1863, two armies clashed in an effort to gain control of vital transportation hubs. The battle was fought over a four square mile area that was covered with dense woods and thick underbush, unlike most battles that occur in open fields. Both sides were winning at different points. After you learn about the battles, be sure to take a walk over to Point Park - site of the famous Battle Above the Clouds (learn why it's called that…two kinds of fog that day) & preserved/interpreted portions of the Chickamauga battlefields - the battles that sealed the fate of the Confederacy. The Visitors Center is home to the large mural, the "Battle of Lookout Mountain" with audio presentation that helps you visually locate the details of this enormous mural painted by an eye-witness. Cravens' House (open for touring) was the site of some of the fiercest fighting, serving as headquarters for both sides. Why did soldiers and reporters take the house apart to stay warm?

MUSEUM CENTER AT 5IVE POINTS

200 Inman Street East (I-75 exit 20 or 25, follow US 11 to Inman St. east)

Cleveland 37311

- ❑ Phone: (423) 339-5745. **Web: www.museumcenter.org**
- ❑ Hours: Tuesday-Friday 10:00am-5:00pm, Saturday 10:00am-3:00pm. Closed holidays.
- ❑ Admission: $5.00 adult, $4.00 senior & students.
- ❑ Miscellaneous: Ask for a treasure hunt paper you complete using clues numbered throughout the museum. Ocoee Players Productions.

A regional history museum of the Ocoee Region. "The River of Time" core exhibit includes seven time periods dating from prehistory to today and interprets how people of this region lived, worked and played. Using video and displayed artifacts, you can meet "Fallen Sky" (an aging Cherokee), a traveling missionary, a child (petrified pants, stiff shoes, swinging washer and butter churn), a railroad conductor (progress), a black teacher, or a TVA carpenter. Great stories with hands-on activities at each station. Did you know Cleveland, Tennessee is the stove capital of the world?

RED CLAY HISTORIC PARK

1140 Red Clay Park Road S.W. (I-75, take exit 3-A (E. Brainerd Rd.) head East about 10 miles)

Cleveland 37311

❑ Phone: (423) 478-0339

Web: www.state.tn.us/environment/parks/parks/RedClay/

❑ Hours: 8:00am-Sunset (March-November). Open until 4:30pm (December-February). Visitors Center closed December 20-January 1. Park closed Christmas.

Being a historic park, Red Clay is dedicated to the preservation and interpretation of Cherokee history. The James F. Corn Interpretive Center, located near the park entrance, houses the park administrative offices, a theater, a resource reading room, and exhibits. This facility contains artifacts and documents that emphasize the 19th-century Cherokee history and culture. Replicas of a Cherokee farmstead (many were farmers) and Council House of the period show how the area might have looked 150 years ago. The Blue Hole spring is located near the Council House and is accessible by a paved trail designed to accommodate the handicapped. The Blue Hole spring is about 15 feet deep, and produces over 504,000 gallons of water a day.

CHEROKEE NATIONAL FOREST

2800 North Ocoee Street (Forest supervisors office)

Cleveland 37320

❑ Phone: (423) 476-9700. **Web: www.r8web.com/cherokee/**

Best known for its rivers along with several lakes which offer more than enough for a vacation of whitewater rafting, floating, canoeing, sailing, fishing and water skiing. Spread throughout the region are trails for biking, horseback riding and hiking trails, with many areas perfect for wildlife watching at designated Watchable Wildlife locations. Also within the forest are several campgrounds and picnic/swimming areas (several nice beach areas near each of the 3 Ocoee Dams). At <u>COKER CREEK</u>, view the falls (FS Road 2138) along the trail that connects to the John Muir Trail (423-261-2157). In town at <u>COKER CREEK VILLAGE</u> you can ride horses or try your hand at gold panning (423-261-2310). The Ocoee River is the site of the Class 3 & 4 rapids (ages 12+). The Hiwassee River has outfitters that rent funyaks, tubes and rafts or people can canoe and kayak on their own. The Hiwassee River is ideal for beginners and families with Class I and 2 rapids. The call (gobble) of the wild turkey in the East Tennessee mountains is an unforgettable sound. Male turkeys (gobblers) usually begin actively attracting female (hen) turkeys by gobbling in early March through mid-May. This thunderous sound is a sure sign that spring is in the air.

CLEVELAND SPEEDWAY

2420 S. Lee Hwy

Cleveland 37320

❑   Phone: (423) 479-8574. **Web: http://clevelandspeedway.com/**

1/3 mile semi Banked Red Clay Oval in Tennessee race Super Late Models every Saturday night, March-August. The other racing divisions at the track include the Claimer Late Models, the Hobby division, the Pony Stock division and the "Anything Goes" Street division. Admission.

CLEVELAND CITY RECREATION DEPARTMENT

Cleveland 37720

❑   Phone: (423) 479-4129

DEER PARK - renovated park turned into a "learning structures" facility with 70 stations that are all age appropriate and can host 160-170 children at a time. Covered pavilion, restrooms. 17th Street.

FLETCHER PARK - 720-acre passive, nature-oriented park contains a five-mile walking trail, old spring house and rock spring, fishing pond, boardwalk, observation walkway, amphitheater and picnic area. TN Nursery Road.

OCOEE WHITEWATER CENTER

Rte. 1, Box 285, Hwy. 64

Copperhill 37317

❑   Phone: (423) 496-5197 or (877) 692-6050

❑   Hours: Monday-Sunday 9:00am-5:00pm (early April-November).
Weekends only (December-March).

❑   Miscellaneous: Conservation Center has various kids' programs
in the summer.

Home of the 1996 Olympic Whitewater Competition, visitors can
also try their hand at rafting the Olympic Race Channel (only
20x/year-level 3 & 4 rapids). There are 10 miles of hiking and bike
trails plus a Native Garden. Swim the "blue hole", just dip your
feet in wading pools or walk out onto the rocks when there aren't
rapids running. The Visitors Center features video footage of the
Olympic races, examples of the construction (before & after) and
how they created "faux" rock. Can you tell the difference?

DAYTON PARKS

Highway 27

Dayton 37321

❑   Phone: (423) 775-6171

CHICKAMAUGA LAKE - offers a variety of sport fishing,
outdoor camping, and family water activities.

LAUREL-SNOW POCKET WILDERNESS & BUZZARD
POINT - Walnut Grove Road, 423-775-7801, This is the first
National Recreation Trail in Tennessee. It provides 10.5 miles of
wilderness trail guiding you to waterfalls, forest and unique rock
formations. They also offer trails for hikers.

HIWASSEE RIVER (SUGARLOAF MOUNTAIN) STATE PARK & OCOEE RIVER

Spring Creek Road (U.S. Hwy. 411, the Ocoee river on U.S. Hwy. 64), **Delano** 37325

❑   Phone: (423) 263-0050 or (423) 263-0060
     Web: www.state.tn.us/environment/parks/hiwassee/
❑   Admission: $3.00 per day per vehicle.
❑   Miscellaneous: Stop by the Webb Brothers Store in Reliance to shop at a 1936 era general store, post office, refreshments and local gossip. Raft and funyak rentals.

Sugarloaf Mountain State Park is situated at the foot of the Ocoee #1 Dam. This state park contains the scale model for the 1996 Olympic Race Course. Especially great to view before you hit the rapids or in lieu of rafting them. Restrooms, picnic area, campsites and canoe put-in. This stretch of river offers canoeing, rafting, fishing, hiking and nature photography. A scenic portion of the John Muir trail winds through the river gorge. The Ocoee River is a premier white-water river in the Southeastern United States possessing Class III, IV, and V rapids.

DUCKTOWN BASIN MUSEUM

(Hwy 64)

Ducktown 37317

❑   Phone: (423) 496-5778
❑   Hours: Monday-Saturday 10:00am-4:00pm. Closed Sundays, Thanksgiving, Christmas, & New Years.
❑   Admission: $3.00 adult, $2.00 senior, $0.50 child

As you drive into the area, look for the copper-colored hills everywhere. Located on the grounds of the historic Burra Burra Copper Mine (best view is from museum's observation platform), the museum exhibits help visitors understand the environmental and cultural history of Tennessee's only copper district. They use a slide show and simulated hard rock copper mine walkthrough. In 1843, a gold prospector discovered rock he thought was gold. It turned out to be red copper oxide. Prospectors, land speculators, and engineers poured into the area from everywhere. By 1860 there were 1,000 people employed here. Today, instead of copper, now companies produce sulfuric acid instead. Ever heard of roasting rock?

L & N DEPOT MUSEUM

P.O. Box 390

Etowah 37331

- ❑   Phone: (423) 263-7840
- ❑   Hours: Tuesday-Saturday 9:00am-4:30pm, Sunday 1:00-4:00pm. Closed major holidays.
- ❑   Admission: Donations accepted.
- ❑   Miscellaneous: Visitors Center is located in the depot also.

This 1906, two-story Victorian rail station has an exhibit "Growing Up With The L&N: Life and Times in a Railroad Town," that tells the story of this town built as a planned community by the Louisville & Nashville Railroad. The museum traces the working class history of the people focused on the railroad business. Also, large artifacts from the depot when it was used as a Canteen during WWII are displayed. An active rail yard is outside where visitors enjoy trains switching, changing crews and passing through. The best view is from the Portico Room observation deck- the circus trains passing thru are a local favorite! Hopefully, a local will be around to tell you some personal stories (lots of townspeople like to hang out here).

HARRISON BAY STATE PARK

8411 Harrison Bay Road (I-75 exit 4, Hwy 153. Exit Hwy 58 N, go 10 miles), **Harrison** 37341

- ❑   Phone: (423) 344-2272
  Web: www.state.tn.us/environment/parks/harrison/
- ❑   Hours: 8:00am-10:00pm.
- ❑   Admission: A $3 per vehicle, per day access fee is charged at this park.

Located along miles of the Chickamauga Reservoir, the park has one of the most complete marine facilities available on any TVA lakes. Many also come for the wildlife viewing. The park has an olympic size swimming pool and a wading pool for small children. The pool is open from Memorial Day through late summer.

FORT MARR

(along US 64)

Ocoee 37317

❑   Phone: (423) 263-7232. **Web: www.tennesseeoverhill.com**

Built in the early 19th century, its most notorious function was during the Cherokee Removal, when it was part of a larger stockade. The Blockhouse, which remains today, can be seen here. Nancy Ward, Beloved Woman of the Overhill Cherokees, is buried nearby, along with her son, Five Killer. The graves overlook the pastoral landscape along the Ocoee River.

HORSIN' AROUND CARVING SCHOOL

302 Walmart Drive (Rte. 153 exit off I-75, to Rte. 27 North, Soddy Daisy exit to Walmart behind past Pizza Hut)

Soddy Daisy 37379

❑   Phone: (423) 332-1111
❑   Hours: Monday-Friday 9:00am-5:00pm, Saturday 9:00am-6:00pm.

The Coolidge Park Carousel features more than 50 animals including horses, tigers, fish, dinosaurs, and even a giraffe! All the animals were hand-carved by students of Horsin' Around carving school. Many people ride by and visit. Some talk to Bud or one of his students who finds it relaxing to craft wooden animals. With sawdust everywhere, you'll see the carousel animals in many stages starting from regular pieces of unfinished wood. With the tap, tap, tap of wooden mallets on chisel handles, pieces of wood fall away to reveal the shape of their creator's vision. Because the work is done by different artists each animal has unique characteristics. Be careful, though, you may fall in love with these animals and want to come back as a student soon!

WATTS BAR DAM AREA

Highway 68 (trails are off of Shut-in Gap Road, northwest of city)

Spring City 37381

❏   Phone: (888) 238-3263 PIN 1318. www.wattsbarresort.com

<u>PINEY RIVER TRAIL, STINGING FORK POCKET WILDERNESS, & TWIN ROCKS NATURE TRAIL</u> - Natural wilderness areas with waterfalls, forests, unique rock formations, deep gorges.

<u>WATTS BAR RESORT</u> - (southeast of town, 800-365-9598) That family vacation you thought was gone still happens here as you stay in one of the resorts cabins, surrounded by picturesque gardens and green hillsides for hiking and wildlife photography. Situated at the lower end of a 39,000 acre lake along the Tennessee River, it is a good spot for fishing, boating, water skiing, house boating and picnicking from your rented pontoon boat or bring your own. Relax and cool off in the resort's swimming pool which also has a wading pool. The restaurant allows you to dine while you view gardens, lake and wildlife.

LOST SEA

140 Lost Sea Road (I-75 exit 60, Rte. 68, between Madisonville & Sweetwater), **Sweetwater** 37874

❏   Phone: (423) 337-6616. Web: www.thelostsea.com

❏   Hours: Open daily 9:00am until 5:00pm (winter), until 6:00pm (September, October, March, April), until 7:00pm (May, June, August), until 8:00pm (July). Closed Christmas Day.

❏   Admission: $12.00 adult, $5.50 child (6-12)

❏   Miscellaneous: Cavern Kitchen, General Store, Trading Post, Blacksmith Shop, picnic facilities and a nature trail. Level walkways on dirt floors, however some steep hills. Stroller / wheelchair accessible. <u>NOTE: Asthmatic persons may experience breathing difficulty.</u> More Adventuresome? Ask about the Wild Cave tour (4 hours) or Overnights. We recommend Best Western Sweetwater Inn with it's indoor tropical pool, family restaurant & Cracker Barrel next door (Hwy. 68, 423-337-3541).

Lost Sea *(cont.)*

Walk thru a metal tunnel into the unbelievable site of the giant Indian council chamber (600 ft x 120 ft). Indians used the calcium deposits as toothpaste and Confederate soldiers mined the cave for saltpeter. "America's Largest Underground Lake" is home to rare Cave Flowers and cascade formations. The earliest known visitor to the cave was a saber-toothed tiger, whose fossilized remains are now in the Museum of Natural History. A guided walk to the bottom of the cavern is rewarded upon entering the lake room, where you will board large glass bottom boats for a trip into the Lost Sea. While on the trip, you will observe some of the largest rainbow trout in the United States (but, why do they taste like liver?) and learn about the 4 acre lake underground. It's hard to believe what you see here!

CHEROHALA SKYWAY

250 Ranger Station Road (Rte. 165)

Tellico Plains 37385

❑   Phone: (423) 253-2520. **Web: www.monroecounty.com**

❑   Hours: Daily, all day. Remember, the roads are winding and snow is common from mid-November thru mid-April, especially in higher elevations.

❑   Admission: FREE

The bulletin board welcomes visitors with general information about the Skyway. It crosses through the Cherokee National Forest into North Carolina. Covering portions of what was once a Cherokee Indian trading route, this 40+ mile, two-lane blacktop road passes crystal-clear rivers and stops at scenic overlooks. Paralleling the Tellico River, the Skyway winds along the river at 1,000 ft. elevation offering canoeing and fishing (mile post 2 & 4). From at least 1650 AD, the Cherokee resided here until 1838 (Removal), when the area was opened for Euro-American settlement. Tellico ("tel-li-quo") means "plains" in Cherokee. At mile post 5, the Skyway begins its ascent through hills and valleys. Stop at mile post 14-16 to view Turkey Creek overlook. Closer to mile post 18, the Skyway passes by a black bear refuge and offers views of many rugged "rock" mountains. Near the Ranger Station (service road 210), you can view Bald River Falls without leaving your car as water cascades over 100 feet onto the rocks below. Further along this road is a state-operated trout hatchery.

FORT LOUDOUN STATE HISTORIC PARK

338 Fort Loudoun Road (Rte. 72 South, off I-75, to Highway 411 North until it intersects Hwy. 360 South, Turn onto 360 South)

Vonore 37885

❑   Phone: (423) 884-6217

      Web: www.state.tn.us/environment/parks/loudoun/index.html

❑   Hours: 8:00am-Sunset. Visitors Center is open daily from 8:00am-4:30pm except Thanksgiving, Christmas or New Years.

❑   Admission: Donations.

❑   Miscellaneous: We recommend Garrison Weekends-A living history program featuring the lives of the soldiers and civilians who originally occupied the fort. While here, the garrison carries out the activities common to frontier outpost. Musket drills, artillery training, cooking in the fireplaces and the bake oven, the sights and smells of frontier America.

This site is the location of one of the earliest British fortifications on the western frontier, built in 1756. Today, the fort and the 1794 Tellico Blockhouse overlook TVA's Tellico Reservoir and the Appalachian Mountains. It's like a giant "playground" of Redcoats and Indians inside the fort. It will inspire children's imagination to play as they wander inside the palisade walls! An interpretive center offers information on the area's history and artifacts that were excavated prior to the Fort's reconstruction. Kids gravitate to the Redcoat "Muppet" display and the diorama showing whites living inside the fort, with Cherokee peering behind bushes on the outside. Also, fishing, hiking and boating recreation opportunities. Feeding the giant carp at the Fort Loudoun Marina is lots of family fun (the carp are numerous and absolutely gigantic and well fed on Calhoun's scraps). Fort Loudon Marina, the largest marina on the Tennessee River, also offers both jet sky and pontoon boat rentals.

SEQUOYAH BIRTHPLACE MUSEUM

P.O. Box 69, Citico Road (across from Fort Loudoun St. Pk.,off
Hwy 411 North, follow signs)

Vonore 37885

- ❑ Phone: (423) 884-6246. **Web: www.sequoyahmuseum.org**
- ❑ Hours: Monday-Saturday 9:00am-5:00pm, Sunday Noon-
  5:00pm. Closed Thanksgiving, Christmas, & New Years.
- ❑ Admission:$3.00 adult, $1.50 child (6-12).
- ❑ Miscellaneous: Nearby are monuments commemorating the
  Overhill towns of Chota and Tanasee, namesake for the State.
  Begin with the video introduction…a good overview. Many easy
  videos & "Hear Phones" are located throughout at different
  stations.

Nearly everywhere you walk around here is prehistoric & historic
Indian land. The museum illuminates 1,000s of years of native
lifeways in the Little Tennessee River Valley and honors
Sequoyah, the inventor of the Cherokee alphabet. Unlike the white
soldiers during the war of 1812, Sequoyah and other Cherokees
weren't able to write letters home, read military orders, or record
events as they occurred. With years of work, he finally reduced the
thousands of Cherokee thoughts to 85 symbols representing
sounds. He made a game of this new writing system and taught his
little girl Ayoka how to make symbols. By the 1820s, Cherokee
were reading and writing documents. The museum also tells of the
history of the Cherokees in their family life, customs, beliefs and
sadness when the Trail of Tears began. Boys love the demos of the
blowgun and bow & arrow used to kill small animals. The one
band of Indians that didn't leave on the Trail of Tears still has a
reservation just over the border into North Carolina. Very
interesting, educational museum about the Cherokee. You'll love
the gift shop - everything is hand-made by Cherokee!

Chapter 6
Area - West (W)

Our Favorites...

* Birdsong Resort & Pearl Farm - Camden
* Casey Jones Village - Jackson
* Pinson Mounds - Pinson (Jackson)
* Graceland & Heartbreak Hotel - Memphis
* Fire Museum of Memphis
* Mud Island River Park - Memphis
* National Civil Rights Museum - Memphis
* Sun Studio - Memphis
* Pickwick Dam & Tennessee River Museum - Savannah
* Reelfoot Lake - Tiptonville

"The Elvis Presley Trio" - Sun Studio

WEST TENNESSEE DELTA HERITAGE CENTER
121 Sunny Hill Cove (I-40 exit 56)

Brownsville 38012

❑   Phone: (731) 779-9000
     Web: www.brownsville-haywoodtn.com/heritage/default.htm
❑   Hours: Tuesday-Saturday 9:00am-5:00pm, Sunday 1:00-5:00pm.
❑   Admission: FREE

Counties in the area have furnished displays to highlight destinations in the region. Other featured sites include the Cotton Museum. Visitors can see and experience the evolution of cotton farming from the time everything was done by hand to today's ultramodern methods of farming. Young and old alike enjoy the hands on exhibit of the stages of field cotton to ginned cotton. The West Tennessee Music Museum spotlights Carl Perkins, Tina Turner and Sleepy John Estes (even the small home of Sleepy John, famous blues musician, is on site) with music and pictures. The Hatchie River Museum focuses on the fragile watershed of the last untouched river west of the Tennessee River in all of the state.

PARIS LANDING STATE PARK
16055 Hwy 79N (east of Paris on US 79)

Buchanan 38222

❑   Phone: (731) 641-4465 or (731) 642-4311 Inn
     Web: www.state.tn.us/environment/parks/paris/
❑   Miscellaneous: Nearby in Paris is the largest replica of France's
     Eiffel Tower, standing proudly with an American flag at the top.

Paris Landing State Park is named for a steamboat and freight landing on the Tennessee River, dating back to the mid 1800's. From here and other landings on the Tennessee River and Big Sandy River, supplies were transported to surrounding towns and communities by ox cart. The 841-acre Paris Landing State Park is situated on the western shore of what is now Kentucky Lake, one of the largest man-made lakes in the world. The 100-plus room Inn has a restaurant, outdoor swimming pool, volleyball and tennis courts and a boat dock. There is a swimming area and beach on Kentucky Lake (along with loads of water recreation). 10 fully-modern cabins and camping facilities are available, too. Summer weekend Music in the Park live entertainment outdoor amphitheater concerts are offered.

BIRDSONG RESORT & PEARL FARM

255 Marina Road (I-40 exit 133 on Scenic Hwy 191N or I-70, Hwy 191S)

Camden (Kentucky Lake) 38320

❑   Phone: (731) 584-7880 or (800) 225-7469
     Web: www.birdsongresort.com
❑   Hours: Monday-Saturday, 8:00am-5:00pm, Sunday, 1:00-4:00pm.
❑   Admission: The mini-theatre & museum are open for walk-in traffic daily, FREE. Best weekdays (45 minutes long). Packages from $30-$50.00 for 2 to 5 hour guided tours. Kids rates run $5.00-$12.00.
❑   Tours: Weekdays. Minimum group size is 15. Families may be added to another group. Meal tours include disposable cameras and coffee mugs. You have the option to take the pontoon boat for the rest of the day for free (if you pay for the full tour).
❑   Miscellaneous: Families can stay at America's only freshwater pearl farm for just over $100 nightly. There are 11 cabins on the property with picnic tables, outdoor grills, full kitchens and some with screened porches & fireplaces. Other resort activities include swimming, basketball, volleyball, shuffleboard, ping-pong, fishing, boating and rentals.

MINI PEARL OF A TOUR (April-November) - Look just below the surface of Kentucky Lake where mussels incubate to eventually process pearls. Freshwater pearl farmers explain how man manipulates the natural process of pearl production with skill and patience (they have to wait 5 years). During the tour, you'll take a boat out to the farm to visit with divers. You'll witness implantation demonstrations and see how mussels are cared for during the cultivation process. The biggest secret - the thickness of the shell grown here. Kids like to help dissect a mussel to get a pearl out! 5 hour tours include a visit to the <u>TENNESSEE RIVER FOLKLIFE MUSEUM & PILOT KNOB CIVIL WAR LOOKOUT</u> (logging, pearl button industry and mussel farming artifacts) and a catered BBQ meal. Did you know the pearl is the official state gemstone? The gem comes in many shapes, too. See many of them set in jewelry, reasonably priced in their gift shop. You'll especially love the friendly, knowledgeable folks who operate the site. This place is absolutely amazing fun…and so-o-o unique!

NATHAN BEDFORD FORREST STATE PARK

1825 Pilot Knob Road (9 miles east of Camden on Hwy 191)

Eva 38333

❑ Phone: (731) 584-6356 or (800) 714-7305 cabins
Web: www.state.tn.us/environment/parks/forrest/
❑ Hours: 7:00am-10:00pm. Center: Wednesday-Sunday 9:00am - 4:30pm.
❑ Admission: $3.00 per vehicle, per day.

This park was named for General Nathan Bedford Forrest, the intrepid Confederate cavalry leader, who on November 4, 1864, attacked and destroyed the federal supply and munitions depot at (Old) Johnsonville at the mouth of Trace Creek. <u>CENTER</u>: When TJ Whitfield retired from a career of musseling on the Tennessee River, he probably never thought his boat, "Old Betsy" would come to rest at this high point. The boat is now a centerpiece of an exhibit on the River Folklife Center atop Pilot Knob. On the deck outside the building is the "Liar's Bench" where recorded interviews can be heard with the press of a button. Listen to the tall-tales and legends of the river people. Also fishing, boating, group lodge and modern cabins.

NATIONAL BIRD DOG MUSEUM & WILDLIFE HERITAGE CENTER

505 W Hwy 57, **Grand Junction** 38039

❑   Phone: (731) 764-2058. **Web: www.fielddog.com**
❑   Hours: Tuesday-Friday 10:00am-2:00pm, Saturday 10:00am-
     4:00pm, Sunday 1:00-4:00pm.
❑   Admission: FREE

You can't miss the museum...kids squeal at the bronze dogs outside. Recognizing over 40 breeds of bird dogs, the museum features numerous exhibits, sporting dog art, wildlife murals, artifacts, and game bird specimens. Among the portraits and exhibits contained in the museum, you will find the National Champions (like the famous Count Noble in full point) which have found glory on the Ames Plantation near Grand Junction (4275 Buford Ellington Rd, 731-878-1067 or **www.amesplantation.org**). Wildlife Room - stuffed wildlife - many you may have never seen. See all the predators that naturally might like a bird for dinner. Even touch many skulls and skins. What happened to the two deer that occupied the interlocked horns? Why are female birds drab in color?

CHICKASAW STATE PARK

20 Cabin Lake (SR 100)

Henderson 38340

❑   Phone: (901) 989-5141
     Web: www.state.tn.us/environment/parks/chicksaw/
❑   Hours: Daily 6:00am-10:00pm. Lodge open April-October. The
     restaurant is open Thursday through Sunday.
❑   Miscellaneous: Cabin Reservation: 800-458-1752

This park and forest was once part of a vast area belonging to the Chickasaw Nation prior to the Jackson Purchase of 1818. Parents like the Bear Trace Golf Course designed by Jack Nicklaus. Miles of roads and trails wind thru the scenic timberlands touching Lake Placid. The park offers vacation cottages, camping sites, group lodge, hiking trails, tennis, badminton, basketball and volleyball courts, a playground, and archery range, ball fields and horseback riding in the summer. A park recreation director, on duty during the summer months, conducts group games, arts and crafts, evening, campfire programs and hayrides. Country dances are held on holiday week-ends.

ALEX HALEY HOUSE AND MUSEUM

200 S. Church Street

Henning 38041

❑   Phone: (731) 738-2240

❑   Hours: Tuesday-Saturday 10:00am-5:00pm, Sunday 1:00-5:00pm. Tours are 30 minutes.

❑   Admission: $2.50 adult, $1.00 student.

This is the boyhood home of Alex Haley, Pulitzer Prize-winning author of "Roots". Visit the burial site of Haley and well-known family members including Chicken George. The front porch of this home is where young Alex heard the stories of his ancestors. Haley's book received international acclaim and spurred millions to research their own ancestry.

FORT PILLOW STATE HISTORIC PARK

Rte. 2, 3122 Park Road (Hwy 87, off Hwy 51, west of town)

Henning 38041

❑   Phone: (731) 738-5581

Web: www.state.tn.us/environment/parks/pillow/

During the spring and early summer of 1862, the Union Navy bombarded Fort Pillow from its mortar boats. Few casualties resulted, but with the increasing danger of being cut-off from the main army, the Confederate Army evacuated Fort Pillow in June of 1862. Union forces immediately occupied the fort and held it for almost two years. The Museum is where visitors will find Civil War artifacts and interpretive displays. There is a 12 minute video on the 1864 Battle shown by request. Fort Pillow State Historic Park has been designated as a Wildlife Observation Area. Interpretive signs identify certain species and their habitat. The park provides sanctuary for deer, turkey, and is frequented by bird watchers. Nature and recreational programs are presented during the summer months or upon request. Other Activities: Playgrounds, Volleyball, Tennis, Horseshoes, Softball, tent camping, canoeing and fishing. The Mississippi River Bike Trail winds its way thru here.

CYPRESS GROVE NATURE PARK

US 70 W

Jackson 38301

❑ Phone: (731) 425-8364
❑ Hours: Daily 8:00am-5:00pm (November-March), 8:00am-7:30pm (April-October).
❑ Admission: FREE

Established to preserve part of Jackson's natural river bottom habitat, the park consists of 165 acres of Cypress forest and features trails, a couple miles of elevated boardwalk, a pond and a lake. The site also features a Raptor Center, a haven for birds of prey that have been injured and cannot survive on their own in the wild. Picnic facilities are here, too.

NC & ST. L DEPOT AND RAILROAD MUSEUM

582 South Royal Street (I-40 exit 80A, south on Hwy 45 bypass)

Jackson 38301

❑ Phone: (731) 425-8223
❑ Hours: Monday-Saturday 10:00am-3:00pm.
❑ Admission: FREE

The N.C. & St. Louis Railroad brought passengers to Jackson's Depot to partake of the town's mineral waters, eat popcorn supplied by a local character named "Popcorn Johnny" and listen to the music. The Depot features a museum, Amtrak dining car, two cabooses, and an elaborate model railroad display reflecting the town's history as West Tennessee's railroad hub.

CASEY JONES VILLAGE

56 Casey Jones Lane (I-40 exit 80Aat US 45 bypass)

Jackson 38305

❑   Phone: (731) 668-1223 or (877) CASEY-100
      Web: www.caseyjonesvillage.com

❑   Hours: Daily 6:00am-10:00pm (except Easter, Thanksgiving &
      Christmas).

❑   Admission: Fee charged for train ride and mini-golf (summers
      10:00am-9:00pm). Fee for House/Museum tour ($3.00-$4.00).

❑   Miscellaneous: Casey Jones Station Inn is where you can sleep in
      a real caboose or at the Station Inn Hotel. The Old Country Store
      Restaurant serves three daily Southern buffets (adult buffets
      reasonably priced between $7.00-$10.00) w/ Little Casey's
      Corner buffets (priced by the age) and features an old-fashioned
      ice cream parlor. Try their cracklin corn bread, for sure.
      AWESOME!

All aboard for Casey Jones Village where your kids will run to
climb on Engine 382 to ring the bell. Train engineer Casey Jones,
heroically stayed with his train and died in a wreck outside
Vaughan, Miss. The Casey Jones Home & Railroad Museum is the
historic 1900s home of America's most legendary railroad man.
Casey died heroically and his story was told in one of the most
popular ballads ever written. The Museum includes railroad
artifacts, original steam locomotive engines and a model railroad
exhibit. How did he get the name, Casey? Learn how Casey loved
the challenge of running faster times on the railroad. If he was
behind, he was skilled to make up time. See a video & mini model
RR showing exactly how the accident happened...the crash heard
round the world...why was he a hero? A Miniature train ride and
Miniature golf operates seasonally. What a family-friendly place
with something for everyone!

WEST TENNESSEE DIAMOND JAXX BASEBALL

Pringles Park, 4 Fun Place (I-40 exit 85)

Jackson 38305

❑ Phone: (731) 644-2020. **Web: www.diamondjaxx.com**
❑ Hours: Schedule includes 70 dates between April and August each year. Most games are Monday-Saturday at 7:05pm or Sunday at 2:05pm.
❑ Admission: $5.00-$9.00

The West Tenn Diamond Jaxx, a Class AA professional baseball team affiliated with the Chicago Cubs, plays in the 6,000-seat Pringles Park. It also offers a variety of amusements and attractions sponsored by Pringles Potato Chips, made in Jackson.

MEMPHIS MOTORSPORTS PARK

5500 Taylor Forge Drive

Memphis 38053

❑ Phone: (901) 358-7223 or (866) 407-7333
Web: www.memphismotorsportspark.com

Hosts NASCAR series, Craftsman Truck Series, as well as NHRA Drag Racing Series. Weekly racing and special events. All seating is general admission except for the Nitro grandstand. Children 12 and under are FREE with a paid Adult. General admission around $13.00. Events spring - early autumn.

BEALE STREET WALKING TOURS

Beale Street Information Center

Memphis 38103

❑ Phone: (901) 527-3427
❑ Hours: Handy House: Tuesday-Saturday 10:00am-5:00pm (summer) and Tuesday-Saturday 1:00-4:00pm (winter).
❑ Admission: Handy House: $1.00-$2.00 per person.

Lining this famous street are some big-name nightspots including B.B. King's Blues Club, Hard Rock Café, or Elvis Presley's

Memphis Restaurant downtown on Beale Street (901-527-6900). The restaurant serves meals made from Elvis' mother's recipes and includes many of his favorite dishes on the menu (maybe the Peanut butter & Banana toasted sandwich or the "Teddy Bear" hamburger). A highlight is the musical performances live on stage as well as special videos produced especially for the club.. Besides hearing music most every evening and some late afternoons, you can also visit various specialty shops or the home of W.C. Handy, who launched his career from here. The small wood-frame house depicts the humble beginnings of the "Father of the Blues". Another popular stop is A. Schwab's, a century-old family-operated dry goods store, where you can find everything from tools to toys. Also check out the Beale Street Police Substation and Museum to see relics from old time police days. On Main Street (intersects with Beale), take a 60c trolley up north towards Mud Island or the Fire Museum.

CIRCUIT PLAYHOUSE

1705 Poplar Avenue

Memphis 38103

❏   Phone: (901) 726-4656. **Web: www.playhouseonthesquare.org**
❏   Hours: Performances for different shows run Thursday-Sunday.

Professional live theater offering Broadway and off-Broadway performances at affordable prices ($12.00-$28.00). Theatre for Youth feature each year plus many Playhouse performances are geared towards families (Purple Purse, Wizard of Oz, Peter Pan).

FIRE MUSEUM OF MEMPHIS

118 Adams Avenue (downtown, a few blocks east of the Mud Island Walkway)

Memphis 38103

❏   Phone: (901) 320-5650. **Web: www.firemuseum.com**
❏   Hours: Monday-Saturday 9:00am-5:00pm. Closed Sunday.
❏   Admission: $5.00 adult, $4.00 senior (60+) & child (3-12).

This downtown museum is housed in the old Fire Station No. 1 and contains a collection of artifacts, including stories and photos of the city's most devastating fires. However, most of the features are for kids: an animated "talking" horse that narrates a video about the role horses played in fire fighting; and, interactive games that teach fire safety and simulate real fires through devices such as hot air, thick smoke, and wrap-around video screens (this will get your attention!); and a 1967 Pumper or modern firetruck cab that children can actually get in and play "fire fighter." Dress up in uniform, turn on the siren or simulate fighting a fire in a skyscraper. There's even a firefighters video arcade to play games on. This is our favorite Kids Fire Museum in the nation!

GIBSON GUITAR FACTORY TOURS (BEALE ST. SHOWCASE)

145 Lt. George W. Lee Avenue in the Beale Street Entertainment District, just a half a block south of Beale Street and Highway 61 (a.k.a. Third Street)

Memphis 38103

- ❑   Phone: (901) 543-0800. **Web: www.gibsonmemphis.com**
- ❑   Admission: $10.00 (ages 12+ only).
- ❑   Tours: Sunday- Wednesday 1:00pm. Thursday - Saturday 11:00am, 12:00pm, 1:00pm, and 2:00pm. Tour lasts 25 minutes.

See Gibson guitars made on a docent-led tour of 16 work stations on the factory floor. Knowledgeable "honest to goodness" musicians lead you along as master craftspeople use the latest technology to hand-craft a guitar from a block of wood. The Les Paul and B.B. King's Lucille are just two of the many prestigious guitars manufactured on-site.

MEMPHIS REDBIRDS (AUTOZONE PARK)

8 S Third Street (Union at Third Street, Riverside Dr. exit, downtown)

Memphis 38103

- ❑   Phone: (901) 721-8050 or (901) 721-6000 box office **Web: www.memphisredbirds.com**
- ❑   Hours: Games April-August.
- ❑   Admission: $5.00-$15.00

For updates visit our website: www.kidslovepublications.com

The AAA affiliate of the St. Louis Cardinals. Baseball, music and fun at the Park. Dominating the park's entry plaza is the 37-foot tall "Nostalgia Man". Kids can join the Rockin Redbirds Club. The Boardwalk is a family-oriented games and amusement area & P.D. Parrot's Playhouse Perch is a playground and fun zone located next to the Bluff. Take a peek "behind the scenes" of the state-of-the-art press box, lighting and see where the players workout. Tours are $3.00-$4.00 per person at 10:00am & 1:00pm on non-game days.

MEMPHIS RIVERKINGS

(DeSoto Civic Center, I-55 towards Jackson, MS. Take the Church Road Exit (#287). Turn right onto Church Rd. then turn left onto Venture Dr)

Memphis 38103

❑   Phone: (662) 342-1755 **Web: www.riverkings.com**

Pro hockey championship team season runs October-April. Tickets packages like 4 for $44.00. Affiliation as the primary AA affiliate of the Toronto Maple Leafs.

MEMPHIS ROCK N SOUL MUSEUM

145 Lt. George W. Lee Avenue (in the Beale Street District just a half a block south of Beale Street and Third St, I-55N exit 12B, east on Beale)

Memphis 38103

❑   Phone: (901) 543-0800 **Web: www.memphisrocknsoul.org**
❑   Hours: Daily 10:00am-6:00pm
❑   Admission: $8.50 adult, $7.50 senior, $5.00 child (5-17).
❑   Miscellaneous: Around the block is the Arcade Diner (540 South Main) where Elvis loved to come for home-cooked breakfasts and their famous cheeseburgers. They even have one booth (in the back) you can sit at that was Elvis' favorite. (daily 7:00am-3:00pm, 901-526-5757)

"In the quest to identify the roots of America's music, all roads lead to Memphis". The Smithsonian's exhibit tells the history of musicians working in the Delta and Memphis area from the 1930s to 1970s and the style of music they developed...from Blues &

Gospel To Rock-And-Roll And Soul. Kids like the CD headset that they can program themselves and customize their tour by listening to songs from certain eras. Start in the cotton fields, then to radio studios and jukebox eras. Then, enter Sun Records and Elvis Rockabilly (white man's words to black man's music) along with Johnny Cash, Carl Perkins or Jerry Lee Lewis...Rebel music crossing the sounds of the blues, soul and country. Next door is the Gibson Factory tour.

MEMPHIS ZOO

2000 Prentiss Place, Overton Park (midtown, off N. Parkway)

Memphis 38103

❑   Phone: (901) 276-WILD. **Web: www.memphiszoo.org**
❑   Hours: Daily 9:00am-6:00pm (March-October), Daily until
        5:00pm (November-February). Closed some holidays.
❑   Admission: $10.00 adult, $9.00 senior, $6.00 child (2-11).

Over 3,000 animal residents occupy areas such as: Cat Country; Primate Canyon; Animals of the Night: Once Upon a Farm; Tropical Bird House; and the new China Exhibit. The star attraction: two giant pandas youth named Le-Le and Ya-Ya. Journey thru the Chinese culture, history and wildlife (like the white-faced gibbons).

MISSISSIPPI RIVER MUSEUM

125 N Front Street (Mud Island)

Memphis 38103

❑   Phone: (901) 678-7230
        Web: www.mississippirivermuseum.org
❑   Hours: Tuesday-Sunday 10:00am-5:00pm (mid April to
        Memorial Day & September, October). Daily 10:00am-8:00pm
        (Memorial Day - Labor Day).
❑   Admission: Includes monorail roundtrip & guided River Walk
        tour, plus museum: $8.00 adult, $6.00 senior (60+), $5.00 child
        (5-12).

This museum of the natural and cultural history of the Lower Mississippi River Valley tells a story. The search for more efficient transportation and the economic impact of river transportation played a vital role in the development of trade routes and the growth of river cities. Walk on a steamboat and hear stories from passengers and crew about life on the river - even go up to the pilothouse. Meet a gallery of famous Showboat folks (Mark Twain, Mike Fink). Now, enter the full-size cannon room of an ironclad and then go on land and fire back. The Theatre of Disasters Gallery has an audio visual presentation of river tragedies, including the great earthquake of 1811, the yellow fever plagues, and steamboat disasters. Next, relax listening to river music. Finally, exit thru the River Room's 4000 gallon aquarium full of river fish (look out for the giant catfish!). Very well done!

MUD ISLAND RIVER PARK

125 N Front Street (walkway or monorail over from Riverside Drive, downtown)

Memphis 38103

- ❑ Phone: (901) 576-7241 or (800) 507-6507
   Web: www.mudisland.com
- ❑ Hours: Daylight hours.
- ❑ Admission: FREE. Fee for boat and bike rentals.
- ❑ Miscellaneous: Monorail ($2.00 per person fee) and Walkway access from downtown riverfront. There are also canoe, kayak, airboat, pedal boat and bicycle rentals. 3 food concession areas.

This combination public park, museum, and entertainment center lies between the Mississippi River and the Wolf River Harbor. The RIVER WALK is a five-block-long scale model of the Mississippi from north to south. Along your journey, you'll revisit historical events and learn about geographical transformations. Walk along the banks or actually wade in the "River" - great family fun! The "1,000" mile journey concludes at the Gulf of Mexico, a one acre enclosure that holds 1.3 million gallons of water. There, visitors can enjoy a leisurely pedal boat ride. The MEMPHIS BELLE PAVILION is home to the WWII famous bomber airplane with a self-guided tour (901-412-8071), and the RIVER MUSEUM (901-576-7230) is on the island (see separate listing). On occasion the Queen Line of famous riverboats docks here.

NATIONAL CIVIL RIGHTS MUSEUM

450 Mulberry Street (downtown, a few blocks from Riverside Dr,
look for the large Lorraine Motel sign)

Memphis 38103

❑   Phone: (901) 521-9699   **Web: www.civilrightsmuseum.org**
❑   Hours: Monday-Saturday 9:00am-5:00pm, Sunday 1:00-5:00pm.
     Closed Tuesdays. Open until 6:00pm (May-August).
❑   Admission: $10.00 adult, $8.00 senior and student, $6.50 child
     (4-17).

The enhanced experience of actually being at the original Lorraine
Motel, site of Dr. Martin Luther King, Jr.'s assassination, is enough
in itself. Begin with an easy video to understand the movement.
Kids and parents get goosebumps seeing where Dr. King died and
all the use of the word "Colored". The letters "C" and "W" were
recognized even by the illiterate. The walk-thru exhibits are very
touching - esp. getting kicked off a bus or seeing the actual motel
room and balcony where Martin Luther King was shot! The
Exploring Legacy exhibit focuses on more recent Civil Rights
struggles as well as revealing additional facts & artifacts
surrounding the assassination (previously classified documents and
evidence). Inspiring feelings of love of freedom here! *Warning:
strong themes and message might scare or intimidate young ones
under 7.*

SLAVE HAVEN UNDERGROUND RAILROAD MUSEUM (BURKLE ESTATE)

826 N Second Street

Memphis 38103

❑   Phone: (901) 527-3427
❑   Hours: Monday-Saturday 10:00am-4:00pm (summer),
     Wednesday-Saturday 10:00am-4:00pm (winter).
❑   Admission: $6.00 adult, $4.00 student.

This former waystation on the Underground Railroad has a secret
cellar and trap doors that reveal the escape route and hiding room
of runaway slaves. Learn hidden code designs sewn into quilts. Get

to know Harriet Tubman as she encouraged slaves to follow her. Mommas had to silence their babies when hiding in the cellar. Startling (a little disturbing for young ones) displays of ads, auctions and artifacts help tell the story of slavery and the escape to freedom.

SUN STUDIO

706 Union Avenue (I-40 exit Rte. 51S, head east on US 70/79/51/64, seven blocks from the River)

Memphis 38103

❑   Phone: (901) 521-0664 or (800) 441-6249
      Web: www.sunstudio.com
❑   Hours: Daily 10:00am-6:00pm
❑   Admission: $9.50 general. FREE for children (12 & under)
❑   Tours: Tours on the 1/2 hour.
❑   Miscellaneous: With computers and CD music to back you up, you can produce your own little song ($20-$30) that says "Recorded at the Legendary Sun Studio Memphis".

This tiny studio (with added museum cafe and gift shop) is where the Rock n' Roll sound started. Elvis Presley, Carl Perkins, Johnny Cash, Jerry Lee Lewis and Roy Orbison all got their start here and stars like U2 and BB King still record here. They made a new sound in this Studio and the walls still feel like they sing and talk to you. Owner Sam Phillips would record anything, anytime, anywhere. Your tour guide showcases memorable moments, out-takes from sessions and you can even touch Elvis' first microphone and hear his first recording as a shy boy with a new sound! Kids like listening to Elvis goofing off on tape and hearing the first radio play of Elvis' "That's All Right". Also, hear the first Rock n Roll song - "Rocket 88" - recorded with a new "distorted" sound, by accident. You must visit this site as part of your exploration of Elvis and rock n roll!

CHILDREN'S MUSEUM OF MEMPHIS

2525 Central Avenue (I-240 East to Airways Exit #23 and travel North to Central Avenue, continue East on Central to Hollywood)

Memphis 38104

- ❑   Phone: (901) 320-3170. **Web: www.cmom.com**
- ❑   Hours: Tuesday-Saturday 9:00am-5:00pm, Sunday Noon-5:00pm. Closed Mondays and some major holidays.
- ❑   Admission: $7.00 adult, $6.00 senior (62+) and child (age 1-12).
- ❑   Miscellaneous: Toddlers Playscape area. Kids Coke Corner vending machines.

Hands-on fun here at a museum designed as a miniature city. Sit in a flight simulator and a real airplane cockpit, explore a Mississippi River model, climb thru the arteries of a giant heart, ride a bicycle...on Mars, create art using recycled items, hop on a real fire engine or shop for groceries. Create performances on stage using the gobs of outfits you can wear and "act" with on a real stage with changing backgrounds. The ever-popular WaterWORKS area is water play while you're learning. Let it Rain room simulates a storm and flood - how do you survive erosion? Your House, My House has endless possibilities of ways to try to build and design your own home or climb up a giant skyscraper!

LIBERTYLAND AMUSEMENT PARK

940 Early Maxwell Blvd. (off East Parkway or I-240 to Airways Blvd North), **Memphis** 38104

- ❑   Phone: (901) 274-1776 or (800) 552-Park
     Web: www.libertyland.com
- ❑   Hours: Wednesday-Sunday Noon-8:00pm. Open early at 10:00am on Saturday (mid-June to mid-August). Weekends only in April, May to early June, & late August to Labor Day.
- ❑   Admission: $8.00 general. Thrill ride wristband additional $10.00 (all rides). Under age 3 and senior (55+) are FREE.

Offers rides for adults and kids, entertainment, games and Fair food. The Double Water Slide delivers wet fun. Other rides include the Tidal Wave (flips and turns), Zippin Rippin (oldest operating wooden roller coaster), the Thriller inflatable slide, the Grand

Carousel, and the ultimate thrill ride, the Kamikaze. The Bicentennial-themed park has replicas of Independence Hall and other buildings.

MEMPHIS BROOKS MUSEUM OF ART

1934 Poplar Avenue, Overton Park (just west of East Parkway and south of North Parkway, and adjacent to the Memphis Zoo)

Memphis 38104

❑   Phone: (901) 544-6200. **Web: www.brooksmuseum.org**
❑   Hours: Tuesday-Saturday 10:00am-4:00pm, Sunday 11:30am-5:00pm.
❑   Admission: $6.00 adult, $5.00 senior, $2.00 student (6+).

The state's oldest and largest fine-arts museum, Brooks offers works dating from ancient times to the latest modern. Throughout the year, the museum hosts a series of Family Days in conjunction with special exhibitions. These fun-filled days are free for everyone and include hands-on art projects and other exciting activities such as: live music, costume contests, films, storytelling, and food. Everyday, families can enjoy self-guided discovery tours and special audio tour stops.

NATIONAL ORNAMENTAL METAL MUSEUM

374 Metal Museum Drive (I-55 exit 12C)

Memphis 38106

❑   Phone: (901) 774-6380 or (877) 881-2326
        Web: www.metalmuseum.org
❑   Hours: Tuesday-Saturday 10:00am-5:00pm, Sunday Noon-5:00pm. Closed Christmas to New Years.
❑   Admission: $4.00 adult, $3.00 senior (62+), $2.00 student.
❑   Tours: Guided tours about 40-45 minutes with minimum 10 people group and at least 2 week reservation.
❑   Miscellaneous: Riverbluff picnic pavilion w/ sculpture garden overlooking Mississippi river.

The only facility of its kind in the country, the museum not only contains a collection of American and European ironworks, metal sculpture, medieval armor and unique metal jewelry, but also presents traveling exhibits, as well. Walk around the garden with one area full of animal sculptures. Metal Art is interesting to look at, but the kids gravitate to the studio workshop where artists perform their craft. Check out the colorful "Four Tops" and "Cornstalk Fence" on your way out.

SOULSVILLE: STAX MUSEUM OF AMERICAN SOUL MUSIC

926 E. McLemore (east of downtown off Crump Blvd, south on Mississippi, east on McLemore)

Memphis 38106

- ❑ Phone: (901) 946-2535. **Web: www.soulsvilleusa.com**
- ❑ Hours: Monday-Saturday 9:00am-4:00pm, Sunday 1:00-4:00pm (March-October). Open at 10:00am, Monday-Saturday (November-February). Closed some holidays.
- ❑ Admission: $9.00 adult, $8.00 senior (62+) and military, $6.00 child (9-12). Under 8 years old FREE.

They celebrate soul music here…the Memphis music made famous by Otis Reading, Isaac Hayes, Al Green, Aretha Franklin, Earth, Wind & Fire and the like. Stax Studios is where it happened in the 1960s and 1970s and this site follows the music's development from local churches to the international stage. Interact with exhibits in the Soul music record label, STAX building. As well as being a historical music mecca, this funky little neighborhood also has some of the best soul food in the world…from the Big S Grill to Ellen's Soul Food.

CHUCALISSA MUSEUM

1987 Indian Village Drive (I-55 exit 9, at edge of Fuller State Park, off Mitchell/Winchester Road, west of Graceland)

Memphis 38109

- ❑ Phone: (901) 785-3160. **Web: www.chucalissa.org**
- ❑ Hours: Tuesday-Saturday 9:00am-4:30pm, Sunday 1:00-4:30pm (summer/spring). Shorter winter hours. Closed Sunday (winter).
- ❑ Admission: $5.00 adult, $3.00 senior and child (under 11).

❑   Miscellaneous: Guided tours, crafts, workshops and storytelling offered on a seasonal basis. Lots of activity at Pow Wows held here every few months.

Built on a Native American Temple Mound complex, this museum and outdoor exhibit features artifacts, an authentic reconstructed pre-Columbia village (w/ thatch roof huts representative of 500 years ago) and an interpretive nature trail. Meaning "abandoned house" (Choctaw), Chucalissa was inhabited by various Indian tribes, who mysteriously deserted the face of the earth in the 1500s. Begin by exploring windows of the ages (starts B.C.)...all the artifacts they found are examples of the periods of different civilizations. Outside, the dioramas inside the huts appear as if you're visiting a family or chief. Can you guess which is the chief's house? You can easily turn your child into an ancient mystery solver here.

T.O. FULLER STATE PARK

1500 Mitchell Rd. (off Hwy 61, south of Memphis)

Memphis 38109

❑   Phone: (901) 543-7581
     Web: www.state.tn.us/environment/parks/tofuller/
❑   Hours: 8:00am-sunset.
❑   Admission: $3.00 per vehicle, per day.

The park was named after Dr. Thomas O. Fuller who had spent his life empowering and educating African-Americans during the late 1800's and early 1900's. Provides: golf, swimming, camping and hiking opportunities.

LICHTERMAN NATURE CENTER

5992 Quince Road, **Memphis** 38111

❑   Phone: (901) 767-7322. **Web: www.memphismuseums.org**
❑   Hours: Monday-Thursday 9:00am-4:00pm, Friday-Saturday 9:00am-5:00pm, Sunday Noon-5:00pm.
❑   Admission: $6.00 adult, $5.50 senior (60+), $4.50 child (3-12).

Lichterman now welcomes you with a large visitors center that has an orientation room (with exhibits and closed-circuit viewing of wildlife) and nature store. On the premises are greenhouses, a backyard wildlife center (interactives, a cutaway pond and meadow habitats, and an elevated boardwalk into the forest), and 3 miles of boardwalks and trails.

MEMPHIS PINK PALACE MUSEUM

3050 Central Avenue [I-240 North to Union Ave. exit east. Go to Hollywood, turn right (south), next light (Central) turn left (east)]

Memphis 38111

❑   Phone: (901) 320-6362. **Web: www.memphismuseums.org**
❑   Hours: Monday-Thursday 9:00am-4:00pm, Friday & Saturday 9:00am-9:00pm, Sunday Noon-6:00pm. Closed on Thanksgiving Day, Christmas Eve, Christmas Day and New Year's Day. Extended summer hours.
❑   Admission: $8.00 adult, $7.50 senior, $5.50 child (3-12).
❑   Miscellaneous: IMAX Theater (901-763-IMAX) with new films every 4 months (IMAX Discovery Room, adjacent, has fun, interactive experiences related to current films). Sharpe Planetarium seasonal sky shows and special Elvis and Holiday laser shows.

The Pink Palace Mansion was Piggly Wiggly founder's dream home, though he never lived in this estate built of pink Georgia marble. The Mansion exhibits tell the historical story of Memphis with name-droppers like Mayor Boss Crump to the King, Elvis and events like the Age of Discovery or the Trail of Tears. See the role wars, women and entrepreneurs played. And then, some exhibits are just plain "to see it is to believe it" (shrunken woman's head and miniature circus). View lifelike dioramas of each time period. The exact replica of the first Piggly Wiggly grocery store is fun to play pretend in. You'll delve into natural regional history, too, as your tykes peer thru microscopes at some tiny things out of the lower Mississippi River Valley. See life-size dinosaur replicas and footprints, mastodon skeletons and teeth, tusks and a display of fossils. They also operate an 1830s historical home, MAGEVNEY HOUSE, downtown (198 Adams Avenue, 901-528-4464, FREE, closed Sundays & Mondays & Jan. & Feb) which was home to one of Memphis' first schoolteachers with original furnishings.

MEMPHIS SYMPHONY ORCHESTRA

3100 Walnut Grove Road, Ste. 501 (performances at Cannon Center)

Memphis 38111

❑   Phone: (901) 324-3627. **Web: www.memphissymphony.org**

Family Concerts and Pops Series interest children the most. Catch Grammy award singers or an evening of Elvis. Also, Memphis Youth Symphony and pre-concert activities occasionally offered.

HEARTBREAK HOTEL

3677 Elvis Presley Blvd. (across from Graceland Mansion, I-55 exit Elvis Presley Blvd.)

Memphis 38116

❑   Phone: (901) 332-1000 or (877) 777-0606
    Web: www.heartbreakhotel.net

Just the mere fact that it's across from Graceland is enough, but, this hotel has many family-friendly features. From the heart-shaped outdoor swimming pool (how fun - great photo ops), to free in-room Elvis movies (all day), to free deluxe continental breakfast to a refrigerator and microwave in every room...this is a fun, comfy place to stay. The Jungle Room Café offers sandwiches and salads...even the famous recipe Peanut Butter and Banana grilled sandwich - YUM! *(we asked for lite on the PB)*. The hotel offers the Elvis Experience that includes package rates to Graceland and Elvis Presley's Memphis restaurant for everything Elvis...at a discount. If you're really into it, rent an Elvis theme suite. After spending a night or two here, you'll be as hooked on Elvis as we were!

MEMPHIS BOTANIC GARDEN
750 Cherry Road (Interstate 240, take exit 20-B)

Memphis 38117

❑   Phone: (901) 685-1566

    Web: www.memphisbotanicgarden.com

❑   Hours: Monday-Saturday 9:00am-6:00pm, Sunday 11:00am-
    6:00pm (March-October). Only open until 4:30pm (November-
    February).

❑   Admission: $5.00 adult, $4.00 senior, $3.00 child (3-12).

As you stroll through 96 acres of gardens, in the heart of East
Memphis, you see horticulture at its best. Check out the Japanese
Garden of Tranquility, Sensory, Wildflower and many other
themed areas. At the heart of the park is the Red Drum Bridge
arching over a koi-filled lake (a kid favorite).

DAVIES MANOR PLANTATION
9336 Davies Plantation Road (I-40East exit 20 north)

Memphis 38133

❑   Phone: (901) 388-0715. **Web: www.daviesmanorplantation.org**

❑   Hours: Tuesday-Saturday Noon-4:00pm (April-early December).

❑   Admission: $5.00 adult, $3.00 student.

An Indian chief built Shelby County's oldest log house in the early
1800s. Later, the Davies moved in and turned the property into a
plantation. The plantation house is a two-story pioneer home and
your 30 minute tour shows you the entry, kitchen, bedrooms and
other parts of the house.

SHELBY FARMS
7171 Mullins Station (I-40 exit 12)

Memphis 38133

❑   Phone: (901) 382-2249

    Web: www.co.shelby.tn.us/todo/parks/index.htm

This 4,500-acre park offers a little nature and a little sporting.
From horseback riding and hiking, to canoeing and wind-surfing,
to wildlife watching or bison roaming on the animal range. The

For updates visit our website: www.kidslovepublications.com

Showplace Arena is where equestrian and other type of events are held. <u>DUCKS UNLIMITED</u> international headquarter's scenic waterfowl propagation lake is here as well as, the <u>AGRICENTER INTERNATIONAL</u> which displays advances in farming technology.

MEMPHIS GRIZZLIES

(home games played at the Pyramid)

Memphis 38173

❑   Phone: (901) 888-HOOP or (866) 479-4667

   Web: www.grizzlies.com

Catch this NBA team in action each October through April. IronKids Grizz Kids Fan Club includes stickers, posters and magazines. Learn about the legend of Grizz and Super Grizz mascots, too. Tickets range $5.00-$30.00+.

MEMPHIS QUEEN LINE

45 Riverside Drive (park at Memphis Harbor, foot of Monroe & Union Avenues at trolley stop)

Memphis 38173

❑   Phone: (901) 527-5694. **Web: www.memphisqueen.com**

❑   Admission: Sightseeing: $10.50-$14.50 (age 4+). Dinner & Music: up to $40.00 per person.

❑   Tours: Sightseeing: Daily afternoons (June-October), additional morning cruise on Friday, Saturday (summer). Other sightseeing cruises offered throughout the week (March-November). Dinner cruises depart Friday & Saturday evenings.

Two hour riverboat cruises on the Mississippi. Take a step back in time with the narrative of past and present river life. A riverboat cruise is a quiet way to learn a little about the river era of Native Americans, explorers, riverboat men like Mark Twain and Mike Fink, highlights of local Civil War river battles and the heritage of the Mississippi River bluffs and delta, plus today's commerce on the river.

WONDERS: THE MEMPHIS INTERNATIONAL CULTURAL SERIES

The Pyramid, **Memphis** 38173

❑ Phone: (901) 312-9161 or (800) 263-6744
Web: www.wonders.org
❑ Hours: Daily 9:00am-9:00pm. Last tour entry at 7:00pm.
❑ Admission: $6.00-$14.00.

This exhibit space produces cultural art and historic shows like: Catherine the Great, Titanic: the Exhibition, and Napoleon. The Imagination Station is a special activity room for children accompanied by an adult. Each visitor is provided a personal MP3 audio guide that is the latest in tour technology. Visitors are free to take the tour at their own pace and stay in the galleries as long as desired.

GRACELAND

3734 Elvis Presley Blvd. (I-55 exit 5B, Elvis Presley Blvd)

Memphis 38186

❑ Phone: (901) 332-3322 or (800) 238-2000. **Web: www.elvis.com**
❑ Hours: Monday-Saturday 9:00am-5:00pm, Sunday 10:00am-4:00pm (March-October). Daily 10:00am-4:00pm, except Tuesdays (November-February). Ticket office opens ½ hour earlier.
❑ Admission: Platinum Tour (all 4 attractions): $13.00-$27.00. Mansion Only: $18.00 adult, $16.20 senior/student, $7.00 child. Other Museums: $6.00-$8.00 adult, $5.40-$7.20 senior/student, $3.00-$4.00 child.
❑ Miscellaneous: A few cafes and grills are in the complex for casual dining. Jump aboard the Elvis Express- your FREE RIDE from Graceland and Heartbreak Hotel to Elvis Presley's Memphis downtown on Beale Street. Arrive early if you want to tour the home first. Plan a 2-4 hour visit.

Experience Elvis' home with the Mansion audio tour (featuring comments from Elvis himself and Lisa Marie) and some new artifacts, not on display until recently. The tour now includes never-before-seen items like the desk from Elvis' personal office and an extensive collection of his stage costumes. Start in the Plaza (across the street) with a **WALK A MILE IN MY SHOES**, presented at the Bijou Theater in the middle of the plaza, this 22-minute film takes guests through highlights of the exciting, fascinating career of Elvis Presley (presented on the hour and the half-hour). After the shuttle takes you over to the home, you'll be one of many to see the insides of the antebellum-style house, including the dining room where Elvis often took a late evening dinner with friends, the kitchen, the TV room and several others. His career is completely unfolded and his "relax time" revealed. You'll go from excitement in the Racquetball Room to the sad story of his last days. Then walk out to his grave before you leave. Cruise through the **ELVIS PRESLEY AUTO MUSEUM**, filled with Elvis' exclusive limited edition and rare vintage vehicles. Wild and colorful cars to look at and even all the golf carts he used to have on the property. See his custom jets...the "**LISA MARIE**" & "**HOUND DOG II**". Get a more intimate glimpse at Elvis' personal life & family in the **SINCERELY ELVIS** exhibit full of candid photos & home-movie clips. You can even touch some of his 70s sample artifacts or watch videos from his tours and see many homemade gifts sent to him. You will leave here knowing so much more about his personal life and really catch "Elvis Fever"!

MEEMAN-SHELBY STATE PARK

910 Riddick Road (13 miles north of Memphis, off US 51)

Millington 38053

❑   Phone: (901) 876-5215 or (800) 471-5293
       Web: www.state.tn.us/environment/parks/meeman/
❑   Hours: 7:00am-10:00pm
❑   Admission: $3.00 per vehicle, per day.

More commonly known as Shelby Forest, this state park sits atop the Chickasaw Bluffs. Bordering on the Mississippi River, the park consists of bottomland hardwood forests and two lakes. Besides hiking trails, camping, and an Olympic-sized swimming pool, the park offers fishing and boating on its Poplar Tree Lake. The park's Nature Center has several exhibits and offers guided tours.

TENNESSEE NATIONAL WILDLIFE REFUGE

3006 Dinkins Lane (along the TN River and Kentucky Lake)

Paris 38242

❑   Phone: (731) 642-2091. **Web: http://tennesseerefuge.fws.gov/**

The Tennessee National Wildlife Refuge combines 25,000 acres of water, 19,000 acres of woodland and 5,000 acres of farmland and pasture to offer irresistible resting and feeding opportunities for migrating waterfowl on one of the nation's major flyways. In addition to being a home to wildlife, the refuge offers many recreational opportunities such as: hunting, fishing, boating, canoeing, wildlife viewing, and photography. Public use areas are open during daylight hours, except as modified by seasonal refuge regulations.

PARKER'S CROSSROADS BATTLEFIELD

(I-40 and Hwy 22, exit 108)

Parker's Crossroads 38388

❑   Phone: (731) 968-4225. **Web: www.parkerscrossroads.com**
❑   Admission: FREE
❑   Tours: Guided tours are available for groups by appt.

This is the site of the famous December 31, 1862 battle by Confederate General Nathan Bedford Forrest. The self-guided driving tour brochure (available at Log Cabin Info Center) takes about one hour, with stops at important points of interest. Every two years (even number years), the association recreates a living history presentation of the battle.

PICKWICK LANDING STATE PARK

Park Road (I-40 to SR 22 south thru Shiloh, then SR 142 south to
SR 57 east)

Pickwick Dam 38365

❏   Phone: (731) 689-3129 or (731) 689-3135 inn

      www.state.tn.us/environment/parks/parks/PickwickLanding/

❏   Hours: Daily 8:00am-10:00pm.

Excellent fishing (the Catfish Capital of the World), a golf course,
a marina and great accommodations (lodge and cabins) are all
available at this State Park. Pickwick Landing was a riverboat stop
dating from the 1840's. In the 1930's, during the depression, the
site was chosen for one of the Tennessee Valley Authority's dams
on the Tennessee River. The new Inn & Restaurant overlook
beautiful Pickwick Lake (offering for skiing, boating, canoeing,
swimming and camping). All 119 rooms have a picturesque view
of the lake. The Inn also has a new gift shop, exercise room with
Nautilus equipment, an indoor and outdoor pool, laundry facilities
and tennis courts. Each cabin has four double beds, for a capacity
of eight people. Linens, dishes, cookware, even firewood for the
fireplace are all provided. Fishing, food and a close-up look at a
large dam and lock system.

PINSON MOUNDS STATE
ARCHAELOGICAL PARK

460 Ozier Road (Hwy. 45 S to Pinson, turn left at the park sign, SR
197 and then follow the signs)

Pinson 38366

❏   Phone: (731) 988-5614

      www.state.tn.us/environment/parks/parks/PinsonMounds/

❏   Hours: Monday - Saturday 8:00am-4:30pm, Sunday 1:00-
      5:00pm. Park trails and picnic shelter are open until dark.

❏   Admission: $3.00 per vehicle fee.

Pinson Mounds consist of at least 15 earthen mounds, a geometric
enclosure and surrounding habitation areas. It is the largest Middle
Woodland period mound complex in the Southeast and dates to

about 1-500 A.D. The Native Americans that built the mounds lived long before historically known Native American tribes, and used the site for ceremonial purposes and burials (see the many skeletons they found). As you enter the building, you walk right into a recreated mound! The museum attempts to replicate a mound with displays, videos and interpretive programs. Families like the open feeling of the grounds, picnic areas, playground, and six miles of hiking trails with a boardwalk along the Forked Deer River. Fieldwork is normally conducted in the summer, and visitors are welcome to watch the archaeologists at work. If they're not digging outside, you can learn and see how a dig is conducted by video and the excellent "Archeology in the Field" exhibit. In this diorama, you'll see a dig with each part of the process separately lit to highlight different features. Can you solve the mystery?

BIG HILL POND STATE PARK

984 John Howell Road (SR 57)

Pocahontas 38061

❑   Phone: (731) 645-7967
     Web: www.state.tn.us/environment/parks/parks/BigHillPond/
❑   Hours: 6:00am-9:00pm.
❑   Admission: $3.00 per vehicle, per day.

The park is located on the junction of the Tuscumbia and Hatchie State Scenic River. Park highlights include:

❑   THE BOARDWALK AND DISMAL SWAMP - ($8/10^{th}$) of a
     mile long, through the scenic Dismal Swamp
❑   THE OBSERVATION TOWER - 70 feet tall, this refurbished
     fire tower offers a panoramic view of Travis McNatt Lake and
     Dismal Swamp.
❑   CIVIL WAR EARTHWORKS - railroad guard post built by
     Union Soldiers.
❑   NATURE WATCHING - waterfowl, including osprey,
     migrations in spring and fall, some year round residence,
     abundant wildlife.

SALTILLO HISTORIC DISTRICT & FERRY

Main Street

Saltillo 38372

❑   Phone: (731) 925-2364 Hardin County CVB

Enjoy a ride on one of Tennessee's remaining river ferries to the charming town of Saltillo, an early river town with homes dating from the 1840s. Styles of architecture range from Greek Revival and Italianate influences to country farmhouses. Two cemeteries and a church pre-date the Civil War. The Saltillo Ferry is open Monday-Saturday 7:00am-4:00pm. Fee charged for ferry crossing. Driving tour map available from Hardin County CVB.

TENNESSEE RIVER MUSEUM

507 Main Street (US 64, downtown)

Savannah 38372

❑   Phone: (731) 925-2364 or (800) 552-3866
❑   Hours: Monday-Saturday 9:00am-5:00pm, Sunday 1:00-5:00pm
❑   Admission: $2.00 adult, Free for children.
❑   Miscellaneous: On Rte. 128S (just a mile south of Rte. 64), you
       might want to grab a bite to eat for lunch or dinner @ Darryl
       Worley's (of fame: "Have You Forgotten?") Worleybirds casual
       restaurant.

The museum has displays of paleontology, archeology, war on the river and the steamboat era. In the exhibits are items from the ironclad gunboats "Cairo" to the riverboats, to musseling (pearl buttons came from mussels, long ago) plus other items concerning the river and its influence on the heritage of the Tennessee Valley. The world famous "Shiloh Effigy Pipe" of a man kneeling is the central archeological item. Be sure to ask for the scavenger hunt sheet - it makes the museum more interesting to follow clues. Hands-on areas include the walk-thru battleship and trying to lift a 6 lb. Cannonball. The collection of fossils is wonderful…many you can touch.

SHILOH NATIONAL MILITARY PARK

1055 Pittsburg Landing Road (Hwy 22 between SR 57 & US 64, on the west bank of the TN River)

Shiloh 38376

- ☐   Phone: (731) 689-5696. **Web: www.nps.gov/shil/**
- ☐   Hours: Daily 8:00am-5:00pm. Closed Christmas.
- ☐   Admission: $5.00 per vehicle per week.
- ☐   Miscellaneous: During fall and spring, ranger-led programs are available on week-ends. Right across from the Military park is Shiloh's Civil War Relics. Browse through the displays and hear some stories, then purchase a relic - some are just $1.00 dug from nearby Civil War campsites (daily, except Tuesday, until 5:00pm, **www.shilohrelics.com** or 731-689-4114).

After bloody Shiloh, fought here in April, 1862, "The South never smiled again". Tours begin with an orientation movie at the visitor center. Now, let the kids touch and try on soldier uniforms (great photo ops). After looking over the museum exhibits, walk outside through the National Cemetery and to Pittsburg Landing on the Tennessee River. Understand and learn about the Hornets nest and temporary hospitals. Along the ten-mile, self-guided auto-tour, stop at each of the fourteen wayside exhibits (audio tour tapes available at the museum). Summertime: Daily rifle firing demos or ranger lead talks meeting at different tour stops. There are also hiking and biking trails in the 4000 acres and SHILOH INDIAN MOUNDS on the bluff overlooking the river. The mounds of Woodland/Mississippian culture prehistoric Indians is one of the best preserved in the Tennessee River valley.

REELFOOT LAKE STATE PARK

Rte. 1 (SR 22 & 78)

Tiptonville 38079

- ☐   Phone: (731) 253-7756

   www.state.tn.us/environment/parks/parks/ReelfootLake/

Created by a series of earthquakes in 1811, this 13,000 acre lake offers great fishing and waterfowl viewing (plus American bald eagles) in the winter. <u>BALD EAGLE TOURS</u> - Eagles can be seen perching, flying/soaring and often snatching fish from the lake. Nearby is the <u>REELFOOT NATIONAL WILDLIFE REFUGE</u> & the <u>REELFOOT LAKE WATERFOWL FESTIVAL DUCK & GOOSE CALLING CONTEST</u>. Naturalists offer <u>PONTOON BOAT CRUISES</u> (May through September, Fees required)- these trips allow visitors to experience the beauty of Reelfoot Lake and learn about this unique area. Three-hour cruises depart daily at 9:00 a.m. and short cruises are offered on weekends and holiday afternoons. Sunset cruises are offered several times per month and moonlight cruises are offered during the full moon (full moon rising through Cypress Trees is an awesome sight). <u>MUSEUM</u> (731-253-9652, 8:00am-4:30pm daily) - exhibits include large aquariums with native fish and a discovery room with a variety of reptiles and amphibians. The boardwalk is especially popular with bird watchers, photographers, and fishermen. <u>DAVY CROCKETT CABIN</u> - (901-665-6195, 219 N Trenton Street, Hwy 45W) Davy Crockett came to Gibson County in the fall of 1822, where he farmed and reportedly killed 105 bears in one winter! The cabin has logs from the original structure plus pieces of furniture from the Crockett Family.

NATCHEZ TRACE RESORT STATE PARK

24845 Natchez Trace Road (I-40, exit 116)

Wildersville 38388

❑   Phone: (731) 968-8176
       www.state.tn.us/environment/parks/parks/NatchezTrace/
❑   Miscellaneous: In nearby Lexington, explore many other lakes
       (Beech, Pine, Sycamore, Dogwood & Redbud) for outdoor
       recreation (731-968-6191). The Beech River Cultural Center &
       Museum houses local geology, settler lifestyle and war history
       (731-967-0306).

Named for the western alternative route of the famous Nashville to Natchez, Miss. Trail of the 18th and 19th centuries. The park includes Pin Oak and Cub Lake and part of the Natchez Trace State Forest. Along with scenic woodlands, the park offers four lakes, miles of hiking trails, a wrangler camp inn, boating, resort lodge, restaurant, playgrounds, a ballfield, 250 miles of horse riding trails, a park store, archery range, and cabins. Picturesque Pin Oak Lodge is situated on the wooded shores of Pin Oak Lake. Support facilities include an exercise room, playground, tennis courts, and adult and kiddie swimming pools. The restaurant at Natchez Trace park over looks the pool and beautiful Pin Oak Lake.

185

Chapter 7

Seasonal &
Special Events

JANUARY

COUNTRY DANCE WORLD CHAMPIONSHIPS

M – Nashville. Gaylord Opryland Resort & Convention Center. (401) 624-7800. Public is invited to the vendor area and free live music stage. Passes are available to purchase for the competition and Learn to Dance workshops. (First week of January)

WILDERNESS WILDLIFE WEEK

ME – Pigeon Forge. www.mypigeonforge.com or (865) 429-7350. Outdoor lovers' activities including guided tours and workshops about the Smoky Mountains and its history. Casual tours or more strenuous hikes. Admission for guided tours. (9 days beginning week after New Years in January)

ELVIS PRESLEY BIRTHDAY CELEBRATION

W – Memphis. Elvis Presley's Graceland. (901) 332-3322 or (800) 238-2000 or **www.elvis.com.** Fun-filled days and nights feature events in celebration of Elvis' birthday. Birthday cake to all Graceland visitors on January 8th. Admission. (5 days leading up to January 8th)

FEBRUARY

SADDLE UP!

ME – Pigeon Forge. Music Road Hotel and various theatres. (865) 429-7350 or **www.mypigeonforge.com**. Features cowboy poetry, Western music and dancing, songwriting workshops and chuckwagon dinners. (Second long weekend in February)

SMOKY MOUNTAINS STORYTELLING FESTIVAL

ME – Pigeon Forge, Country Tonite Theatre & Grand Resort Hotel. (865) 429-7350 or **www.mypigeonforge.com**. Master storytellers carry on the Appalachian tradition of spinning tales indoors, theater-style, or outdoors alongside a blazing bonfire. Evening trolley rides. Admission. (mid-February long weekend)

MARCH

OLD-TIME FIDDLER'S CHAMPIONSHIP

M – **Clarksville.** (931) 648-0761 or **www.tnfiddlers.com**.
Admission (12+). Annual state championship that features
authentic old-time music. (Last Friday & Saturday in March)

IRISH CELEBRATION "WEARING OF THE GREEN"

M – **Erin**, downtown. (931) 289-5100. For over 40 years this town
has had the traditional "Wearing of the green" and proclaimed Irish
heritage with a grand parade, carnival, crafts, music, and a fish fry.
(March 17th, St. Patrick's Day)

A VICTORIAN EASTER

M – **Nashville.** Belle Meade Plantation. (800) 270-3991, (615)
356-0501 or **www.bellemeadeplantation.com**. See this elegant
Southern mansion decorated for the season in the full spirit of the
19th Century. Special Easter brunch served in the restaurant. (mid-
March – mid-April).

APRIL

EASTER EVENTS

EASTER EGG HUNTS

ALL AREAS – Tennessee State Parks (most all).
www.state.tn.us/environment/parks. Three age divisions for
children ages Toddler thru 10 years old. Grand prize (savings
bond) and little treats can be found. (Easter Saturday)

EASTER BUNNY TRIP

M – **Nashville**. Tennessee Central Railway. (615) 244-9001 or
www.tcry.org. Departs at 9:00am to Watertown, 90 mile trip. Ride
along with the Easter Bunny and join the egg hunt during the
layover in Watertown. Admission. (Two Saturdays before Easter
Sunday)

Easter Events *(cont.)*

EGGSTRAVAGANZOO

M – Nashville. Nashville Zoo at Grassmere. (615) 833-1534 ext. 39 or **www.nashvillezoo.org**. Games, egg hunts, and children's activities. Bunny Breakfast by reservation only. (Easter Saturday)

EASTER SUNRISE SERVICE

ME – Gatlinburg. Ober Gatlinburg. (865) 436-5423. Free tram rides, a breakfast buffet offered, Easter egg hunt for children 2-10, and a special sunrise worship service. FREE. (Easter morning beginning at 6:30am)

SPRING COLORS / EASTER TRAINS

ME – Oak Ridge. Secret City Scenic Excursion Train. (865) 241-2140. Admission. (Easter Saturday, 1:00 & 3:00pm)

EASTER BOAT CRUISES

SE – Chattanooga. Southern Belle Riverboat. (423) 266-4488 or **www.chattanoogariverboat.com**. Easter cruises with families are available on Easter weekend. Kids love their breakfast cruise, which includes a visit from the Easter Bunny. Admission. (Easter weekend in April)

GREAT EGG CAPER

SE – Chattanooga. Audubon Acres. (423) 892-1499. Kids dye eggs with natural dyes made from nuts, greens, and berries. Egg hunt on the trails followed by a picnic. Small admission. (Saturday before Easter)

APRIL - GENERAL EVENTS

NATIONAL CORNBREAD FESTIVAL

EM – South Pittsburg. Downtown Historic district. (423) 837-0022 or **www.nationalcornbread.com**. Celebrate cornbread and small town hospitality at this event that includes a Championship cookoff, carnival, puppet shows, magicians, cloggers, storytellers, entertainment and trolley rides. (Last weekend in April)

For updates visit our website: www.kidslovepublications.com

DOVE AWARDS

M – Nashville. Grand Ole Opry House. (615) 242-0303 or **www.doveawards.com**. Personally experience the nationally televised award show that recognizes excellence and achievement in gospel music. Admission varies. Tickets go on sale in January – call for details. (mid-April)

DOLLY SPRING PARADE

ME – Pigeon Forge Parkway. (865) 429-7350 or **www.mypigeonforge.com**. Join Grand Marshal Dolly Parton as she leads the city's annual spring kick-off parade. FREE (First Weekend in April)

WORLD'S BIGGEST FISH FRY

W – Paris. (800) 345-1103 or **www.paris.tn.org**. More than 10,000 pounds of catfish will be served along with large parades, auto shows, a rodeo, all-you-can-eat dinners and catfish races. Admission. (Last full week of April)

MAY

GOSPEL MUSIC JUBILEE

M – Clarksville. (931) 648-0001. Celebration that features musical entertainment from world-renowned gospel musical groups. You'll also see pioneer activities, appearances by local music groups, and historic home tours. Weekend passes and day rates available. (Third weekend in May)

COLONIAL FAIR

M – Goodlettsville. Mansker's Fort. (615) 859-7979. Travel back in time to 18th century times complete with music, food, crafts and games. Every artist and merchant must adhere to 1750-1790 attire. Watch artisans demonstrate their craft. Purchase colonial foods such as pork chops w/ sizzle sauce, bratwurst, roast corn, beans, or fried pies cooked over a fire. Also, Scottish dancing, live music, puppets, beggars, preachers and Indians. Admission. (First weekend in May)

May *(cont.)*

TENNESSEE RENAISSANCE FESTIVAL

M – Nashville (Triune). Castle Gwynn, a full size replica of a 12th century castle. (615) 395-9950 or **www.tnrenfest.com**. Step back in time to 16th Century England and enjoy the colorful pageantry of costumed villagers, musicians, and artisans. Games of human skill, full armored joust and man-powered rides. Admission varies. (Every weekend in May)

STRAWBERRY FESTIVAL

M – Portland. Downtown. **www.portlandtn.com** or (615) 325-9032. Parade, storytelling, bluegrass music, games and the Middle TN Strawberry Parade. At the peak of the strawberry business, this small town was shipping out 30 railroad carloads a day. You can still visit local strawberry patches. (Mid-May for five days)

SCOTTISH FESTIVAL & HIGHLAND GAMES

ME – Gatlinburg. Mills Park. (865) 436-5346 or **www.gatlinburg.com**. More than 60 clans gather with activities including pipe & drum bands, pro and amateur Highland athletics, Highland dancing, border collie demos, entertainers and food. Admission. (Third long weekend in May)

DAY OUT WITH THOMAS

SE – Chattanooga. Tennessee Valley Railroad. (866) 468-7630 or **www.tvrail.com**. Welcome Thomas the Tank Engine – ride on a vintage, full-size train led by Thomas himself, meet with Sir Topham Hatt, watch Thomas & Friends videos, coloring books, funny clowns and lots of extra food and entertainment. Admission (age 1+). (First and second long weekends in May)

STRAWBERRY FESTIVAL

SE – Dayton. Main Street. **www.tnstrawberryfestival.com** or (423) 775-0361. Pie and cake baking contests, carnival, parade, block party, children's area, entertainment, local entertainers, the Strawberry Crunch Demo Derby (rodeo grounds in Evensville), and Strawberry Shortcake at the Courthouse. (Mid-May for nine days)

STRAWBERRY FESTIVAL

W – Humboldt. 1200 Main Street. (731) 784-1842 or **www.humboldtchamber.tn.org.** Includes parades, walking horse show, car show, carnival, gospel singing, country western dancing, checker's tournament, and the Strawberry Recipe Contest. The Festival Museum includes memorabilia of past festivals dating back to 1934 and displays of local culture (authentic strawberry packing shed, early telephone switchboard). FREE. (Mid-May for eight days)

FORKED DEER RIVER FESTIVAL

W – Jackson. Fairgrounds Park. (901) 427-1565 or **www.forkeddeerfestival.com.** A fun family event that showcases the arts in TN. Visit artists or join a class, enjoy live entertainment or visit the Animal kingdom. KidzFest is an interactive creative station with a carnival and midway. Admission. (Mid-May long weekend)

ITALIAN FESTIVAL

W – Memphis. Marquette Park. (901) 685-1378 or **www.memphisitalianfestival.com.** Authentic Italian cuisine, arts, crafts, games and music. Includes a spaghetti gravy contest. (Memorial Day weekend)

MEMPHIS IN MAY

W – Memphis. Tom Lee Park & various locations. (901) 543-5303 or **www.memphisinmay.org.** This is a celebration of business and fun with events including the Beale Street Music Festival, International Week, and World Championship Barbeque Cooking Contest (all shapes and sizes of cookers made to resemble everything from fire trucks to piggy banks – 90,000 pork lovers sample and view demos of BBQ). Check schedule. (Entire month of May)

JUNE

RC & MOON PIE FESTIVAL

M – Bell Buckle. Town Square. (901) 389-6547. A day of crafts, carnival, live music, games, the world's largest Moon Pie, Moon Pie toss, synchronized wading, Superman and Wonder Woman of Bell Buckle contest. (Third Saturday in June)

CELTIC MUSIC FESTIVAL

M – Nashville. Travellers Rest Plantation and Museum. (615) 832-8197 or **www.travellersrestplantation.org**. A celebration dedicated to exploring the musical heritage of the Scots-Irish with bagpipes, step-dancers, highland dancers, and Celtic music. Complimentary tours available. (Second Sunday in June)

FAN FAIR, THE WORLD'S BIGGEST COUNTRY MUSIC FESTIVAL

M – Nashville. The Coliseum, Nashville Convention Center and Riverfront Park. (866) FAN-FAIR or **www.fanfair.com**. Over 40 hours of live entertainment but the real fun is the picture and autograph sessions with the stars. Admission varies – call or visit website for details. (First long weekend in June)

NATIVE AMERICAN DANCE THEATRE

M – Nashville. Ryman Auditorium. (615) 889-9636 or **www.NativeAmericanDance.net**. Authentic Native American drum and dance. Traditional music. Performances by CMA recording artists. (Second Sunday in June)

NATIVE AMERICAN FESTIVAL & MUSTER

NE – Elizabethton. Sycamore Shoals State Historic Area. (423) 543-5808. An emphasis on Cherokee culture includes native music, dance, encampments, musket drills, tomahawk throwing, flint-napping and campfire cooking. (Third weekend in June)

RIVERBEND FESTIVAL

SE – Chattanooga. Ross Landing & Downtown. (423) 756-2242 or **www.friendsofthefestival.com**. This nine-day festival draws hundreds of thousands of spectators each year. It features country, blues and rock musical performances, sporting events, family activities, food and a spectacular fireworks display. Admission. (Second week of June)

FRONTIER DAYS

W – Henderson. Chickasaw State Park. (731) 989-5141 or **www.state.tn.us/environment/parks/chicksaw**. This event honors the frontier spirit of the early settlers of West Tennessee. Live band, street dance, old time games, and parade. (second weekend in June)

JULY

JULY 4TH CELEBRATIONS

Our Nation's Birthday Party featuring live music, exhibits, concessions and fireworks show.

- ❑   **M – Franklin**. Downtown. **www.williamscvb.org**
- ❑   **M – Goodlettsville**. Mansker's Station. (615) 859-3678.
- ❑   **M – Nashville**. Riverfront Park. (615) 862-8400. Nashville's largest one-day event. Science of fireworks and chemical reactions at Adventure Science Center.
- ❑   **ME – Gatlinburg**. Strike of Midnight Parade. The first Independence Day parade in the nation each year.
- ❑   **ME – Kingston**. Fort Southwest Point & Walt's Bar. Lakefront. **www.southwestpoint.com**. Living history, boat races.
- ❑   **ME – Knoxville**. Volunteer Landing. (865) 215-4248.
- ❑   **ME – Norris**. Museum of Appalachia. (865) 494-0514. Anvil shoot. "Fireworks" with black powder.
- ❑   **ME – Pigeon Forge**. Patriot Festival. (800) 251-9100.
- ❑   **NE – Elizabethton**. Roan Mountain State Park. (423) 772-0190.
- ❑   **NE – Jonesborough**. Downtown. (423) 753-5281 or (423) 753-9580.

July 4th Celebrations *(cont.)*

- ❑ **SE – Chattanooga**. Coolidge Park. Creative Discovery Museum & Winnepesaukah Amusement Park. (423) 424-4430 or **www.chattanoogacvb.com**. Fireworks downtown and at Winnepesaukah. Red, White, & Blue Day, scavenger hunt, crafts, ice cream.
- ❑ **SE – Spring City**. Veteran's Park. (423) 365-6441.
- ❑ **W – Jackson**. Fairgrounds Park. (731) 425-8640.
- ❑ **W – Memphis**. Beal Street & Tomlee Park. (901) 529-0999. Fireworks on the Mississippi River.
- ❑ **W – Pickwick Dam**. Pickwick Landing State Park. (800) 552-3866 or (731) 925-8181.

OFFICIAL STATE & NATIONAL CHAMPIONSHIP SMITHVILLE FIDDLERS' JAMBOREE

EM – Smithville. Town Square. (615) 597-8500 or **www.dekalbtn.com**. State and National championship in 24 categories plus seven categories for beginners. Continuous jam sessions and crafts. (First weekend in July)

NORTH TENNESSEE STATE FAIR

M – Clarksville. Clarksville Fairgrounds Park. (931) 920-5568. Agricultural & livestock exhibits, tractor & truck pulls, carnival rides, demolition derby, beauty pageant. Admission. (mid July)

CEDARFEST

M – Lebanon. James E. Ward Agricultural Center. (800) 789-1327 or **www.cedarfest.com**. The "Appalachian Square Dance Capital of the World" hosts this celebration of music and dance in bluegrass, square dance, round dance, buck dance and clogging. (Second weekend in July)

UNCLE DAVE MACON DAYS FESTIVAL

M – Murfreesboro. Cannonsburgh Village. (615) 893-2361. Visit the free village with buildings open to view/discuss with period-costumed docents. Take your picture by the World's Largest Cedar bucket, then listen in on the Championship old-time banjo, clogging and buckdancing performances. This festival is broadcast on the original Opry radio station, WSM, where Uncle Dave developed his roots in music. FREE. (Second weekend in July)

WATAUGANS OUTDOOR DRAMA

NE – Elizabethton. Sycamore Shoals Historic Area. (423) 543-5508. 18th Century settlement comes to life thru local outdoor drama. Watch them form the Watauga Association, the Transylvania Purchase, the siege of Fort Watauga, and the Muster of the Overmountain Men before the Battle of Kings Mountain. You might learn some 18th century lingo or get to know interesting regional characters. Admission ($5.00-$8.00). (Last three weekends, Thursday-Saturday, in July. Performances begin at 7:30pm)

FUNFEST

NE – Kingsport. Fort Henry Drive/Memorial Drive. (423) 392-9600 or **www.funfest.net**. Begin with Farm Fest @ Exchange Place. Now, check out the top-name contemporary concerts or Kids Central at the elementary school. Strolling magic shows, balloon animals, obstacle course, splash dance, petting zoo, moonwalk, gymnastics demos, and a fishing derby. FREE admission. Some activities require a fee. (Third week of July)

SCOPES TRIAL PLAY & FESTIVAL

SE – Dayton. Rhea County Courthouse, downtown Hwy 27. (423) 775-7801 or **www.rheacounty.com/scopes.html**. This restored courthouse was the scene of the Scopes Monkey Trial. The Scopes Evolution Trial started after the passing of a statute by the Tennessee legislature which made it unlawful for any teacher in any public school "to teach any theory that denies the story of the divine creation of man as taught in the Bible, and to teach instead, evolution". Local businessmen and one teacher conspired a publicity stunt. Up to 10,000 reporters and onlookers came to this small town to observe the most famous lawyers and orators of the time debate the case against the alleged teacher's violation. How does it end? Watch the play and visit the historic sites to put it all together. Admission for play, FREE for festival. (July)

July *(cont.)*

NO TILL FIELD DAY

W – Milan. West TN Agricultural Museum, US 45E/70 & 79. (901) 686-8067. The nation's largest such event, this is a good opportunity to visit the Ag Museum and the extensive collection of farming tools spanning two centuries of farming development. FREE. (July)

NATIONAL CATFISH DERBY KIDS FISHING RODEO

W – Pickwick Dam. Pickwick Landing State Park. (800) 552-3866 or (731) 925-8094. Join other anglers (age 4-16) at the "Catfish Capitol of the World." and fish for prizes for the biggest catfish. Record fish from these waters have exceeded 100 lbs! (Third Saturday in July)

TOMATO FESTIVAL

W – Ripley. Ripley Park, Lauderdale County. (901) 635-9541 or **www.lctn.com**. Tomato tastings from famous Ripley tomato growers. Live entertainment, carnival, food, barbecue cookoff and pet show, too. Admission. (First weekend in July)

AUGUST

TENNESSEE WALKING HORSE NATIONAL CELEBRATION

M – Shelbyville. Calsonic Arena. (931) 684-5915 or **www.twhnc.com**. The premier showcase for the Tennessee Walking Horse breed. The champion is crowned plus hosting of horse shows, rodeos and concerts. The history of the breed and horse industry is featured in exhibits and videos at the Tennessee Walking Horse Museum. Admission. (Ten days in August)

OAK RIDGE RENAISSANCE FAIRE

ME – Oak Ridge, Bissell Park. (865) 425-0717 or **www.oakridgevisitor.com**. Enjoy fun and merriment with minstrels, live chess matches (where onlookers are invited to be chess pieces), a theatrical troupe with elaborate costumes,

Renaissance era food vendors, craftsmen, and puppetry. FREE, donations accepted. (Last three weekends in August)

CELEBRATE FREEDOM! – PIGEON FORGE SALUTES AMERICA'S VETERANS

ME – Pigeon Forge. (865) 429-7350. This award winning festival is a tribute to all Americans that have served in the armed forces. Historical exhibits, military book fair, special guest speakers, and star entertainment. (Previous performers have been Lee Greenwood, Aaron Tippin) (Second Saturday in August)

CHEROKEE DAYS OF RECOGNITION

SE – Chattanooga. Red Clay State Historic Area. (423) 478-0339. Authentic Cherokee food, crafts, dance, and music. FREE admission. (First weekend in August)

INTERNATIONAL ROCKABILLY REUNION

W – Jackson. 531 Riverside Dr. (731) 423-5440 or **www.rockabillyhall.org.** Celebrate the heritage and continued interest in rockabilly music throughout the world. Features national and international stars from current years and the past. (Second weekend in August)

CHOCTAW HERITAGE FESTIVAL

W – Memphis. Chucalissa Village. (901) 785-3160 or **www.chucalissa.org.** Bring the family and come watch a pot being made, or point being flint-knapped, throw a spear with an atlatl or shoot a blowgun. Listen to a storyteller or watch a traditional dance. Admission. (First weekend in August)

ELVIS WEEK

W – Memphis. Graceland. (800) 238-2000 or **www.elvis.com.** Elvis fans from around the WORLD gather to remember the music, the magic and the memories associated with the legacy of Elvis Presley. A full week of music, dance, sports and charitable events. Candlelight vigil on August 15. Admission. (Week of Elvis' death in mid-August)

August *(cont.)*

MUSIC & HERITAGE FESTIVAL

W – Memphis. Center for Southern Folklore. (901) 525-3655 or **www.southernfolklore.com**. Celebrating the arts, music and food of the region. (Labor Day weekend)

SEPTEMBER

SOUTHERN HERITAGE DAY

M – Burns. Old Spencer Mill (30miles west off I-40 exit 182). (615) 412-5169 or **www.oldspencermill.com**. Civil War demos with period food and music. Tours of grist mill, living history demos (broommaking, basketweaving, weaving, spinning), farm animals. (Saturday after Labor Day in September)

RIVERFEST

M – Clarksville. McGregor Park, Cumberland River Walk. (931) 648-6124 or **www.clarksvilleriverfest.com**. Celebrate Clarksville's river heritage. Children's activities, arts and crafts, entertainment, boat races. Admission. (First Friday & Saturday in September)

AFRICAN & CARIBBEAN STREET FESTIVAL

M – Nashville. TSU Main Campus. (615) 299-0412. Exotic food concessions. Stage show featuring gospel, reggae, rap, blues, jazz, R&B and drama. Children's storytelling. Free admission. (Third long weekend in September)

APPLE FESTIVAL

M – Nashville. Nashville Farmer's Market. (615) 880-2001. Apple samples, square dancing, and country music singing contest. Kids will also enjoy a farm animal petting zoo, craft projects, and games. Free admission. (Second Saturday in September)

DAY OUT WITH THOMAS

M – Nashville. Tennessee Central Railway. (615) 244-9001 or **www.tcry.org**. Welcome Thomas the Tank Engine – ride on a vintage, full-size train led by Thomas himself, meet with Sir Topham Hatt, watch Thomas & Friends videos, coloring books, funny clowns and lots of extra food and entertainment. Admission (age 1+). (Labor Day weekend and possibly the next weekend)

FALL FEST

M – Nashville. Belle Meade Plantation. (800) 270-3991, (615) 356-0501 or **www.bellemeadeplantation.com**. Mansion tours, arts and crafts, music, children's activities. Harvest baked goods and pumpkins. (Third weekend in September)

GREEK FESTIVAL

M – Nashville. Holy Trinity Greek Orthodox Church. (615) 333-1047. Enjoy music and dancing, exhibits, shopping, and the fabulous Greek food and drink. Admission. (First long weekend in September)

TENNESSEE STATE FAIR

M – Nashville. Tennessee State Fairgrounds. (615) 862-8980. See over 10,000 livestock, agricultural and creative arts exhibits, free concerts from stars, Midway KidsTown free children's area (age 12 and under). Admission. (9 days – begins weekend after Labor Day).

FALL FESTIVAL

ME – Townsend. Smoky Mountain Convention and Visitors Bureau. (800) 525-6834 or **www.smokymountains.org**. The festival is a family-oriented event that includes a variety of events that celebrate Appalachian heritage and culture, including bluegrass music, arts and crafts, storytelling ("old cornstalk, hillbilly stories") and historic re-enactments. FREE. (Last weekend in September)

September *(cont.)*

OVERMOUNTAIN VICTORY TRAIL CELEBRATION

NE – Elizabethton. Sycamore Shoals State Historic Area. (423) 543-5808. Annual encampment by the Company of Overmountain Men celebrating and re-creating the muster of the Overmountain Men before the battle of King's Mountain in 1780. Witness the historic march crossing the river. (Third weekend in September)

CULTUREFEST

SE – Chattanooga. (423) 267-1218. Held at Coolidge Park, this event celebrates cultural, ethnic and national diversity in the city and the arts. Enjoy and engage in performances, food and art indigenous to various cultures within the community. (September weekend)

WAR BETWEEN THE STATES SPECIAL TRAIN

SE – Chattanooga. Tennessee Valley Railroad. **www.tvrail.com**. Steam power ride to Chickamauga for an extended layover during the annual Civil War Days activities including reenactments, artillery demos and entertainment. All Day. Admission. (Third Saturday in September)

OCOEE RIVER DAYS FESTIVAL

SE – Ocoee. Whitewater Center. (423) 496-5197 or **www.southernregion.fs.fed.us/ocoee**. Celebrate the anniversary of the opening of the Center with big name entertainment, food, fun, exhibits, games and activities. Admission. (Water Release Saturdays in September)

SEQUOYAH FESTIVAL

SE – Vonore. Sequoyah Birthplace Museum. (423) 884-6246 or **www.sequoyahmuseum.org**. Native American festival interpreting history, crafts, food, dance, painting and clothing. Cherokee Artist demos. Admission. (First weekend in September)

18TH CENTURY TRADE FAIRE

SE – Vonore, Fort Loudoun Historic Park. (423)-884-6217 or **www.state.tn.us/environment/parks/loudoun/events.htm** The park's largest event hosts about 200 re-enactors and 5000 visitors at the recreation of the Trade faires of old. Visitors walk the streets of the faire and shop for period wares, sample food and enjoy entertainment of the times. Indian Camp. Admission. (Weekend after Labor Day)

TENNESSEE RIVER FOLKLIFE AND MUSIC FESTIVAL

W – Eva. Nathan Bedford Forrest State Park. (731) 584-6356. Includes crafts, food, live music, folk heritage demos, children's games and the annual Patsy Cline sing-a-like contest. (Third Saturday in September)

ARCHEOFEST

W – Jackson. Pinson Mounds State Park. (731) 988-5614 or **www.state.tn.us/environment/parks/pinson/archfest.htm.** A celebration of Native American culture and archeology. Traditional Native American storytellers, music, dancers, and artisans. Hay wagon tours, demonstrations, and films are available. (Third weekend in September)

MID-SOUTH FAIR

W – Memphis Fairgrounds. **www.midsouthfair.com** or (901) 274-8800. Regional state fair with over 60 rides, over 150 food vendors, 200 exhibitors, free mainstage concerts, rodeo, livestock shows, creative arts and student competitions. Admission. (Last ten days of September)

INTERNATIONAL GOAT DAYS

W – Millington. USA Stadium and Arena. (901) 872-4559 or **www.internationalgoatdays.com.** Rustic fun featuring goat shows, contests, & games. Rural craft demos reflect gentler times of the past. (First full weekend in September)

SEPTEMBER / OCTOBER

SANGO MILLS FARM

M – Clarksville. 154 Towes Lane, Madison St. Extension. (931) 358-2637. Apples and sorghum on a working farm. Watch the sorghum cooking process or view fresh cornmeal being ground. FREE. (September-October, Tuesday-Saturday, daytime)

COMER'S FARM

M – Lebanon. 692 Walnut Grove Road. (I-40 to Rte 231S) (615) 453-2023. Farm animals, honey pot educational exhibit, pumpkin patch and an 8-acre corn maze. Admission. (September-October)

AMAZING MULE MAZE

M – Spring Hill. Rippavilla Plantation, 5700 Main Street (Hwy 31 south). (931) 486-9037 or **www.rippavilla.org**. 2.5 miles of twisting, turning fun as visitors match wits with two of the most cantankerous mules to come out of Middle Tennessee. It's challenging in the daylight ..... but we dare you to try it after nightfall, in the shadows of the tall corn and faint light of a flashlight or glow stick. Admission. (Thursday thru Sunday, September-October)

SMOKY MOUNTAIN HARVEST FESTIVAL

ME – Gatlinburg, Pigeon Forge, Sevierville. (800) 251-9100 or **www.mypigeonforge.com**. City and businesses decorate in autumn themes with a decorating contest, craft shows, pumpkins, fall flowers, cornstalks, scarecrows and a gospel jubilee. (Mid-September thru October)

AMAZING CORN MAZE

ME – Greenback. Maple Lane Farms. (865) 856-3511 or **www.maplelanefarms.com**. The 8 acres of fully grown corn is a labyrinth of pathways you walk thru past twists and turns and 85 decision points (takes at least one hour). Also food, hayrides, entertainment, and a pumpkin patch. Admission. (September-October)

MYERS PUMPKIN PATCH & CORNFIELD MAZE

NE – Bulls Gap. 3415 Gap Creek Road (I-81 exit 23 towards Greeneville). (423) 235-4796. Kids' games and crafts, hay rides, and a 24-acre corn maze. (Daily, September-October)

BLACKBURN FARM & OLD MILL PUMPKIN PATCH

NE – Jefferson City. 443 E. Dumplin Valley Road. (865) 397-9841. Old-fashioned working dairy farm with pick-your-own pumpkin and gourd patches, hayrides, hay play area and a corn maze. Admission. (September-October)

SHULTZ FARM FOODS

SE – Athens. 245 County Road 603, Hwy 30 to CR 750, left on CR 603. (423) 745-4723. Educational farm tour, sample products sold offering everything from assorted veggies to pumpkins and apples. (Daily, September-October)

ROCK CITY'S ENCHANTED MAIZE MAZE

SE – Chattanooga. Lookout Mountain. (706) 820-2431 www.enchantedmaze.com Cornfield maze, hay rides, kiddie hay maze, hay pyramid, pumpkin patch, fun barn, food. Checkpoints along the trail post questions that *(if answered correctly)* will steer you in the right direction to find the way through the maze. Admission. (September-October)

MASON'S CORN MAZE

SE – Niota. CR 361. (423) 568-2498 or www.mayfielddairy.com. Sponsored by Mayfield Dairy, the maze is full of turns, dead ends and choices along the way. Answer dairy questions correctly at the checkpoints and you'll complete the maze the fastest. Admission. (September-October)

MAIZE QUEST CHEROKEE INDIAN ADVENTURE

SE – Riceville. 522 CR 67. www.cornmaze.com or (423) 336-9896. Follow the pathways of the 8-acre corn maze to complete puzzles and games related to the Cherokee culture. Flashlight nights, giant straw bale maze for young ones, petting barn, country store and wagon rides out to pumpkin patch. Admission. (September-October)

OCTOBER

OLD SPENCER MILL DAYS

M – Burns. Old Spencer Mill (30 miles west off I-40 exit 182). (615) 412-5169 or **www.oldspencermill.com**. Tours of the grist mill plus living history demos of crafts such as basket weaving, using farm tools, tending to farm animals, children interpreters, horse and wagon rides and lots of ground meal foods and dulcimer music. (Last weekend in October)

FALL PILGRIMAGE & OKTOBERFEST

M – Clarksville. Historic Collinsville and downtown. (931) 647-0243 or (931) 648-9141 or **www.historiccollinsville.com**. Battle of Riggins Hill re-enactments, Pioneer Activities: weaving, candlemaking, blacksmithing, spinning, soapmaking, ropemaking, broommaking, woodcarving, rughooking and singing. Open house in historic homes with costumed tour guides and concessions. Special Children's Day, hayrides, face painting and games. Look for the Chicken Dance and polka music and food at the Oktoberfest activity sites. Admission. (First weekend in October)

PUMPKINFEST

M – Franklin. (615) 595-1239. Children's carnival area, craft vendors, entertainment, costume contest, hay rides, games, music, food, and pumpkin painting. Admission. (Fourth Saturday in October)

PUMPKIN FESTIVAL

M – Lewisburg. Fox Cave Park. (931) 359-5520. Pumpkin patch, hayrides, exotic animals, picnic & playground area, trails. Admission. (Every weekend in October)

FALL FEST

M – Nashville. Nashville Farmer's Market. (615) 880-2001. Hear bluegrass music as the kids have fun with carnival games, seasonal craft projects, and decorate their own pumpkin for a competition. Free admission. (Second Saturday in October)

MUSIC & MOLASSES FESTIVAL

M – Nashville. Ellington Agricultural Center. (615) 837-5197 or **www.picktnproducts.org/agmuseum**. See molasses making done the old-fashioned way. Cooking and tasting at the sorghum mill. Children's activities, crafts, carriage rides, outdoor kettle cooking, grist mill, clogging, and bluegrass music. Admission & hours vary, call for details. (Third weekend in October)

NAIA POW-WOW

M – Nashville. (615) 726-0806. A gathering of Native Americans from throughout the U.S. and Canada. Storytelling, competitive dancing, traditional food from various tribes, demonstrations, and fine art displays. Admission. (Third long weekend in October)

OKTOBERFEST

M – Nashville. Historic Germantown. (615) 256-2729. Hear live German music, see polka dancing, and enjoy the authentic German food and beverages. Free admission. (Second Saturday in October)

SOUTHERN FESTIVAL OF BOOKS

M – Nashville. War Memorial Plaza. (615) 320-7001 or **www.tn-humanities.org**. Meet authors from around the country. Readings, children's authors and activities, discussions, book signings and sales. Free admission. (Second long weekend in October)

HERITAGE DAYS

M – Smyrna. Sam Davis Home. (888) 750-9524 or (615) 459-2341. A living history celebration with activities such as spinning, weaving, quilting, and blacksmithing. (First weekend in October)

BATTLE OF MURFREESBOROUGH RE-ENACTMENT

M – Spring Hill. Rippavilla Plantation, 5700 Main Street (Hwy 31 south). (931) 486-9037 or **www.rippavilla.org**. Military & civilian re-enactors (North South Alliance) create an authentic view of life during this significant time in America's Civil War. Civilian exhibits & wares of the period merchants (called sutlers). Watch a period cricket match. Stroll through the camps & stop by the demonstration tent to feel the rhythm of 1860s military & civilian life. Admission. (Last weekend in October)

October *(cont.)*

BATTLE OF BOYD'S CREEK

ME – **Sevierville**. Sevier County Fairgrounds. (888) SEVIERVILLE. Annual reenactment of the Revolutionary War Battle involving Native American, Tennessee and US history. FREE admission. (Last weekend in October)

MUSEUM OF APPALACHIA TENNESSEE FALL HOMECOMING

ME – **Norris**. Museum of Appalachia. (865) 494-0514. The event is a celebration of the culture and heritage of the Appalachian pioneer, mountain and rural life. Four stages of music, demos of early pioneer activities include cane grinding with a mule-powered mill, molasses boiling, saw milling, sheep herding, soap making and rail splitting. Hundreds of craftspeople make and sell their wares plus smell the kettles of sassafras tea, cider and other country food cooked over fires in iron kettles. (Second weekend in October)

FALL COLOR TRAIN

ME – **Oak Ridge**. Secret City Scenic Excursion Train. (865) 241-2140. Scenic Fall Color tours by train. 2-3 times daily. (Last three weekends in October)

APPLE FESTIVAL

NE – **Erwin**. Downtown. (423) 743-3000. Hundreds of vendors line the streets offering handmade crafts and delicious homemade apple products/treats. (First long weekend in October)

NATIONAL STORYTELLING FESTIVAL

NE – **Jonesborough**. International Storytelling Center, 116 W. Main Street & Festival tents. (423) 753-2171 or (800) 952-8392 or **www.stroytellingcenter.net**. Celebrate the power of storytelling during the showcase of the world's stories, storytellers, and storytelling traditions in the most dynamic event dedicated to the oral tradition. Admission $25-$80 per day, ~$100.00 weekend. (First long weekend in October)

AUTUMN STEAM EXCURSIONS

SE – Chattanooga. Tennessee Valley Railroad Museum. (423) 894-8028. Ride behind an authentic steam locomotive on scenic trips through Chattanooga and North Georgia. Some of the interesting points along the way include: Chattanooga /Chickamauga National Military Park, Missionary Ridge, and small towns of Chickamauga, Trion, Summerville, Rock Spring, and Lafayette. Eat lunch in the train's dining car. Call for rates and departure times. (October – early November, some weekdays, most weekends)

BOO AT THE ZOO

SE – Chattanooga. Chattanooga Zoo. A fun, non-scary event where you can make a scarecrow, paint a pumpkin, ride on a wagon or a pony. Carnival, too. **http://zoo.chattanooga.org**. Admission. (Last weekend in October)

FALL COLOR CRUISE & FOLK FESTIVAL

SE – Chattanooga. Ross' Landing & Southern Belle Riverboat. (423) 892-0223. See the grand canyon at its height of fall color by boat, car, or bus. Sample genuine southern cuisine and enjoy traditional, country, and gospel music folk festival. (October)

INDIAN SUMMER DAYS

SE – Chattanooga. Audubon Acres. (423) 892-1499. Learn Indian and pioneer history through crafts, games, dances, storytelling, and music. Baby animals, Indian food (fry bread). Admission. (First weekend in October)

KETNER'S MILL COUNTRY FAIR

SE – Chattanooga.   (423) 267-5702 or (423) 821-3238. Children's activities, living history, and fine crafts. (October)

CHOCTAW INDIAN FESTIVAL

W - Henning. Choctaw Reservation. (901) 635-9541. Learn about the Native American culture, skills, and traditions on a 160 acre reservation owned by the Choctaws. (Last weekend in October)

October *(cont.)*

GREAT CASEY JONES BALLOON CLASSIC

W – Jackson. McKellar Sipes Regional Airport. (731) 660-1088 or **www.tnballoonclassic.org**. TN's largest Hot Air Balloon event has 35 hot air balloons and an air show plus a carnival. (Second weekend in October)

FALL FOLKLORE JAMBOREE

W – Milan. West TN Agricultural Museum, #3 Ledbetter Gate Road. (901) 686-8067. Local folks exhibiting trades and entertainment. The Ag Museum presents a dioramic view of early settler life with displays of equipment and materials. (Third Saturday in October)

DAVY CROCKETT DAYS

W – Rutherford City Hall & historic Crockett log cabin. (731) 665-7166. Full week of celebration includes contests, parade, country music and a visit inside a replica of Davy's log cabin (when he lived in the area). (First week in October)

NOVEMBER

COMMEMORATION OF 11TH PRESIDENT JAMES K. POLK BIRTHDATE

M – Columbia. (931) 388-2354. Honor the 11th President by visiting his historic home on his birthday. Free admission. (November 2).

TURNIP GREEN FESTIVAL

M – Nashville. Nashville Farmer's Market. (615) 880-2001. Sample turnip greens, cornbread, sweet potatoes, and Cajun-fried turkey. Children's activities.   Hot sauce and turnip eating competition. Free admission. (Second Saturday in November)

HOLIDAYS AT THE HUNTER

SE – Chattanooga. Hunter Museum. **www.huntermuseum.org**. Watch a boat parade and fireworks from the Sculpture Garden. (Thanksgiving Friday)

For updates visit our website: www.kidslovepublications.com

NOVEMBER / DECEMBER

CHRISTMAS ON THE CUMBERLAND

M – Clarksville. Riverwalk. See over 3 million lights transform Clarksville's Riverwalk into a holiday festival of sights and sounds. In-ground speakers feature the "sounds of the season" during your walking tour. Free admission. (Last weekend in November – January 1st)

TRINITY CHRISTMAS CITY

M – Hendersonville. Trinity Music City USA. (615) 826-9191 or **www.tbn.org**. Tour by car and by foot, the more than one million lights, Virtual Reality Theatre, recording studios, home and gardens. FREE. (Daily, November-January)

A COUNTRY CHRISTMAS

M – Nashville. Opryland Resort. (877) 456-OPRY or **www.gaylordhotels.com**. A Christmas Spectacular (often featuring the Radio City Rockettes), Enchanted Holiday Dinner, and Fantasy in Ice (theatre full of life-size sculptures in ice). Admission. (mid-November thru Christmas)

CHEEKWOOD'S TREES OF CHRISTMAS

M – Nashville. Cheekwood Gardens. (615) 353-2150. More than two dozen trees decorated with handmade ornaments featuring countries and Christmas lore from around the world. Admission. (Saturday before Thanksgiving thru New Years Eve)

CHRISTMAS AT BELMONT

M – Nashville. Belmont Mansion. (615) 460-5459 or **www.belmontmansion.com**. A Victorian land of garland, fruit, flowers and tussie-mussies while on tour of the mansion. Admission. (Thanksgiving weekend thru New Years Eve)

November / December *(cont.)*

HOLIDAY MORNING CRUISE

M – Nashville. General Jackson Showboat. (615) 871-6100 or **www.gaylordhotels.com**. Festive cruises begin with a breakfast followed by a fun-filled holiday show. Cruise departs at 8:15am and returns at 10:15am. Admission. (Thanksgiving thru mid-December)

PRESIDENTIAL CHRISTMAS

M – Nashville. The Hermitage, Home of President Andrew Jackson. (615) 889-2941 or **www.thehermitage.com**. Special holiday exhibits at the mansion feature early traditions and decorations of the 1800s. Café and gift shop open, also with holiday theme. Admission. (mid-November thru weekend after New Years)

SEASON OF CELEBRATION

M – Nashville. Cheekwood Botanical Garden & Museum of Art. (615) 356-8000 or **www.cheekwood.org**. Showcase of multi-cultural traditions of Christmas, Hanukah, and Kwanzaa. (Thanksgiving weekend thru New Years Eve)

CHRISTMAS 1860

M – Smyrna. Sam Davis Home. (615) 459-2341 or (888) 750-9524. Learn about Christmas traditions before the Civil War. Admission. (Thanksgiving weekend thru New Years Eve)

SMOKY MOUNTAIN CHRISTMAS

ME – Gatlinburg, Pigeon Forge, Sevierville. (865) 429-7350, (800) 267-7088 or **www.mypigeonforge.com**. The gateway towns to the Smokies turn into a winter wonderland with over 7 million lights and fantastic displays throughout every town. Special activities include: Hayrides with Santa, Theatre holiday productions, Dollywood Appalachian Christmas, and Trolley Tour of Lights w/ pickup at various trolley depots (weekdays and evenings, 865-453-6444). FREE to drive thru. Individual admission for activities. (First Saturday in November thru past New Years)

CHRISTMAS IN THE CITY

ME – Knoxville. Gateway Regional Visitor Center. (800) 727-8045. (Mid-November thru New Years Eve)

DIXIE STAMPEDE, DOLLY PARTON'S CHRISTMAS AT DIXIE

ME – Pigeon Forge. (800) 356-1676 or (865) 453-4400. A seasonal twist to a night at the Stampede with a friendly rivalry between the North and South. Specially designed skating platform and holiday music enhance the show. Audience participation games like wreath tossing and reindeer riding. Highlight celebration of the Christmas story of Jesus' birth. Santa makes an appearance in his reindeer drawn sleigh as Dixie's arena is turned into a Southern winter wonderland of fresh fallen snow. Admission. (First weekend in November thru New Years Day)

SPEEDWAY IN LIGHTS

NE – Bristol. Bristol Motor Speedway & Dragway. (423) 764-1161. Admission. (Mid-November thru early January)

ROCK CITY'S ENCHANTED GARDEN OF LIGHTS

SE – Chattanooga. Lookout Mountain. (706) 820-2531 or **www.seerockcity.com** . An enchanting outdoor walk that features 25 holiday scenes in a garden nocturnal fantasyland with over a quarter of a million lights. Hot chocolate, gingerbread cookies, carolers, Santa. Daytime hours feature the Legends of Christmas. Admission. (Mid-November-early January, nighttime except Christmas Eve)

RUBY FALLS – "DECK THE FALLS"

SE – Chattanooga (Lookout Mountain). (423) 821-2544. See the majesty of the 145 foot underground falls transformed with enchanting holiday lights and sound effects. (November - early January)

November / December *(cont.)*

WINTER DAYS AND LIGHTS

SE – Chattanooga. (423) 265-0771. Downtown Chattanooga puts on its Christmas best at the Grand Illumination. Festivities include: An Appalachian Christmas, Christmas on the River (parade of floats & marching bands, food at Ross' Landing, and a lighted boat parade with fireworks), Holiday Nightlight Parade, and New Year's Eve Block Party (laser countdown, Big Band music, and fireworks). Southern Belle Riverboat offers A Christmas Carol, Ho Ho Ho Children's Santa and 'Tis the Season Luncheon Cruises. Most land activities FREE, fee for boat cruises. (November-December)

CHRISTMAS AT GRACELAND

W – Memphis. Graceland. (800) 238-2000 or **www.elvis.com**. In all its holiday splendor 24 hours a day, 7 days a week on GracelandCam. In person, visit the estate filled with holiday trees, decorations. Outside on the front lawn Elvis always had a large Santa, sleigh and reindeer. Plus, the lawn also displays a life-size Nativity scene, along with lighted aluminum trees and a winding driveway outlined in hundreds of blue lights. Admission. (Thanksgiving weekend thru Elvis' birthday in early January)

DECEMBER

CHRISTMAS PARADES

Usually the weekend after Thanksgiving or the first Saturday in December. Look for lots of floats, candy and Santa.

- ❑ **M – Franklin**, **www.franklinkiwanis.com**
- ❑ **M – Lebanon**, (615) 453-9655
- ❑ **ME – Gatlinburg** Fantasy of Lights, (800) 267-7088
- ❑ **NE – Elizabethton**, (423) 547-3850
- ❑ **SE – Chattanooga** (downtown), (423) 265-0771
- ❑ **SE – Dayton** Old-fashioned Christmas, (423) 775-0361
- ❑ **W – Camden**, (731) 584-8395
- ❑ **W – Germantown**, (901) 757-7382
- ❑ **W – Memphis**, (901) 826-0000 (Jingle Bell Ball at the Peabody)

NUTCRACKER BALLET

Both young and old will enjoy the magic of the season with this holiday favorite for family and friends. A great way to kick off your holiday season! Music accompaniment by The Symphony. Admission. (December – call for dates)

❑   **M – Nashville**. Jackson Hall, Tennessee Performing Arts Center. (615) 255-9600.

❑   **ME – Knoxville**. Civic Auditorium on Church Avenue. (865) 544-0495.

❑   **W – Memphis**. Orpheum Theatre. Ballet Memphis. (901) 737-7322.

DECEMBER (GENERAL)

CANDLELIGHT TOURS

M – Clarksville, Historic Collinsville. (931) 648-9141. Enjoy caroling in the village while you experience the peacefulness of the spirit of Christmas of the past. Reservations required. (December evenings – call for details)

PLANTATION CHRISTMAS

M – Columbia, Spring Hill & Mt. Pleasant. (888) 852-1860 or (931) 381-7176. Town & country antebellum homes decorated for the holidays. Costumed guides and holiday foods. Admission. (First long weekend in December)

AN 1860 CHRISTMAS

M – Dover. Fort Donelson National Park, Dover Hotel (Surrender House). Members of the History Guild portray a pre-civil war family trying to enjoy the holiday season. FREE. (Second weekend in December)

December *(cont.)*

DICKEN'S OF A CHRISTMAS

M – Franklin. Historic Main Street. (615) 595-1239 or **www.historicfranklin.com**. Free admission. A historic Christmas right out of a Charles Dickens's classic. Living windows of craftsmen demonstrating 19th century arts, Victorian costumes, and strolling minstrels. (Second weekend in December).

YULEFEST

M – Goodlettsville. Historic Mansker's Station Frontier Life Center. (615) 859-3678. Experience Christmas during the Colonial Days of the 1770s. Docents in period dress re-enact the customs of the time period. Evening programs have candle lanterns illuminated everywhere. Refreshments are offered and horse-drawn wagon rides carry visitors between the sites. Traditional carols, period music and dancing. Admission daytime, FREE Saturday. (First weekend in December)

CHILDREN'S CHRISTMAS SHOW

M – Nashville, Chaffin's Barn Dinner Theatre. (800) 282-BARN or **www.dinnertheatre.com**. For the 6 - 10 year old age group. It's always a fun-filled time for the kids with Santa and his elves trying to get Christmas "off-the-ground" so to speak! The shows are presented as 'brown bag' matinees, and usually last about 40 - 45 minutes. Admission. (December shows with details on website)

NATIVITY EXHIBIT

M – Nashville. The Upper Room Chapel and Museum. (615) 340-7207. Annual Nativity scenes (more than 100) representative of many styles and cultures. Admission. (December and January)

PLANTATION CHRISTMAS

M – Nashville. Traveler's Rest Plantation & Museum. (615) 832-8197 or **www.travellersrestplantation.org**. Experience an 1830s Christmas with costumed docents and Candlelight tours. Enjoy some hot wassail, learn the true story of Twelfth Night and hear about special holiday guests from the past. Occasional kids activities include dancing the Virginia Reel or make a holiday craft. Admission. (December)

SANTA EXCURSIONS

M – Nashville to **Watertown**. Tennessee Central Railway. (615) 244-9001 or **www.tcry.org**. Ride the train with Santa for "Christmas in the Country". Live entertainment and a joyous holiday feeling with a visit to the Santa Post Office Train. Departures at 8:00am & 3:00pm. Admission. (Second and third Saturdays in December)

POLAR BEAR EXPRESS

ME – Knoxville. Volunteer Landing at the Waterfront. (865) 525-9400. All aboard the Three Rivers Rambler Passenger Train. Admission. (Second weekend in December)

CHRISTMAS IN OLD APPALACHIA

ME – Norris. Museum of Appalachia. (865) 494-7680 or **www.museumofappalachia.com**. The Christmas tree in the schoolhouse is adorned with traditional paper chains, the Daniel Boone cabin's tree bears strings of popcorn and balls of cotton. Mark Twain's cabin features sweet gum and sycamore balls. Musicians, carol singing and stockings hung by the fire. Admission. (First weekend thru New Years Eve in December)

SANTA TRAIN

ME – Oak Ridge. Secret City Scenic Excursion Train. (865) 241-2140. Santa himself rides along on the train ride past historic WWII secret sites. 2-3 tours offered each day. (Second weekend in December)

CHRISTMAS AT CARTER MANSION AND THE FORT

NE – Elizabethton. Sycamore Shoals State Historic Area. (423) 543-5808. Decorated for Christmas in the style of the late 1700s. Costumed interpreters, candlelight tours, refreshments and music. Living history demos of the 18th century in the backwoods of Colonial America. Admission. (Second long weekend in December)

December *(cont.)*

1818 CANDLELIGHT CHRISTMAS PARTY

NE – **Kingsport**. Netherland Inn. (423) 246-7986 or **www.netherlandinn.com**. 1818 Christmas Party. Decorations and fiddle/dulcimer/violin music. Admission. (Second long weekend in December)

COUNTRY CHRISTMAS

NE – **Kingsport**, Exchange Place. (423) 288-6071. Includes Christmas-related crafts, seasonal and 1850s traditional crafts demonstrated and home-baked goods made and sold. Admission. (First weekend in December)

19TH CENTURY CHEROKEE CHRISTMAS

SE – **Chattanooga**. Red Clay State Historic Area. (423) 478-0339. Authentic Cherokee food, crafts, dance, and music. (First Sunday in December)

CHATTANOOGA CHOO CHOO'S VICTORIAN HOLIDAY PACKAGES & POLAR EXPRESS TRAINS

SE – **Chattanooga**. (423) 266-5000. See the historic Chattanooga Choo Choo Hotel in full dress for the holiday season. Victorian Nights is a selection of four inclusive holiday packages that include one or more nights' accommodations and discount tickets to attractions. Polar Express steam train rides feature hot chocolate and cookies, storytelling, Santa, and lots of holiday cheer to bring on the spirit of the season. (December)

CHRISTMAS CAROL & HO HO HO SANTA CRUISE

SE – **Chattanooga**. **www.chattanoogariverboat.com** or (423) 266-4488. Either dinner cruises with live band, DJ, Santa, magic show & singing crew or shorter (1½ hour), cruises with Santa, a magic show and characters. (December)

HOLIDAY LIGHTS

SE – Chattanooga. **http://zoo.chattanooga.org.** The most beautiful place to be in winter. The zoo draped in lights with entertainment everywhere. Admission. (Mid-December for one week)

MEMORIES OF CHRISTMAS PAST

SE – Chattanooga. Audubon Acres. (423) 892-1499. Pioneer Christmas with hearth cooking, decorated live trees, old-time Christmas crafts, music. (First Saturday in December)

CHRISTMAS AT FORT LOUDOUN

SE – Vonore, Fort Loudoun Historic Park. (423)-884-6217 or **www.state.tn.us/environment/parks/loudoun/events.htm.** Fort Loudoun celebrates an 18th Century Christmas with decorations, period carols sung and games played. Evening highlight of candlelight tour of the fort (weather pending) and concluded with a night firing of the cannon. Admission. (First full weekend in December)

CHRISTMAS LIGHTING

W – Henderson. Chickasaw State Park. (731) 989-5141 or **www.state.tn.us/environment/parks/chicksaw.** On one weekend, the park comes alive with electric lights and candle luminaries. Drive-thru with several special displays and Santa. (Evenings, second long weekend in December)

ENCHANTED FOREST FESTIVAL OF TREES

W – Memphis. Pink Palace Museum. (901) 320-6362. Designed and decorated trees displayed along with kids activities and a holiday laser show at the Planetarium. Kwanzaa Festival after Christmas. Admission. (Month-long in December)

HOLIDAYS AT THE MEMPHIS ZOO

W – Memphis. Zoo. (901) 276-Wild. Christmas treats, lighted displays and breakfast with Santa. Admission. (First three weeks in December)

December *(cont.)*

LIBERTY BOWL

W – Memphis, Liberty Bowl Memorial Stadium. (901) 795-7700 or **www.libertybowl.org**. College football game where the champion of the Conference USA plays the champion from the Mountain West Conference. Parade on Beale Street on December 30th. Admission. (Late December)

VICTORIAN CHRISTMAS

W – Savannah. Historic District. (800) 552-3866 or **www.tourhardincnty.org**. Begin with "Dickens Alley" on Courthouse Square where period food, crafts, carolers and actors bring the time of Dickens to life. Activities include horse and carriage rides, walking tours led by "Father Christmas" and decorated home tours. Admission. (First Saturday in December)

NEW YEAR'S EVE

FIRST NIGHT KINGSPORT

NE – Kingsport, Downtown. (423) 246-2017. Alcohol-free celebration of the arts offering music, games and activities for the family. Admission. (New Years Eve)

NEW YEAR'S AT NOON

W – Memphis. Children's Museum. (901) 458-2678. Celebrate New Years, kid-style, early at 12:00 Noon. Admission. (New Years Eve)

Master
Index

For updates visit our website:	www.kidslovepublications.com

Activity Index

PROUDLY

MADE IN THE USA

AMUSEMENTS

ANIMALS & FARMS

MUSEUMS

OUTDOORS

EM - Crossville, *Cumberland Mountain State Park*, 4

EM - Crossville, *Ozone Falls*, 5

EM - Hilham, *Standing Stone State Park*, 6

EM - Jamestown, *Pickett State Park*, 7

EM - Manchester, *Old Stone Fort State Archaeological Park*, 7

EM - McMinnville, *Cumberland Caverns*, 8

EM - Monteagle, *South Cumberland State Recreation Area*, 8

EM - Pikeville, *Fall Creek Falls State Park Resort*, 9

EM - Rock Island, *Rock Island State Rustic Park*, 10

EM - Silver Point, *Edgar Evins State Park*, 10

EM - Sparta, *Burgess Falls State Natural Area*, 11

EM - Sparta, *Virgin Falls State Natural Area*, 11

EM - Winchester, *Tims Ford State Park*, 13

M - Adams, *Port Royal State Park*, 17

M - Burns, *Montgomery Bell State Resort Park*, 17

M - Chapel Hill, *Henry Horton State Park Resort*, 19

M - Clarksville, *Cumberland Riverwalk & "As The River Flows" Exhibit*, 21

M - Clarksville, *Dunbar Cave State Natural Area*, 21

M - Dover, *Cross Creeks National Wildlife Refuge*, 23

M - Dover, *Land Between The Lakes National Recreation Area*, 24

M - Gallatin, *Bledsoe Creek State Park*, 27

M - Lawrenceburg, *David Crockett State Park*, 32

M - Lebanon, *Cedars Of Lebanon State Park*, 35

M - Linden, *Mousetail Landing State Park*, 36

M - Nashville, *Cheekwood Botanical Garden & Museum Of Art*, 45

M - Nashville, *Radnor Lake State Natural Area*, 54

M - Nashville (Hermitage), *Long Hunter State Park*, 60

ME - Caryville, *Cove Lake State Park*, 67

ME - Gatlinburg, *Great Smoky Mountains National Park*, 69

ME - Jellico, *Indian Mountain State Park*, 74

ME - Kingston, *Watts Bar Lake,* 75

ME - Knoxville, *Ijams Nature Center*, 82

ME - Maynardville, *Big Ridge State Park*, 86

ME - Norris, *Norris Dam State Park*, 87

ME - Sevierville, *Forbidden Caverns*, 100

ME - Townsend, *Cades Cove*, 102

ME - Townsend, *Tuckaleechee Caverns*, 103

ME - Wartburg, *Frozen Head State Park*, 104

NE - Bristol, *Bristol Caverns*, 107

NE - Kingsport, *Bays Mountain Park & Planetarium*, 113

NE - Kingsport, *Warriors' Path State Park*, 115

NE - Morristown, *Panther Creek State Park*, 117

NE - Roan Mountain, *Roan Mountain State Park*, 118

SE - Chattanooga, *Booker T. Washington State Park*, 133

For updates visit our website: www.kidslovepublications.com

SPORTS (cont.)

W - Memphis, *Memphis Grizzlies*, 175

W - Memphis, *Memphis Motorsports Park*, 160

W - Memphis, *Memphis Redbirds,* 162

W - Memphis, *Memphis Riverkings*, 163

TENNESSEE HISTORY

EM - Byrdstown, *Cordell Hull Birthplace & Museum State Park*, 3

EM - Hartsville, *Civil War Tour/ Battle Of Hartsville Preservation*, 5

EM - Hartsville, *Living History Museum Of Trousdale County*, 6

EM - Pall Mall, *Alvin C. York State Historic Area*, 9

M - Castalian Springs, *Historic Cragfont*, 18

M - Castalian Springs, *Wynnewood*, 18

M - Castalian Springs, *Bledsoe's Fort Historic Park*, 19

M - Clarksville, *Customs House Museum & Cultural Center*, 20

M - Clarksville (Southside), *Historic Collinsville*, 22

M - Columbia, *James K Polk Home*, 22

M - Dover, *Fort Donelson National Military Park*, 24

M - Franklin, *Carnton Plantation*, 26

M - Franklin, *Carter House & Franklin Civil War Museum*, 26

M - Goodlettsville, *Historic Mansker's Station Frontier Life Center*, 27

M - Hendersonville, *Rock Castle*, 28

M - Hohenwald, *Lewis County Museum Of Natural & Local History*, 30

M - Hohenwald, *Natchez Trace Parkway Historic Sites*, 30

M - Lebanon, *Fiddlers Grove Historic Village*, 34

M - Lebanon, *Lebanon Museum And History Center*, 34

M - Murfreesboro, *Cannonsburgh Village*, 37

M - Murfreesboro, *Stones River National Battlefield/ Fortress Rosecrans*, 38

M - Nashville, *Bicentennial Capitol Mall State Park*, 57

M - Nashville, *Tennessee State Capitol*, 57

M - Nashville, *Tennessee State Museum*, 58

M - Nashville, *Travellers Rest Historic Home*, 55

M - Nashville (Hermitage), *Hermitage, Home Of President Andrew Jackson*, 59

M - New Johnsonville, *Johnsonville State Historic Park*, 60

M - Pulaski, *Sam Davis Trail*, 61

M - Smyrna, *Sam Davis Home*, 62

M - Spring Hill, *Rippavilla Plantation*, 63

ME - Kingston, *Fort Southwest Point*, 75

ME - Knoxville, *Blount Mansion*, 77

ME - Knoxville, *East Tennessee History Center*, 76

ME - Knoxville, *Gateway Regional Visitor Center*, 80

ME - Knoxville, *James White Fort*, 81

ME - Knoxville, *Marble Springs State Historic Farmstead*, 83

For updates visit our website: www.kidslovepublications.com

GROUP DISCOUNTS & FUNDRAISING OPPORTUNITIES!

We're excited to introduce our books to your group! These guides for parents, grandparents, teachers and visitors are great tools to help you discover hundreds of fun places to visit. Our titles are great resources for all the wonderful places to travel either locally or across the region.

We are two parents who have researched, written and published these books. We have spent thousands of hours collecting information and *personally traveled over 20,000 miles* visiting all of the most unique places listed in our guides. The books are kid-tested and the descriptions include great hints on what kids like best!

Please consider the following Group Purchase options: *For the latest information, visit our website·* **www.kidslovepublications,com**

- ❑ **Group Discount/Fundraising** – Purchase books at the discount price of $2.95 off the suggested retail price for members/friends. <u>Minimum order is ten books</u>. You may mix titles to reach the minimum order. Greater discounts (~35%) are available for fundraisers. <u>Minimum order is thirty books</u>. Call for details.

- ❑ **Available for Interview/Speaking** – The authors have a treasure bag full of souvenirs from favorite places. We'd love to share ideas on planning fun trips to take children while exploring your home state. The authors are available, by appointment, *(based on availability)* at (614) 792-6451 or **michele@kidslovepublications.com**. A modest honorarium or minimum group sale purchase will apply. Call or visit our website for details.

<u>**Call us soon at (614) 792-6451 to make arrangements!**</u>
Happy Exploring!

YOUR FAMILY MEMORIES!

Now that you've created memories with your family,
it's time to keepsake them by scrapbooking
in this unique, family-friendly way!

Check Out These Unique Features:

* **The Book That Shrinks As It Grows!** - Specially designed pages can be removed as you add pictures to your book. This keeps your unique travel journal from becoming too thick to use.

* **Write Your Own Book** - The travel journal is designed to get you started and help you remember those great family fun times!

* **Design Your Own Book** - Most illustrations and picture frames are designed to encourage kids to color them.

* **Unique Chapter Names** - help you <u>simply</u> categorize your family travel memories.

* **Acid Free Paper** - was used to print your book to keep your photos safe for a lifetime!

Writing Your Own Family Travel Book is This Easy...

Step 1 - Select, Cut and Paste Your Favorite Travel Photos

Step 2 - Color the Fun Theme Picture Frames

Step 3 - Write about Your Travel Stories in the Journal (We get you started...)

Step 4 - Specially Designed Pages are removed to reduce thickness as you add photos

Remove This Page
(to reduce binding thickness as you add personal photos)

The Perfect Companion to the Best-Selling "Kids Love" Travel Series!

Create Your Family Travel Book Today!

Visit your local retailer,

use the order form in the back of this book,

or our website: www.kidslovepublications.com

Attention Parents:

All titles are "Kid Tested". *The authors and kids personally visited all of the most unique places* and wrote the books with warmth and excitement from a parent's perspective. Find tried and true places that children will enjoy. No more boring trips! Listings provide: Names, addresses, telephone numbers, websites, directions, and descriptions. All books include a bonus chapter listing state-wide kid-friendly Seasonal & Special Events!

❑ **KIDS LOVE INDIANA** - Discover places where you can "co-star" in a cartoon or climb a giant sand dune. Over 500 listings in one book about Indiana travel. 8 geographical zones, 213 pages.

❑ **KIDS LOVE KENTUCKY** - Discover places from Boone to Burgoo, from Caves to Corvettes, and from Lincoln to the Lands of Horses. Nearly 500 listings in one book about Kentucky travel. 5 geographic zones. 186 pages.

❑ **KIDS LOVE MICHIGAN** - Discover places where you can "race" over giant sand dunes, climb aboard a lighthouse "ship", eat at the world's largest breakfast table, or watch yummy foods being made. Almost 600 listings in one book about Michigan travel. 8 geographical zones, 229 pages.

❑ **KIDS LOVE OHIO** - Discover places like hidden castles and whistle factories. Over 800 listings in one book about Ohio travel. 9 geographical zones, 260 pages.

❑ **KIDS LOVE PENNSYLVANIA** - Explore places where you can "discover" oil and coal, meet Ben Franklin, or watch your favorite toys and delicious, fresh snacks being made. Over 900 listings in one book about Pennsylvania travel. 9 geographical zones, 268 pages.

❑ **KIDS LOVE TENNESSEE** – Explore places where you can "discover" pearls, ride the rails, "meet" Three Kings (of Rights, Rock & Soul). Be inspired to sing listening to the rich traditions of Country music fame. Over 500 listings in one book about Tennessee travel. 6 geographical zones, 235 pages.

❑ **KIDS LOVE THE VIRGINIAS** – Discover where ponies swim and dolphins dance, dig into archaeology and living history, or be dazzled by record-breaking and natural bridges. Over 900 listings in one book about Virginia & West Virginia travel. 8 geographical zones, 262 pages.

ORDER FORM

KIDS LOVE PUBLICATIONS

1985 Dina Court
Powell, Ohio 43065
(614) 792-6451

Visit our website: **www.kidslovepublications.com**

#	Title		Price	Total
	Kids Love Indiana		$13.95	
	Kids Love Kentucky		$13.95	
	Kids Love Michigan		$13.95	
	Kids Love Ohio		$13.95	
	Kids Love Pennsylvania		$13.95	
	Kids Love Tennessee		$13.95	
	Kids Love the Virginias		$13.95	
	Kids Love Travel Memories!		$14.95	
	Combo Discount Pricing			
	Combo #2 - Any 2 Books		$23.95	
	Combo #3 - Any 3 Books		$33.95	
	Combo #4 - Any 4 Books		$42.95	
			Subtotal	
(Please make check or money order payable to: KIDS LOVE PUBLICATIONS)		*(Ohio Residents Only – Your local rate)*	Local/State Sales Tax	
☐ Master Card		*$2.00 first book $1.00 each additional*	Shipping	
☐ Visa			**TOTAL**	

Account Number ☐☐☐☐-☐☐☐☐-☐☐☐☐-☐☐☐☐

Exp Date: ☐☐/☐☐ (Month/Year)

Cardholder's Name _____

Signature *(required)* _____

Name: _____
Address: _____
City: _____ State: _____
Zip: _____ Telephone: _____

All orders are shipped within 2 business days of receipt by US Mail. If you wish to have your books autographed, please include a legible note with the message you'd like written in your book. Your satisfaction is 100% guaranteed or simply return your order for a prompt refund. Thanks for your order. Happy Exploring!

"Where to go?, What to do?, and How much will it cost?", are all questions that they have heard throughout the years from friends and family. These questions became the inspiration that motivated them to research, write and publish the "Kids Love" travel series.

This adventure of writing and publishing family travel books has taken them on a journey of experiences that they never could have imagined. They have appeared as guests on hundreds of radio and television shows, had featured articles in statewide newspapers and magazines, spoken to thousands of people at schools and conventions, and write monthly columns in many publications talking about "family friendly" places to travel.

George Zavatsky and Michele (Darrall) Zavatsky were raised in the Midwest and have lived in many different cities. They currently reside in a suburb of Columbus, Ohio. They feel very blessed to be able to create their own career that allows them to research, write and publish a series of best-selling kids' travel books. Besides the wonderful adventure of marriage, they place great importance on being loving parents to Jenny & Daniel.